BYSTANDERS

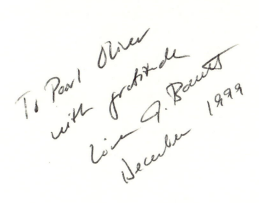

To Pearl Oliner
with gratitude

Eva G. Bossett

December 1999

Recent Titles in
Christianity and the Holocaust—Core Issues

BYSTANDERS

Conscience and Complicity During the Holocaust

Victoria J. Barnett

Contributions to the Study of Religion, Number 59
Christianity and the Holocaust—Core Issues
Carol Rittner and John Roth, *Series Editors*

GREENWOOD PRESS
Westport, Connecticut • London

Library of Congress Cataloging-in-Publication Data

Barnett, Victoria J.
   Bystanders : conscience and complicity during the Holocaust /
Victoria J. Barnett.
      p. cm.—(Contributions to the study of religion, ISSN
0196-7053 ; no. 59. Christianity and the Holocaust-core issues)
   Includes bibliographical references and index.
   ISBN 0–313–29184–5 (alk. paper)
   1. Holocaust, Jewish (1939–1945)—Moral and ethical aspects.
2. Holocaust, Jewish (1939–1945)—Social aspects. 3. World War,
1939–1945—Collaborationists. 4. Apathy. I. Title. II. Series:
Contributions to the study of religion ; no. 59. III. Series:
Contributions to the study of religion. Christianity and the
Holocaust-core issues.
   D804.3.B356 1999
   940.53'18—dc21   98–51641

British Library Cataloguing in Publication Data is available.

Library of Congress Catalog Card Number: 98–51641
ISBN: 0–313–29184–5
ISSN: 0196–7053

First published in 1999

Greenwood Press, 88 Post Road West, Westport, CT 06881
An imprint of Greenwood Publishing Group, Inc.
www.greenwood.com

Printed in the United States of America

The paper used in this book complies with the
Permanent Paper Standard issued by the National
Information Standards Organization (Z39.48–1984).

10 9 8 7 6 5 4 3 2 1

Copyright Acknowledgments

The author and publisher gratefully acknowledge permission for use of the following material:

Excerpts from Zygmunt Baumann: *Modernity and the Holocaust*. Copyright © 1989 by Zygmunt Baumann. Used by permission of the publisher, Cornell University Press.

Excerpts from *The Tremendum*, by Arthur Cohen. © Copyright 1981, by Crossroad Publishing. Reprinted by permission of The Continum Publishing Company.

Reprinted with the permission of The Free Press, a Division of Simon & Schuster from *In The Shadow of Death: Living Outside the Gates of Mauthausen* by Gordon J. Horwitz. Copyright © 1990 by Gordon J. Horwitz.

Excerpts from *The Roots of Evil: The Origins of Genocide and Other Group Violence* by Ervin Staub. Copyright © 1989 by Cambridge University Press. Used by permission of Cambridge University Press.

Excerpts from Minutes, November 5, 1934. Federal Church papers, *RG18 Box 3 F 12 "American Committee for Christian Refugees January 1934–December 1937."* Presbyterian Church (USA). Used by permission of the Department of History and Records Management Services, Philadelphia.

Excerpts from *Guiding principles for the treatment of the Jewish problem in post-war Germany*. Papers of Henry Smith Leiper, Series I, Box 3, Folder 3. Archives of the Burke Library Union Theological Seminary in the City of New York. Used by permission of the Burke Library Union Theological Seminary in the City of New York.

Contents

Series Foreword

The Holocaust did not end when the Allies liberated the Jewish survivors from Nazi Germany's killing centers and concentration camps in 1945. The consequences of that catastrophic event still shadow the world's moral, political, and religious life.

The "Christianity and the Holocaust—Core Issues" series explores Christian complicity, indifference, resistance, rescue, and other responses to the Holocaust. Concentrating on core issues such as the Christian roots of anti-Semitism, the roles played by Christian individuals and groups during the Holocaust, and the institutional reactions of Christians after Auschwitz, the series has a historical focus but addresses current concerns as well.

While many of the series' authors are well-known, established Holocaust scholars, the series also features young writers who will become leaders in the next generation of Holocaust scholarship. As all of the authors study the Holocaust's history, they also assess the Holocaust's impact on Christianity and its implications for the future of the Christian tradition.

Victoria Barnett is a Protestant Christian scholar whose earlier book, *For the Soul of the People: Protestant Protest Against Hitler* (Oxford University Press, 1992) examines questions such as: How should moral people behave under systematically evil regimes like that of the Nazi Third Reich?; What lessons, if any, can we learn from those Germans who tried to oppose Hitler?; and Who then tried to learn from their mistakes of the past after 1945? *For the Soul of the People* is a frank revelation of the choices people were forced to make during a ghastly dictatorship, and the stinging moral consequences of those choices.

Bystanders: Private Conscience and Public Complicity in the Holocaust
expands the issues and raises additional questions about how moral people
should behave under systematically evil regimes. In this book, Barnett
brings the figure of the bystander out of the shadows of history. She struggles with an issue that also confounded Elie Wiesel: "This, this was the
thing I had wanted to understand ever since the war. Nothing else. How a
human being can remain indifferent." According to Barnett, the bystander
is central to what happened in the Holocaust, and much of our growing
fascination with the Holocaust revolves around questions that arise about
bystanders. *Who were they? Where were they? Why did they do nothing?*

What we do know is that bystanders were neither perpetrators nor victims. They were ordinary people who simply went about their daily lives
in the midst of a ghastly dictatorship. Their behavior raises troubling questions about human nature, about the very foundations of human ethics and
morality. Did these ordinary people have choices? Did they have the power
to change what was happening? Did they want to? In many societies there
are people who are prepared to turn against other groups, but it is the
population as a whole who provides or denies the support such people need
to take action. Do dictatorships like that of the Nazi Third Reich induce a
kind of mass psychosis that transformed some people into brutes and others
into passive marionettes?

In *Bystanders: Private Conscience and Public Complicity in the Holocaust*, Victoria Barnett explores and analyzes factors that shaped the behavior of "ordinary people" during the Holocaust. She raises profound
questions about the threads that bind us together in the human community.
During the Holocaust, these threads did not hold firm. Institutions that
should have exemplified the human face of God in a suffering world—
Christian churches—failed to live out their founder's highest ideals. Those
who should have recognized the human face of God in their persecuted
Jewish brothers and sisters—Christians—failed to do so. As a result, too
few resisted the Nazis, too few helped the Jews, and too many remained
indifferent. Barnett forces us to ask the question, What about today? What
does it take to move "ordinary people" from indifference to action on
behalf of others? Places like Cambodia, Bosnia, and Rwanda compel us to
admit that this is a question we cannot afford to ignore.

Carol Rittner and John K. Roth

Acknowledgments

I am grateful to a number of friends and colleagues for their ideas, insights, and assistance. Professor John Roth and Sister Carol Rittner, editors of this series, have been encouraging throughout my work on this book. At key points, Carol asked the important questions that helped me past various mental stumbling blocks. Another ongoing and stimulating conversation partner has been Dr. Mary Johnson of Facing History and Ourselves; her own ideas about bystanders helped me focus and organize the material. Professor Dan Bar-On read the completed manuscript and offered important corrections and insights which will continue to shape my thinking on bystanders and related issues. Despite their busy schedules, professors Doris Bergen, Susannah Heschel, and Pearl Oliner all graciously read the entire manuscript and helped with comments and corrections; as did my colleague, Margaret Obrecht of the Church Relations Department at the United States Holocaust Memorial Museum.

I also owe a tremendous debt to the students of the seminar I taught in summer 1997 on "Bystanders in an age of genocide," at Wesley Theological Seminary, Washington, D.C. Their courage in confronting the material and honesty in sharing their own experiences led me to rethink several central issues and rewrite portions of the book.

Finally, it is with profound gratitude that I thank my husband, Ulrich Wolf-Barnett, and our children. They helped, tolerated, and humored me in numerous ways as I worked on this difficult topic. Most importantly, each of them has taken my work on this book as an occasion for family conversations about the kind of people we would like to be and the kind of society we would like to live in. Despite the depressing nature of most of the material I was working with, their presence and support sustained me and gave me hope.

Introduction

No Man is an Iland, intire of it selfe; every man is a peece of the Continent, a part of the maine; if a Clod bee washed away by the Sea, Europe is the lesse, as well as if a Promontorie were, as well as if a Mannor of thy friends or of thine owne were; any mans death diminishes me, because I am involved in Mankinde; and therefore never send to know for whom the bell tolls; It tolls for thee.

—John Donne

In recent years, the literature of the Holocaust has become a distinct genre. There are generalized studies of the European Jews and the rise of Nazism in Germany, as well as more specialized books about various aspects of the Holocaust. Some scholars have examined the history of different regions and nations during the Nazi period. Others have focused on the history of specific groups such as doctors, women, Christians, or homosexuals. Scholars have traced the development of the Nazi bureaucracy and the concentration camp system. There are detailed and horrifying accounts of what the Jews and others endured in the concentration camps. There are psychological studies of the personalities of those who created and governed the camps. Other writers have chosen to focus on the victims and survivors, and to pay tribute to them by preserving the memory of their lost world.

But there remains one group that is seldom studied as a separate phenomenon, although it appears throughout the literature. In the shadows of virtually every book about the Holocaust are the bystanders: millions of human beings conspicuous not by their absence, but by their silence. They are often recalled obliquely, as in these words by a survivor of Mauthausen:

I try to repress much, but one thing lodges especially in my memory, very deep in memory. These were the marches, the daily marches upon which we shifted from the camp to work in the tunnels, and, especially later in the afternoons, tired, utterly exhausted, dehumanized, on the way from work in the tunnels into the camp. On the left side, on the right side these white houses. I was so frightfully cold. I tried to dream of all that lay behind these walls. And I tried to think, perhaps a mother and children live in this house, but always I was awakened by the shouts of the SS: "Move on! Move on!" But again and again, every day when I left the camp, I tried to have these momentary dreams. That has remained so alive in my memory.[1]

Bystanders: the people who lived in those white houses, not-so-distant witnesses to horror. The Mauthausen prisoner thought of them almost longingly, as a link to the normal life that had been brutally denied him. On another level, however, the silent spectators in the white houses epitomized one of the most horrifying realities about the Holocaust: it was not just carried out by other human beings, but tolerated by countless others. To those suffering in the camps, these anonymous witnesses were invisible, almost unimaginable. Who were they? the victims asked themselves. More importantly: Where were they? Why did they do nothing?

These questions have become more urgent as time has passed, because it has become clear how extensive the ranks of bystanders were. The residents of the white houses had been joined by millions of people throughout the world who knew, but did not want to know, what was happening to the European Jews and other victims of Nazism. Some, as citizens of Nazi Germany or the Nazi-occupied countries, actually witnessed the persecution of the Jews. Others lived far away, and knew of the genocide through press reports. Some were helpless to do anything. Others were people in power who might have been able to do something.

None of these people were unusual. Human history is filled with terrible examples of brutality, cowardice, complicity, and indifference to suffering. There have always been bystanders: people in various walks of life who might have changed the course of history, had they chosen to become more actively involved.

In a unique fashion, however, the figure of the bystander is central to what happened in the *Shoah*. We will never know whether the Jews of Europe might have been saved by mass demonstrations in Germany opposing the Nuremberg laws, or by a serious international effort to take in more refugees from Nazi-occupied Europe. Yet many people hold bystanders as accountable as the perpetrators for what happened; they believe that Auschwitz is what happens when good people choose to do nothing. Elie Wiesel has offered a scathing summary of what happened between 1933 and 1945: "There was no freedom, and there was no conscience. The killers killed. The slaughterer slaughtered. And the victims died. The world was silent."[2]

The literature about the Holocaust is filled with bystanders. Whether the topic is Vichy France, the medical profession, the behavior of Polish villagers or German soldiers, the issue of bystander behavior arises. The term usually refers to someone immediately present, an actual witness, someone for whom involvement was an option. It implies a certain form of behavior.

It also presupposes a certain detachment; bystanders are not automatically involved. The term "bystander" does not apply to leading Nazis or guards in concentration camps, but to "ordinary" citizens. In some fashion, these people simply went about their daily lives during one of the ghastliest dictatorships the world has ever known. They continued to work and raise their children. Those who lived near concentration camps tended their gardens and had regular dealings with those who worked and ran the camps. After November 9, 1938, when thousands of Jewish-owned businesses in Germany suddenly had new owners, people continued to shop in them as though nothing had changed.

They were people who, to their vast relief, were convinced after 1945 that they had not been directly involved in the genocide of the Jews. And if we consider how the world must have looked to these people, they are not really that difficult to understand. People throughout the world adjust to their political circumstances. Most people are far more preoccupied with maintaining the normal rhythms of their lives than with the wish to become involved—perhaps at some risk—to alleviate the suffering of others.

Yet in the post-Holocaust awareness that "normal" life was proceeding while millions of people were murdered, the bystander becomes an especially haunting figure. As the narrator of Wiesel's 1964 novel, *The Town beyond the Wall*, says:

This, this was the thing I had wanted to understand ever since the war. Nothing else. How a human being can remain indifferent. The executioners I understood; also the victims, though with more difficulty. For the others, all the others, those who were neither for nor against, those who sprawled in passive patience, those who told themselves, "The storm will blow over and everything will be normal again," those who thought themselves above the battle, those who were permanently and merely spectators—all those were closed to me, incomprehensible.[3]

How *do* we comprehend and judge such attitudes, in ourselves and in others? Our response to this question depends partly on our own judgments about the circumstances that bystanders faced. Did they have choices? Did they have the power to change what happened? Do dictatorships induce a kind of mass psychosis that transforms some people into brutes and others into passive marionettes? Were they ideologically conditioned, blinded by prejudice to the suffering of those who didn't belong to their religious or ethnic group? What factors move people to altruistic behavior; what factors keep people passive? What is the nature of the sin we are addressing here: political? moral? all too human? What does the Holocaust tell us about ourselves and God? How, particularly within the Christian and Jewish traditions, do we wrestle with the questions it raises?

As all these questions suggest, the bystanders are not just a historical phenomenon. They raise troubling questions about human nature and the very foundations of human ethics. If we decide that a Holocaust should never happen again, we must think about the behavior of those who were present, but did nothing to stop the evil or help its victims.

This book attempts to explore and analyze some of the factors that shaped the behavior of "ordinary people" during the Holocaust. It is not a historical documentation of bystanders during the Holocaust. Although I will draw upon the existing literature in many fields for examples of bystander behavior, I do not intend to make a list of who fits the category of bystander. My emphasis is on the factors that fostered passivity and complicity in Nazi Germany and in other countries, with the hope of understanding the relationship between bystanders and other issues that arise in Holocaust scholarship.

While many of the examples in this book will focus on behavior in Nazi Germany, the bystander, of course, was not just a German phenomenon. The parallels between bystander behavior in Germany and elsewhere may give us some insights into human behavior on the individual and collective levels. There were varying degrees of complicity. We will be examining the different factors that influenced human behavior *not in order to exonerate the bystanders, but to grasp how they moved from one point on the spectrum to another.* If there is an underlying thesis here, it is that human beings are connected to the world around them in numerous ways and on numerous levels. No single factor explains the passivity and complicity of the bystanders. Indeed, the Third Reich was powerful precisely because of the many levels on which people became involved in what was going on. Even people who were unhappy with some aspects of Nazism supported other policies of the regime. Ultimately, very few people were able to extricate themselves entirely from the web of complicity.

The goal of this analysis is to develop a framework by which we can understand the significance of bystanders during the Holocaust, with the hope that this can yield more insight into the relevance of such behavior today. Indeed, I believe that these lingering questions about human behavior and ethics are one reason for the growing interest in Holocaust studies. Genocide is not a phenomenon unique to Nazi Germany, and many analogies have been drawn between the genocide of the European Jews and other events. The term "Holocaust" has been applied to the bombings of innocent civilians in the Vietnam War, the Cambodian genocide under Pol

Pot, and the atrocities committed during the civil war in Yugoslavia. African Americans sometimes speak of the age of slavery as their Holocaust; Native Americans, too, look back on a history of genocide. Some gay activists have spoken of an "AIDS Holocaust."

Many of those who survived the Nazi death camps oppose such analogies, fearing that any universalization of the Holocaust trivializes this event. With good reason, they worry that if the discussion about the Holocaust becomes more generalized, there will be less focus upon the specific factors, like anti-Semitism, that led to it. It is possible for victims, perpetrators, and bystanders alike to become lost in vague clichés like "man's inhumanity to man." As Alvin Rosenfeld of Indiana University once observed, "To generalize or universalize the victims of the Holocaust is not only to profane their memories but to exonerate their executioners, who by the same line of thinking pursued above also disappear into the mist of a faceless mankind."[4]

A closer look at the parallels drawn to the Holocaust, however, reveals a central assumption that is crucial to any understanding of bystanders. Morally, such comparisons to the Holocaust serve as an exclamation mark. They often represent a claim to absolute moral justification, and, almost always, they are an appeal to the outside world to act. In other words, the real comparison being drawn is not between different classes of victims, but between bystanders. With respect to Bosnia, Cambodia, or other situations, we are saying that the rest of humanity has been put into the same position as the bystanders during the Holocaust. We are being called upon to respond, to do something. Or we are being summoned to acknowledge our own connection to past injustice—for example, our part in the legacy left by slavery.

It is morally repugnant to compare the "qualifications" of different groups of victims. But it may be helpful if we understand the analogies made to the Holocaust as a call to examine the parallels between the behavior of bystanders, then and now. These parallels are an indication that, if we do not want something similar to happen again, something has to change. The prevention of future Holocausts may depend not upon identifying and protecting potential victims, but upon our learning—as bystanders—to respond differently to the plight of victims everywhere. If the bystander has become a modern archetype, it is because of the considerable evidence, in the final years of the 20th century, that there is really very little that distinguishes most of us from the silent bystanders of the 1930s.

For this reason, bystander behavior is an intrinsic part of the ethical and theological dilemmas that have emerged since the Holocaust. The belief in an orderly universe, in which each person had his or her divinely ordained place, has virtually dissolved in modern Western society. The religious philosopher Arthur Cohen attributes this to the Holocaust, which he describes as a "tremendum"—a historical break with deep philosophical and religious consequences. "Historical catastrophe," he writes, "ends certain intellectual options as surely and powerfully as it ends lives."[5] In a post-Holocaust age, Cohen believes, concepts of "both God and man are in need of rethinking and redescription."[6]

Cohen's words are echoed in Elie Wiesel's observation that what perished in the flames of the *Shoah* was "not only man . . . but the idea of man."[7] The grim, altered view of human nature that emerged after Auschwitz seems impossibly far from the 16th-century idealism of John Donne. Yet we may draw some hope from the fact that most who study the Holocaust emerge conscious of the responsibility that we bear for one another, and wrestle with how to practice that responsibility in modern life. Above all, it is my hope that this book will contribute to that consciousness.

NOTES

1. Horwitz, *In the Shadow of Death*, 3.
2. Wiesel, "Freedom of Conscience: A Jewish Commentary," 639.
3. Elie Wiesel, *The Town beyond the Wall* (New York: Avon Books, 1969), 159.
4. Rosenfeld, *A Double Dying*, 160.
5. Cohen, *The Tremendum*, 61.
6. Ibid., 34.
7. Quoted in Willis, "The Burden of Auschwitz: Rethinking Morality," 278.

CHAPTER 1

Who Is a Bystander?

His presence is evasive, and commits him less than his absence might
. . . He says nothing. He is there, but he acts as if he were not. Worse:
he acts is if the rest of us were not.
                              —Wiesel, *The Town beyond the Wall*[1]

TWO VILLAGES

Sonderburg

In 1980, Canadian anthropologist Frances Henry paid a series of visits to
a small town in Germany. She hoped to recapitulate the town's history
during the Nazi era, but her interest in the town she called "Sonderburg"
was more than professional. Sonderburg was her birthplace; her family had
lived there for generations. After the November 1938 pogrom (the so-called
"Kristallnacht"), Henry's father was taken to Dachau and released only
after he liquidated his bank account. Her parents were able to emigrate to
Canada in 1939, when Frances was seven. The rest of the family, including
her grandparents, were killed in the concentration camps.

In addition to examining town records and accounts of town life during
the Nazi era, Henry interviewed thirty-one people still living in Sonderburg.
All had known some or all of the Jewish community; one-third of them
had been employees of Jewish-owned businesses. Four of her interviewees
had been civil servants and Nazi party members; all thirteen men she in-

terviewed had been drafted into the German military in World War II. None had been leading Nazis or members of the SS. Henry was also able to interview nineteen Jewish former residents of Sonderburg, all of whom had emigrated to the United States. For a number of reasons, Henry's portrait of ordinary life in a German town under Hitler offers many insights into the changes that occurred in the relationships between the ordinary citizens of Sonderburg—Jews and non-Jews—after January 1933.

At the beginning of the Nazi era, Sonderburg had 4,000 residents, 150 of whom were Jewish. Many of its residents were small farmers or tradesmen. Most of the town's businesses were owned by Jews, a legacy of the not-so-distant era when other avenues of employment had been barred to them. Neither the Jews nor the non-Jews who had lived in Sonderburg recalled many difficulties between the two groups before 1933. "Even Jewish respondents," notes Henry, "commented that before Hitler they had no real problems living amongst German non-Jews; only occasional incidents of anti-Semitism marred an otherwise comfortable style of life."[2] Indeed, there was more social tension between the town's Catholics and Protestants than between Jews and Christians, and local Jews recalled having cordial relationships with their non-Jewish neighbors.

Some of the cultural patterns Henry uncovered in pre-1933 Sonderburg existed in other parts of Germany. The legal emancipation of the Jews during the 19th century had led to greater assimilation in German society. Freed to enter professions previously closed to them, many Jews also embraced German culture; their contributions led to a German renaissance in the fine arts and sciences. In retrospect, however, full assimilation seems to have been an illusion; many invisible boundaries between Jews and non-Jews remained. German Jews retained a sense of "being different," and the views of most non-Jewish Germans showed some degree of anti-Semitism.[3]

In Sonderburg, there was very little intermarriage between Jews and non-Jews (less than the German national average for the period),[4] and a number of social clubs barred Jews from membership. Contacts between Jews and non-Jews occurred primarily in the workplace. The non-Jews relied upon the Jews for jobs and goods; the Jews upon the non-Jews for employees and customers.

In some respects, the Jews of Sonderburg were more integrated in their community than elsewhere in Germany. The population was small enough that "class segregation was not especially evident," and there was no residential segregation.[5] Christian and Jewish children attended the same schools, and all the citizens of Sonderburg "participated in the same political structures and shared some, if not all, recreational pursuits."[6]

At the beginning of the Third Reich, then, Sonderburg was a stable community. Relationships among the different groups in the town were uncomplicated by any marked political, ethnic, or religious tension. Even at the height of the Nazi era, Sonderburg was not a Nazi stronghold. Only 600

Sonderburg citizens joined the Nazi party; after researching party files and town records, Henry estimated that only 100 of these were hard-core members.

Nonetheless, within days of January 30, 1933, when Adolf Hitler became the German chancellor, the Jewish residents of Sonderburg were feeling the cold wind of Nazism—and much of it came from the actions of their neighbors. One of Henry's interviewees was Joshua Abraham, a Jewish villager who, for years, had met with a group of men twice a week to play cards. "As soon as the Nazis came to power," he recalled, "I was no longer told when they were playing cards. Everything stopped. I would see them on the street and we pretended we didn't see each other. Not one of them spoke to me."[7]

What happened in Sonderburg—and throughout Germany during the early months of the Third Reich—was the *Gleichschaltung* (synchronization) of German society into a Nazified one. Under the direction and leadership of the Nazi party, new organizations were created for Germans in all walks of life, from schoolchildren to tradespeople to hobby gardeners. *Gleichschaltung* essentially meant Nazification, and it served two purposes. In a nation that had been torn apart by the social and economic tensions of the Weimar years, it rapidly created a new sense of common purpose and camaraderie. But it was also an ominous way of establishing who belonged in the new German Reich and who did not. The process of isolating the Jews from the rest of society had begun.

What Joshua Abraham experienced was not official Nazification, however, but the immediate and spontaneous accommodation of his old friends to the new rules of their society. With striking suddenness, the non-Jewish citizens of Sonderburg began treating their Jewish neighbors and co-workers differently.[8] Like Abraham, many Jewish interviewees recalled neighbors who, literally from one day to the next, stopped speaking to them. Others had friends who visited them privately, embarrassed, to apologize. In general, the Jews of Sonderburg discovered that they had few friends who were brave or principled enough to display public solidarity with them.

Those who were schoolchildren at the time were suddenly divided by the different possibilities open to them. The non-Jews interviewed by Henry recalled the Hitler Youth programs and other Nazi events for children as innocent fun that they didn't take too seriously (or so they claimed in retrospect, at least). But their Jewish classmates—excluded from these activities, and belittled by their teachers and former friends as inferior—suffered silently.[9]

The non-Jewish residents of Sonderburg remained part of the community; their Jewish neighbors had become a nonentity, invisible and irrelevant. In the early months of Nazism, non-Jews who maintained contacts with Jews were harassed and discriminated against; as time went on, the potential punishment for contacts between Jews and non-Jews became more severe. (Still, Henry discovered only two cases in which people who helped Jews or openly criticized Nazi policies were punished.)[10]

The break in relationships was supported by both sides: "many of the Jews, through fear, rapidly complied with the rules and were the ones to discourage contact with Gentiles."[11] They halted relations with non-Jewish friends and discouraged their non-Jewish customers from entering their businesses. "Starting in 1933, most Sonderburg Jews conducted their social life outside of Sonderburg."[12] Many began to take short trips to nearby Frankfurt, where they could shop or go to the cinema without being identified as Jews.

As time passed, the patterns of silence, obedience, and conformity became more insidious as non-Jews actually began to benefit from the persecution of their neighbors. Non-Jews were able to buy Jewish businesses and homes for far less than their actual value. Some Sonderburg Jews used this money to buy their way to freedom abroad.

Where it did exist, solidarity with the Jews was shown privately. In fact, Henry discovered that a "significant minority" helped the Sonderburg Jews secretly, "without committing themselves to any action which could have landed them in trouble."[13] "As oppression from the top increased, local acts of kindness similarly increased . . . Obviously, not all Germans complied with the dictates of the regime."[14] After 1939, for example, the twelve Jews left in Sonderburg were aided by friendly neighbors who brought them food, letters, and other necessities until all twelve were deported in 1942.[15] All such help came from individuals, not institutions. The Catholic and Protestant churches in Sonderburg did nothing to aid the Jewish community.[16] Those individuals who aided Jews were either neighbors or business acquaintances.

Of particular interest in Henry's study were the attitudes of the Jews and non-Jews at the time she interviewed them. Most of the Jews she interviewed (all had left Germany) were bitter and had no intention of ever returning. They felt "considerable ambivalence" between their tendency to condemn all Germans and their recollections of neighbors and acquaintances who had helped them.[17] "Discussion surrounding the German people's ostensible knowledge of the genocide," found Henry, was "crucial to understanding how surviving Jews perceive their old Gentile friends even today. Jewish survivors are convinced that all Germans had this knowledge."[18]

The non-Jewish residents of Sonderburg, on the other hand, had convinced themselves that the past was irrelevant. Henry and the few other Jews who returned to visit were overwhelmed by the warm hospitality initially shown them by the townspeople, who hoped to reestablish their pre-1933 relationships. Under the surface of this hospitality, however, was considerable discomfort and tension. Henry had the impression that the townspeople wanted only to forget the Nazi period; they couldn't understand why this was impossible for Jews who had lived through Nazism. When the townspeople did discuss the Nazi era, "the word *machtlos* [powerless] occurred over and over in our conversation."[19] They had been powerless, the non-Jews told Henry, paralyzed by fear and the threat of retribution (although, as Henry noted, there was very little actual retribution against people who did refuse to comply with Nazi policies). Most non-Jews expressed bewilderment, even today, at what had happened to their former neighbors: they "were never sure why" the Jews had been persecuted and claimed that they still didn't understand it.[20]

Although "Sonderburg" means "special town" in German, there was nothing special about this village, even during the Third Reich.[21] It was not a center of Nazi activity; there was no concentration camp there. The residents interviewed by Henry were puzzled and hurt by the suggestion that they might have been responsible for Nazi crimes in any way. In their minds, Sonderburg had continued to be a decent, upstanding community between 1933 and 1945.

In the normal course of events, as Willy Brandt noted in his foreword to Henry's book, its residents would have continued to get along with each other, "to live and let live." Under Nazism, the non-Jews of Sonderburg became bystanders to the Holocaust. These people, who had gotten along fine with their Jewish neighbors before 1933, had simply proceeded with their own lives after that date—not completely oblivious to what was happening to their Jewish neighbors, but oddly uninvolved, as though it had nothing to do with them. Many continued to feel this way even after 1945, and this was the barrier that separated the citizens of Sonderburg long after the *Shoah*.

The ethical question raised by the story of Sonderburg, as Brandt put it, is: When does tolerance become " 'minding one's own business'? At what point does laissez-faire turn into indifference, indifference into disrespect?"[22] When, by implication, do disrespect and indifference contribute to something far more malignant?

Mauthausen

The attitudes of indifference and disrespect indicate varying degrees of distance between individuals and their immediate society. According to Gordon Horwitz, the noninvolvement of bystanders is achieved only by creating and maintaining such distance, either physically or psychologically. Horwitz's insightful book about the villages surrounding the Austrian concentration camp of Mauthausen is a study of the dynamics by which local residents maintained their distance from the horrors occurring in their midst.[23]

The village of Mauthausen was smaller than Sonderburg; 1,772 of its

1,813 residents were Catholic; none were Jewish.[24] It was a farming community, far removed from the political events of Nazi Germany until August 1938, when the Nazis decided to build a concentration camp near the stone quarries there. In the years that followed, Mauthausen and the surrounding bucolic countryside became a center of murder. The infamous Hartheim Castle, one of the euthanasia centers, was located nearby, and several smaller concentration camps were opened in the region during the final years of the war.

Initially, the residents of the area seem to have viewed the concentration camp as an intrusion. The SS staff and the camp commandant, Franz Ziereis, were viewed as disruptive thugs who got involved in drunken brawls and desecrated local religious shrines.[25] Eventually, however, these "initial tensions . . . were resolved in the camp's favor . . . The camp and the town were enmeshed in such numerous ways that the killings in and around the camp were never a secret to the population."[26]

How did this happen? Fear seems to have been one factor. From the beginning, Mauthausen was a brutal camp, and this was evident to nearby residents. Horwitz's research shows the extent to which the villagers suddenly found themselves in a reign of terror. The Nazis dealt decisively with the few cases of protest or resistance they encountered. One civilian employee in the stone quarries who protested the mistreatment of the inmates there was fired; after he complained to other townspeople, he was sent to Buchenwald for eight months.[27]

Yet there were few such people who complained or protested, and it soon became clear to local residents that they had nothing to fear if they simply conformed to their new circumstances. The villagers of Mauthausen were not the Nazis' intended victims. All that was required for them to continue their lives was that they remain bystanders.

The process of creating and maintaining the necessary distance to what was taking place in the camp began. In a community that small, the possibility of physical distance was limited. Both Mauthausen and the smaller surrounding camps offered jobs to local people; day laborers and local suppliers from the region were needed to keep the camps going. In addition, a number of townspeople were hired as assistants and secretaries at the nearby euthanasia center at Hartheim.[28]

These people soon learned what was going on in the camp. Indeed, Horwitz's account reveals how visible the suffering of those in the camps was to most of the surrounding population, even those who did not work there. During the first few years of the camp's operation, inmates were frequently tortured, shot, or thrown into the rock quarry. Almost 119,000 died in the Mauthausen area camps (39,000 of them were Jews; the rest were political prisoners and, during the war, Russian prisoners of war).[29] Especially during the final months before the liberation of the camp in May 1945, prisoners were often murdered "within sight of, and often with the active complicity of, wide sections of the civilian population."[30]

Where physical distance to horror is not possible, psychological distance is the next recourse. Soon after the camp opened, the SS posted warnings to townspeople to ignore whatever they saw. The townspeople, "although cognizant of the terror in the camp . . . learned to walk a narrow line between unavoidable awareness and prudent disregard."[31]

That line was indeed narrow when one considers how immediately the citizens of Mauthausen were confronted by the reality of what was happening in the camps. One farmwoman filed a formal complaint in 1941, noting that she often could see shootings from her farm, which overlooked the rock quarries: "I am anyway sickly and such a sight makes such a demand on my nerves that in the long run I cannot bear this. I request that it be arranged that such inhuman deeds be discontinued, or else done where one does not see it."[32]

The stance of local residents, in other words, was to accept the camp as an unpleasant but unchangeable reality. Accordingly, they arranged their lives and psyches—and their ethics—so they did not have to deal with what was going on there.

This was true even among people who actually worked in one of the camps or at Hartheim, where hundreds of the physically and mentally disabled were murdered. Horwitz cites the case of Matthias Buchberger, a local Nazi party member chosen to help renovate Hartheim for the euthanasia program. Once the murders of patients began, Buchberger continued to work at Hartheim as a maintenance man, but refused to work in the crematorium because of his "abhorrence of corpses." He saw "the line separating innocence and complicity . . . at the point of being on hand to view the mass executions. By remaining absent when persons were killed and their corpses disposed of, Buchberger kept his conscience clear."[33]

It was a common pattern among all those who lived in the area. Because these simple countrypeople had not ordered the murders, they felt no personal responsibility for them. This distinction was deliberately upheld by the leaders of the camps and the Hartheim institution. In Hartheim, for example, nurses hired to undress patients for the gas chamber had no further contact with them, and did not witness the gassings. As one nurse recalled, the presiding doctor "took strict care seeing to it that we not come in contact with these things."[34] Murder was compartmentalized into "a series of coordinated, separate, divisible steps implemented by individuals with little personal regard, not to say indifference, for the victims they helped create."[35] This made it easier for those who worked in the camps or at Hartheim to convince themselves that they had nothing to do with what was going on. They—and the residents of the area in general—shared "a common delusion that their individual actions were not instrumental to the entire process."[36]

This delusion, of course, was a retreat, a form of rationalizing away whatever misgivings people may have had. Fear, reinforced by warnings that those who protested would themselves be sent to the Mauthausen

camp, effectively convinced people that nothing could be done. They concluded that any resistance would be "pointless" and "without result"—
phrases that "reinforced passivity. These expressions comprised a framework and guide to mental categories of moral paralysis."[37]

The experience in Hartheim, writes Horwitz, teaches us "that when acting under coercion and fear of personal harm individuals are capable of
doing their jobs with diligence, insuring in no small way that the plans of
their superiors are carried out fully. It also becomes clear that under these
circumstances persons can effectively satisfy their conscience through a conviction that their cooperation has been forced contrary to their personal
will."[38]

In April 1944, another small camp was opened at the nearby village of
Melk; over one-third of its inmates had died by May 1945. Before the
crematorium at Melk was built, their bodies were taken to Mauthausen.
Every day, the inmates of Melk were marched through the town to the
train station; the townspeople maintained "observant passivity."[39] Here,
"as in Mauthausen, the bystander wore blinders, kept a stiff neck, and
peered straight ahead . . . The angle of noninvolvement was forward."[40] In
February 1945, when 495 prisoners (all of them Russian prisoners of war)
managed to escape the camp and tried to hide in the area, only 3 found
refuge with local families. More than 300 of them were recaptured, but
only 57 were captured alive. Local farmers and residents joined the SS in
hunting down and brutally murdering the escapees.

It was now, during the final months of Nazi terror, that the real effects
of the residents' "distance" to the camp became evident. The lines of de-
marcation between town and camp broke down completely. There were
bloodstains on the streets and crude graves beside the roads. Inmates were
beaten or shot before peoples' eyes. One woman recalled that, when she
went shopping, "the edge of the street which I used for walking was sometimes so blocked by persons lying on the ground that I did not know how
I was supposed to get by."[41]

By denying what was taking place in the camp, the people who lived
near Mauthausen had become an extension of it, clearly aligned with the
murderers, not with their victims. "In marching the inmate remnant across
the countryside, in killing indiscriminately, and enacting their work of human destruction in the open, the SS had at last cut the wire that otherwise
neatly separated the world of death from the world of life . . . In the end
the killing was broad and open and mobile."[42]

It was at this stage that the last pretenses of morality or courage dissolved. The townspeople had acquiesced to the laws of barbarism, and
those laws now governed them. The local priest recalled how he and the
townspeople watched the death marches go by: "The others anyway did
not dare say anything. I as a priest stood there and gave them all general
absolution. There was absolutely nothing more anyone could do."[43]

The survivors of Mauthausen later remembered their sense of invisibility. Even when they were forcibly led through the village streets, the townspeople never acknowledged their presence. "Internalizing their invisibility, the inmates came to identify themselves as men without substance or shadow. In their own eyes they had become beings as unreal as their rulers said they were."[44] The villagers' indifference toward the suffering of the inmates left permanent scars on those who survived. But, as Horwitz's account makes clear, it also utterly dehumanized the villagers themselves, who had thought they could escape the consequences of evil by ignoring them.

WHO IS A BYSTANDER?—SOME DEFINITIONS

The residents of Mauthausen and Sonderburg became bystanders to the Holocaust. To some extent, this was an accident of history. Born in Germany and Austria at a certain time, they found themselves in historical and political circumstances over which they had limited control. The sense of "powerlessness" described by the villagers of Sonderburg was shared by many people throughout Europe between 1933 and 1945.

Yet the outcome of this historical accident was that the residents of Sonderburg and Mauthausen behaved in certain ways, held certain convictions, and changed. Chance may have placed them at a particular point in history, but other factors influenced their individual responses. In turn, the behavior of these bystanders shaped the course of history. In seeking to understand their behavior and motives, we must begin by establishing who they were.

Who is a bystander? What combination of outside circumstances and internal tendencies creates a bystander? In most dictionaries, the meaning of the word "bystander" is based upon its linguistic components: literally, to stand by or be present. A standard legal definition of a bystander, for example, is "One who stands near; a chance looker-on; hence one who has no concern with the business being transacted. One present but not taking part, looker-on, spectator, beholder, observer."[45]

This definition distinguishes a "bystander" from someone who is actively involved. The bystander is not the protagonist, the person propelling the action; nor is the bystander the object of the action. In a criminal case, the bystander is neither victim nor perpetrator; his or her legally relevant role is that of witness—someone who happened to be present and could shed light on what actually occurred.

But the implications of words like "witness" and "bystander" are altered by human experience. A witness does not merely see something; a bystander is not just physically present. People are changed by what they see and do, and they are often moved to act. A definitive part of human experience is the way in which we react to outside circumstances: either involuntarily (such as withdrawing one's hand from a hot stove) or deliberately (such as deciding whether or not to respond to a cry for help). It is tempting, as theologian Miroslav Volf writes, to think of the bystanders' world as "neutral territory, suspended above the agonistic world of noninnocence"; that is certainly how bystanders like to think of it! In reality, however, they are "immersed in that same large world inhabited by the parties in conflict. They themselves are perpetrators and victims, often both at the same time, and they project their own struggles, interests, and expectations onto the conflict they either observe or try to resolve."[46]

Throughout human history, religious and philosophical thinkers have wrestled with the deeper significance of how we interact with our world and one another. In both the Judaic and Christian traditions, for example, the word "witness" connotes a more active role. The witness exists and acts within what Helen Fein has called the "universe of obligation," and there are clear consequences when this obligation is denied and when victims are excluded from this universe.

As a result, most of us have certain expectations about bystanders or witnesses to an event. Depending on the circumstances, we usually make assumptions about their behavior. We may try to establish, for example, whether involvement was an option for them; and we may make moral judgments about the consequences of their noninvolvement or passivity.

The term "bystander" not only identifies a person's status with regard to a particular event, but implies a certain form of behavior, including the decision to become involved or remain uninvolved. Most definitions of bystander behavior deal with these two levels of meaning. Samuel and Pearl Oliner, in their study of rescuers and altruism, simply define "bystanders" as people who did nothing to help others or to resist.[47] Psychologist Ervin Staub, who has examined the phenomenon in great depth, defines bystanders as "those members of society who are neither perpetrators nor victims, or outside individuals, organizations, and nations."[48] But, he continues, the "support, opposition, or indifference" of these people "largely shapes the course of events."[49]

In other words, bystanders are confronted by a wide range of behavioral options, and they bear some responsibility for what happens. They may intervene to change the course of events. They may be apathetic, feeling that what is occurring has nothing to do with them. Or their emotions may be in turmoil: they may feel torn with anxiety, caught between a strong desire not to become involved and the sense that they should do something. Other factors may influence their failure or readiness to help: the presence and behavior of people around them; feelings of powerlessness or fear; and a sense of identification with the victim or, conversely, indifference or active prejudice against the victim.[50]

Because so many of these factors are subjective and immeasurable, judgments about bystander behavior vary according to the circumstances. In a U.S. court of law, for example, an uninvolved bystander is usually cleared of criminal liability by definition. In the fields of sociology or psychology, objective judgments about bystander behavior will take into account the various factors (e.g., poverty or a family history of mental illness) that may have influenced that behavior.

All these aspects are only a starting point for any in-depth examination of bystanders—particularly with respect to the Holocaust, which raises more problematic issues. This is because the exclusion of Jews from German society depended upon the passivity of people like the villagers of Sonderburg; the smooth running of death camps throughout Europe would not have been possible without the complicity of villagers like those in Mauthausen.

The genocide of the European Jews would have been impossible without the active participation of bystanders to carry it out and the failure of numerous parties to intervene to stop it. The Holocaust did not occur in a vacuum. There was a general failure—among individuals, institutions, and the international community—to acknowledge and stop the genocide. Moreover, the genocide was preceded by years of intensifying anti-Jewish persecution, which much of Europe's non-Jewish population either witnessed or participated in.

For that reason, whereas we might exonerate bystanders of all responsibility in some situations, the issues are not so straightforward in the Holocaust. As I noted in the introduction, we don't refer to concentration camp guards or leading Nazis as "bystanders"; these were people in positions of power who acted deliberately and knew the consequences of their actions. But it is interesting to note how similar the characteristics of bystander and perpetrator behavior are in much of the literature—and how apologists for both groups tend to offer the same excuses for their behavior. It was typical of both groups, for example, to make an ethical distinction between the public and private realms, or to use subservience to authority as grounds for exonerating individuals of responsibility.

Psychologically and historically, bystanders, perpetrators, and rescuers stood at different points along the same continuum. Some individuals who began as bystanders later became actively involved in the genocide. A minority of people moved in the opposite direction, and became rescuers or members of resistance groups.

As a result, many scholars assume that bystanders and perpetrators not only stood on the same side, but were manifestations of the same phenomenon—that bystanders are simply somewhat more passive perpetrators. Theologian David Gushee, for example, writes that "from a moral point of view there may be no such thing as a bystander. If one is present, one is taking part."[51]

This assumption deserves closer examination if we are to understand the ethical significance of bystander behavior. Was the passivity of ordinary citizens simply a less extreme form of the behavior we find among leading

Nazis and concentration camp guards? Is the culpability of different groups during the Holocaust merely one of degree? Or are there significant differences between the factors that make some people bystanders and those that lead others to active participation?

These are important ethical issues. While many of the bystanders in Nazi Germany and elsewhere would not be found guilty in a court of law, most Holocaust scholars assume that they bear some responsibility for what happened. But how do we define that responsibility? This ethical question influences how we decide who was a bystander historically, and what judgments we make as a result. Any examination of the role of bystanders during the Holocaust must focus on the links between intent, actual behavior, and moral accountability. The usual definitions are insufficient to absolve bystanders of all responsibility in the actual genocide.

A central problem in this link between the historical and the ethical is that we are dealing with what historian Michael Marrus calls "negative history," with what did not happen: "the history of inaction, indifference, and insensitivity."[52] As Marrus observes, this is easier to condemn than to explain. Moreover, the task of identifying bystanders in the Holocaust raises some difficult historical questions in addition to the ethical ones. Any definition of a "bystander" during the Holocaust will produce a long list of people. Ordinary German citizens, church leaders inside and outside of Germany, German civil servants, foreign relief organizations, Allied leaders, and even some members of the international Jewish community have been described as bystanders.[53] The list lengthens even after May 1945, when, as Elie Wiesel has noted, thousands of concentration camp survivors remained in displaced persons' camps because no country would take them in.[54]

The obvious danger is that this renders the term "bystander" meaningless, ethically and historically. If practically everyone was a bystander, then how do we speak meaningfully about the specific responsibilities of certain individuals and institutions? If we contend that the bystanders were essentially perpetrators, then how do we define "perpetrator"? Can we really use the word "bystander" to describe such diverse groups as the American Jewish community, residents of areas that bordered concentration camps, and international aid officials? Objecting to a "universalistic" portrayal of the victims of the Holocaust, the novelist Cynthia Ozick once wrote, "Blurring eases. Specificity pains. We have no right to seek a message of ease in Auschwitz, and it is moral ease to slide from the particular to the abstract."[55] Her admonition could also apply to the danger of universalizing the identity and accountability of bystanders. There were indeed many of them, from all walks of life. Precisely for that reason, it is important to make some distinctions if we are to understand the various factors that moved them.

The most obvious distinction that can be made about "bystander behavior" concerns the different levels on which bystanders became involved in the Holocaust or were affected by it. In looking at the behavior of perpetrators, psychologist Ervin Staub differentiates among three levels of involvement: the individual, the institutional, and the international. This continuum of involvement—which essentially describes the levels of all human behavior—can be applied to bystanders as well. Each of these levels offers insight into a particular aspect of bystander behavior during the Holocaust. Some ethical issues arise specifically at each level; other ethical questions arise from the conflicting or interacting demands of different levels. An analysis of the continuum of involvement—from individual to institutional to international—is the first step in examining the dynamics of complicity in the Holocaust.

NOTES

1. Elie Wiesel, *The Town Beyond the Wall* (New York: Avon Books, 1969), 161.
2. Henry, *Victims and Neighbors*, 38.
3. Ibid., 154.
4. Ibid., 150. Around 10 percent of German Jews either converted or left Judaism to become completely secularized. "As late as 1933, 44 percent of all Jews who married chose partners of a different religion." The children of such marriages were usually not raised as Jews (from Sarah Gordon, *German Opposition to Nazi Anti-Semitic Measures between 1933 and 1945 with Particular Reference to the Rhine-Ruhr Area*, dissertation, SUNY, 23).
5. Henry, *Victims and Neighbors*, 158.
6. Ibid., 159.
7. Ibid., 95.
8. This was the case throughout Germany. Hans-Bernd Gisevius, a 1933 Gestapo officer who later joined the German resistance and became the main German informant of U.S. intelligence officer Allen Dulles, described the "individual *Gleichschaltung*" prevalent in 1933: people "understood that they could no longer hang back" (cited in Gellately, *The Gestapo and German Society*, 11).
9. Henry, *Victims and Neighbors*, 62.
10. Ibid., 100.
11. Ibid., 93.
12. Ibid., 82.
13. Ibid., 98.
14. Ibid., 10.
15. Ibid., 84.
16. Ibid., 101–102.
17. Henry relates one particularly haunting example of a Jewish woman who did consider resettling in Sonderburg and made several visits to the town. On her last visit, something happened—Henry was unable to discover what—that made clear that she was not really welcome; the woman committed suicide (*Victims and Neighbors*, 125).

18. Ibid., 137–138.

19. Ibid., 136.

20. Ibid., 175.

21. Other works that describe similar findings include Allen, *The Nazi Seizure of Power*; Broszat, ed., *Bayern in der NS-Zeit*; Koshar, *Social Life, Local Politics, and Nazism*; Hecht, *Invisible Walls*; and Marion Kaplan, *Between Dignity and Despair: Jewish Life in Nazi Germany* (New York: Oxford University Press, 1998).

22. In Henry, *Victims and Neighbors*, vii.

23. Horwitz, *In the Shadow of Death: Living Outside the Gates of Mauthausen*, 1992.

24. Ibid., 28.

25. Ibid., 32.

26. Ibid., 52.

27. Ibid., 39.

28. Ibid., 55.

29. Ibid., 22.

30. Ibid., 21.

31. Ibid., 35.

32. Ibid., 35.

33. Ibid., 70–71.

34. Ibid., 76.

35. Ibid., 82.

36. Ibid., 81.

37. Ibid., 80.

38. Ibid., 80.

39. Ibid., 112.

40. Ibid., 92.

41. Ibid., 146.

42. Ibid., 162–163.

43. Ibid., 151.

44. Ibid., 89.

45. *Black's Law Dictionary* (St. Paul, MN: West Publishing Co, 1990), 201.

46. Volf, *Exclusion and Embrace*, 83.

47. Oliner and Oliner, *The Altruistic Personality*, 4.

48. Staub, *The Roots of Evil*, 20.

49. Ibid.

50. Ibid.

51. Gushee, *The Righteous Gentiles of the Holocaust*, 62.

52. Marrus, *The Holocaust in History*, 157.

53. See, for example, Raul Hilberg's comprehensive list in *Perpetrators, Victims, Bystanders: The Jewish Catastrophe 1933–1945*. As Michael Marrus notes, "murder on such a colossal scale involved the entire organized society to one degree or another and depended on a measure of support everywhere" (Marrus, *The Holocaust in History*, 83).

54. Wiesel, "Freedom of Conscience: A Jewish Commentary," 643.

55. In Rosenfeld, *A Double Dying*, 198.

CHAPTER 2

Individual Behavior

It might seem that any discussion of bystanders could be confined to the level of individual behavior. Ultimately, it is individuals, not institutions or nations, who make moral decisions and act upon them. One of the principles established by the 1946 Nuremberg trials of Nazi war criminals (and in subsequent war crimes trials as well) was that individuals can be held accountable for their actions, even when these are carried out under the orders of an institution or national government.

In looking at the broad canvas of the Holocaust, however, it is difficult to focus solely on individual responsibility. The diversity of individual situations makes it difficult to draw general conclusions about individual behavior and its underlying motivations. The situation of a Polish farmer who lived five miles from Auschwitz, for example, differed from that of a Swiss relief official in Geneva, a Protestant minister in Berlin, or a civil servant in France. Yet each of these people could have faced an identical situation: that of being approached by a Jew in desperate search of refuge. In other words, people from different backgrounds, operating in very different circumstances (or acting on behalf of an institution or foreign country), often confronted similar choices that demanded an immediate individual response.

A more significant problem is that the very nature, scale and duration of the Nazi crimes raise troubling questions about the interplay between individual and group behavior. When we hold individuals accountable for their actions, we are affirming that the roots of human morality—even on the collective level—are ultimately based upon the freedom of each individual to decide for good or evil.

But, even if we recognize the link between the free choices of the individual and the values enforced in the public sphere, it is often difficult to identify where one realm begins and the other ends. To some degree, even individual values and notions of morality are the product of socialization. Traditional sociological interpretations stress that the development of morality is a social construct.[1] "Moral behavior," writes sociologist Zygmunt Bauman, "is conceivable only in the context of coexistence, of 'being with others,' that is, a social context."[2] Values supported by collective society create certain expectations about individual behavior. In any society, writes Ervin Staub, "people have not only individual but also collective self-concepts. Their 'societal' self-concept includes shared evaluation of their group, myths that transmit the self-concept and ideal self, goals that a people set for themselves, and shared beliefs (e.g., about other groups)."[3]

Existing studies of Nazi Germany illustrate how powerfully Nazi ideology, with its emphasis on an ethnically defined national identity, influenced the behavior of individual Germans. This ideological context makes it easier to see how the subordination of private convictions to the collective will of the *Volk* led to passivity and complicity among individuals. Outside Nazi Germany, the pressures of Nazi occupation, the anti-Semitism of the population, and the cautious priorities of international organizations were also factors that shaped the behavior of individuals.

Thus, individual behavior during the Holocaust may reflect a number of factors: the significance of the action itself and its immediate consequences; the numerous personal factors that may have been involved; and the extent to which this behavior was affected by institutional or international connections. Many scholars attribute the complicity of individuals primarily to the social, cultural, and political influences on individual behavior. These scholars emphasize the ways in which social and cultural factors, such as nationalism and anti-Semitism, encouraged individuals to follow orders blindly or to subjugate traditional ethical constraints (e.g., against murder) to the ideological dictates of Nazism. Because individual behavior in Nazi Germany was characterized by the transfer of responsibility from the individual to the collective, it is important to understand how totalitarian systems and large bureaucracies "relieve" individuals of responsibility for their actions.

An example of this in Horwitz's study of Mauthausen was the Hartheim nurse, whose only job was to help victims undress. Since she was not otherwise involved in the killings of patients, she did not consider herself responsible for the actual deaths. Nazi Germany offers numerous such examples. The compartmentalization of mass murder, in which many of those directly involved either never saw their victims or did not directly witness their murders, is certainly a contributing factor to the passivity of some individuals.

Zygmunt Bauman's *Modernity and the Holocaust* emphasizes this aspect of the Holocaust. Bauman sees strong parallels between the passivity and apathy of Germans under Hitler and the qualities frequently observed in modern industrialized societies. He cites the growth of urban areas and the corresponding disintegration of small intact communities, the pace and mobility of modern life, its dependence upon technology, and the development of "mass society" as factors that have eradicated the social fabric necessary for a traditional sense of individual ethical responsibility to survive. These developments make individuals less capable of withstanding a totalitarian ideology like Nazism—not only in Germany, but throughout the modern world. "We live in a type of society that made the Holocaust possible," Bauman writes, "and that contained nothing which could stop the Holocaust from happening."[4]

Still, many aspects of bystander behavior during the Holocaust cannot be explained solely as the outcome of modernity or 20th-century industrial society. A closer examination of what happened under Nazism reveals the disturbing degree to which people in intact, smaller communities became passive bystanders or even active murderers. The villagers of Mauthausen, for example, were not officials of a large impersonal bureaucracy, yet their behavior mirrors the phenomenon described by Bauman. Indeed, many of the regions surrounding the large death camps could be described as pre-industrial. Socially and economically, life in those areas during the 1930s and 1940s was much as it had been for centuries.

Thus, other scholars who study the Holocaust, while acknowledging societal influences on individual behavior, stress the role of individual responsibility, morality, and prejudice. The case studies cited above, by Frances Henry and Gordon Horwitz, fall into this category. Many studies of the altruistic behavior of rescuers or resisters fall into this category as well, since such behavior was predominantly individual, not collective, behavior. Other studies, notably Daniel Goldhagen's book *Hitler's Willing Executioners* (1996), emphasize the dual effects of individual and collective anti-Semitism.

Under normal circumstances, of course, viewing morality as a social construct does not deny the ethical independence of individuals. Most studies of the Holocaust recognize that the behavior of bystanders, like that of perpetrators, is ultimately the behavior of individuals. It is in extreme situations like Nazi Germany that individuals may appear to be cogs in a machine, lacking all free choice. Because this aspect is one of the striking characteristics of modern totalitarianism, it is all the more important to examine the influences that help shape individual notions of responsibility, even when we are looking at what appears to be collective behavior.

Ervin Staub lists four primary kinds of motivation for human behavior: personal goals; biological needs; social customs, rules, and standards; and unconscious motivation.[5] These categories include more specifically individual factors like personality and family or religious influences. The key to understanding what happened in Nazi Germany is seeing how these personal factors were shaped by greater social, political, and historical forces.

The rise of Nazism in Germany is a classic example of the interplay between the microcosm of the individual realm and the macrocosm of a political movement. An examination of the turbulent years between Germany's defeat in 1918 and the beginning of the Nazi regime in 1933 offers many insights into why German citizens, torn by economic and political insecurity, welcomed a strong Führer.

But the Germans did not embrace Nazism just as a political solution to economic chaos. Part of Nazism's widespread appeal was its use of traditions that had deep roots in German history and culture—such as militarism and nationalism—and its support for traditional teachings about the family and the role of women.[6]

By invoking such traditional values, Nazism created the foundation for a totalitarian ideology that exerted powerful pressure upon individual citizens. Two central concepts of this ideology were the *Führerprinzip* (the principle that the Führer was the ultimate authority of German life) and *Gleichschaltung*—the synchronization of every level of German society, similar to the way in which different parts of a machine are connected to a central circuit.

Skillful propaganda portrayed both these concepts as the political embodiment of traditional values. At the same time, the enactment of these political principles erased a sense of individual responsibility. Every form of power rested in the state and its offices, and this was described as the "collective will" of the German *Volk*. The Nazis dealt brutally and decisively with the early political opposition to these principles that did emerge from individual dissidents, the German labor unions, the Social Democrats, and Communists.

As a result, many Germans retreated into a world of their own and felt profoundly powerless on a social or political level. It was typical of individual Germans to deny having any real power over their fate and, therefore, to deny any degree of personal responsibility, even for their own actions—as Frances Henry discovered among the citizens of Sonderburg, who spoke of their "powerlessness" during the Third Reich.

This "powerlessness," however, is a complex phenomenon. As we will see in subsequent chapters, it was a widespread characteristic of many bystanders in the Holocaust—not just in Germany, but elsewhere. To what extent did "powerlessness" actually reflect the realities of the situation; to what degree did it mask implicit approval for what was happening, or serve as a rationalization for passivity? Many studies suggest that, far from being imposed by the Nazi regime, "powerlessness" was actually embraced by many German citizens. They were eager to abandon individual uncertainty for the sake of a collective identity. The quickness with which the citizens of Sonderburg voluntarily conformed to their new situation (and in this they were typical) suggests that a new, Nazified identity was hardly forced upon them.

Still, the issue of "powerlessness" cannot be discussed without some analysis of the role of free will, or individual moral decision, in the Nazi context—particularly over a period of time. It will become clear that, just as bystanders moved along a spectrum of behavior during the Nazi era, their political and social circumstances changed with time as well. Finally, the question of "powerlessness" also raises psychological and ethical questions: To what extent did individuals recognize that what was being done was evil; to what extent did they "redefine" their ethical systems in order to view the persecution of Jews as a "good"?

These questions will be examined more deeply in subsequent chapters, but they are central to any analysis of the behavior of individual bystanders. They show how "powerlessness" can either represent actual reality or serve as an escape from responsibility. As the phenomena of rescue and resistance remind us, other options did exist. Any analysis of the factors that created "powerlessness" among bystanders must be balanced by the insights we glean from the behavior of those who supported Nazism and those who resisted it.

The resisters (whose stories we will examine in the final section of this book) illustrate that it was possible for individuals to be more than cogs in a machine, even in Nazi Germany. They show that, beneath the surface of apparently universal complicity, the potential for individual freedom of thought and action remained. Although it is clear that groups exercise power over their individual members, the assumption that individual behavior merely reflects the larger values of a society evades the question of what constitutes *moral* behavior. Even in a dictatorship, we can find instances of independent thought and action. Likewise, "collective will" is never completely imposed from above; it is created and reinforced by the complicity and passivity of individual citizens. A fundamental precept that emerged from the Nuremberg trials was that human morality is not solely the creation of social constructs and norms. As Zygmunt Bauman said, there is a "moral responsibility for resisting socialization."[7] When the Nazis claimed, for example, that the killing of Jews was necessary for the cultural rehabilitation of Germany, they—and other Germans—should and could have known that this was evil. Social and political factors may shape individual behavior, but ultimately it is the individual who decides what is moral, and acts accordingly.

In the second section of this book, we will examine some of the historical and ethical factors that influenced individual behavior during the Holocaust. First, however, we must confront the issue of what the Holocaust tells us about innate human behavior. Its disturbing message is not only that human beings are capable of such terrible things; the Holocaust raises the question as to whether the potential for such evil exists in all of us.

POST-HOLOCAUST STUDIES OF HUMAN BEHAVIOR

Ethically, historically, and psychologically, the death camps mark a break in human history. Atrocities in wartime are nothing new; history is also replete with examples of dictatorship, brutality, and torture. Yet what happened under Nazism does not really fit any of these patterns. The persecution of the Jews was not the effect of war or territorial disputes. It began in peacetime; its first victims were German citizens who had previously felt secure in that society. It was utterly unnecessary and self-defeating. The exclusion of the Jewish citizens of Germany robbed that society of some of its most brilliant and loyal citizens, and Nazi Germany's rampage throughout Europe ultimately destroyed the German nation itself.

The most fundamental question, however, is what the Holocaust tells us about human behavior and the forces that shape it. Was the horrifying cruelty and apathy toward others' suffering during the Holocaust the product of a unique convergence of historical and political circumstances? Or does the Holocaust tell us something about the innate tendencies of human beings, with respect to both the evil of perpetrators and the passivity of bystanders?

Some of the first scholars to confront these questions were psychologists. Two early works were by Theodor Adorno and his colleagues (*The Authoritarian Personality*, 1950) and Viktor Frankl (*Man's Search for Meaning*, 1959). Adorno had fled Nazi Germany during the 1930s and Frankl had survived the concentration camps; thus, both works were shaped by professional insight and personal experiences. The authors of the essays in Adorno's book focused on the psychological traits of individuals, analyzing factors (such as prejudice and an authoritarian upbringing) that may have predisposed Nazi perpetrators and others to become "fascistic individuals." Frankl's book, which lay the groundwork for his theory of logotherapy, attempted to grasp the deeper meaning of the experience under Nazism, particularly for its victims. Another survivor, psychologist Bruno Bettelheim, also began to focus on the powerful hold that Nazi totalitarianism had over human behavior and personality—of victims and perpetrators alike.[8] Two other books from the same era, *The Nature of Prejudice* (1954), by American psychologist Gordon Allport, and *Dynamics of Prejudice*, by Bettelheim and Morris Janowitz (1950), dissected the sociological, religious, psychological, and individual factors that foster prejudice in individuals and societies.

To a degree that may strike us as odd today, these works are nonhistorical; the psychological dynamics they analyze appear universal. The Holocaust is portrayed as one example of the human struggle between good and evil; but it appears to be a struggle that could have happened anywhere, at any time. These early analyses explored the determinants of human behavior, not on the basis of the historical details of the Holocaust, but according to the principles of human psychology. Frankl's work, for example, was driven by his passionate conviction that "if there is a meaning in life at all, then there must be a meaning in suffering."[9] He concluded that all individuals—even victims—had a choice as to whether they would be controlled by circumstance. People who rose above their circumstances were those with an "inner hold on their moral and spiritual selves."[10] Free will—not history, politics, or social pressure—was the force that determined behavior and its consequences.

This nonhistorical emphasis indicated the professional leanings of a psychologist, but it also reflected the era in which these books were written. A detailed history of the Holocaust had not yet emerged. The death camps and the persecution of the Jews were widely seen as only one aspect of the historical period of Nazism and World War II. While many scholars today view the Holocaust as the definitive event of that era, this was not the case in the 1950s and 1960s. In those early decades, most scholars who studied the Holocaust at all viewed it as an aberration of human behavior within a larger historical context.

For a number of reasons, this focus shifted in the following decades. Survivors of the camps like Elie Wiesel, Charlotte Delbo, Paul Celan, and Tadeusz Borowski began to write and reflect on their experiences. It took even longer for the historical details about the records of different nations and institutions to come to light—a process that continues to the present day.

An important turning point was the trial of Nazi henchman Adolf Eichmann and the publication of Hannah Arendt's account of the trial, *Eichmann in Jerusalem*. The testimony at the Eichmann trial confronted many people with the historical details of the genocide of the Jews for the first time. The trial itself revealed inevitable conflicts between the psychological interpretations that had been more common during the 1950s and the historical realities of what had actually happened. The details that emerged from the Eichmann trial made the earlier books on human psychology under Nazism seem almost naïve. By challenging traditional understandings about good and evil, history, human culture, and civilization, the terrible details of the Nazi genocide also undermined the capability of scholars to understand this experience in traditional terms. Viktor Frankl, for example, had written:

Even in the concentration camps, man *can* preserve a vestige of spiritual freedom, of independence of mind, even in such terrible conditions of psychic and physical stress . . . Every day . . . offered the opportunity to make a decision . . . which determined whether or not you would become the plaything of circumstance, renouncing freedom and dignity to become molded into the form of the typical inmate.[11]

Frankl, we must recall, wrote from his firsthand experience as a survivor of the camps. Yet, while his words reflected the reality he experienced, the kinds of details that emerged during the Eichmann trial (as well as subsequent recollections from other survivors) offered a different perspective. For many victims, "a vestige of spiritual freedom" had been impossible. Sick, starving, and exhausted, they had endured, not triumphed; and the notion that they had possessed any control over their fates seemed a bitter illusion. Lawrence Langer wrote that Frankl's book "provides millions of readers with a solace that blurs the true painful nature of the death camp ordeal."[12] In a similar fashion, Zygmunt Bauman later criticized Theodor Adorno for focusing almost exclusively on individual personality as a determinant of behavior, ignoring the social and political forces.[13]

In *Eichmann in Jerusalem*, Arendt recognized this caesura, the break between the past and the present, between what could be understood using traditional philosophical and psychological tools and what demanded new paradigms. But she interpreted this break primarily in political terms, viewing the "ordinary" individual, Adolf Eichmann, against a much greater historical and political background. In contrast, Frankl and others believed that the confrontation with evil demanded an existential decision from the individual, who had to draw upon inner resources to withstand it.

Yet the evil Arendt observed in the Jerusalem courtroom seemed utterly different from that described by Frankl. In her words, it was a matter "of small legal relevance" but "of great political interest to know how long it takes an average person to overcome his innate repugnance toward crime, and what exactly happens to him once he has reached that point."[14] Looking at Eichmann, Arendt asked: What happens to human beings in this situation? What makes them capable of acting in such ways? Her shocking conclusion was that, on a very existential level, nothing had happened to him at all. Eichmann—and, by extension, others like him—had remained "ordinary," an example of "the banality of evil." He was not a monster; like the vast majority of Germans, he had simply conformed to his political circumstances. The judges in Jerusalem, Arendt decided,

missed the greatest moral and even legal challenge of the whole case. Their case rested on the assumption that the defendant, like all "normal persons," must have been aware of the criminal nature of his acts, and Eichmann was indeed normal insofar as he was "no exception within the Nazi regime." However, under the conditions of the Third Reich only "exceptions" could be expected to react "normally." This simple truth of the matter created a dilemma for the judges which they could neither resolve nor escape.[15]

The Eichmann trial acquainted a wide audience with the horrific details of the Holocaust for the first time. These details revealed the close connection between individuals like Eichmann and what had happened historically. The "ordinariness" and "banality" of people's daily lives under Nazism could not be separated from the terrors of the Holocaust. The routines described in the Eichmann trial introduced the world to the phenomenon of mass murder carried out not in passion or in the heat of battle, but with cool bureaucratic exactitude. The most chilling aspect of Eichmann's defense was the contention that his activities were incidental and thereby, on some level, unintentional. He was simply doing his job, his lawyer argued; had his superiors ordered him to oversee the manufacture of windows for hospitals, he would have done that.

Because it implied that what had happened under Nazism was neither unique nor unrepeatable, Arendt's phrase "the banality of evil" provoked controversy; to many survivors, it even seemed to minimize the crime. Arendt may have been one of the first to note that the Holocaust was carried out by "ordinary people," a phrase that has now become standard in much of the literature. The phrase "ordinary people," however, signifies a number of things. In much of the historical literature (e.g., Christopher Browning's *Ordinary Men*), it simply establishes that the genocide was carried out by people who were not ideological fanatics or party activists, but ordinary citizens. Despite their differences on other points, most scholars agree that the Nazi perpetrators were "normal by conventional standards of mental health."[16] The same holds true for bystanders as well. Whatever the psychological mechanisms that emerge under totalitarianism (which will be discussed in a subsequent chapter), they did not render most people incapable of functioning or of making decisions.

The widespread complicity of "ordinary people" in the genocide suggests that what we see in Holocaust is not an anomaly, and that the potential for such evil exists in us all. And it raises a deeper question about the *nature* of individual responsibility within a totalitarian system, which was actually the focus of Arendt's book. Arendt was not questioning Eichmann's individual responsibility for his actions. The nature of Eichmann's role was what made him "banal." As George Kateb observes, Arendt saw him as an "agent" of political power, not the "actor"[17]; his crimes were the product of "thoughtlessness rather than an intoxicated sadism."[18] Arendt's thesis was that the Nazi leaders "were unique in what they caused to be done, not in what they were."[19]

Eichmann, of course, was not a bystander in any sense of the word. But it is striking to note that his defense, like that in several war crimes trials, was based on portraying him as a kind of bystander. This was what Arendt observed and reflected on. The debate about her conclusions underscored issues that continue to be crucial in any analysis of bystanders today. The fundamental issue at stake was not just the principle of individual respon-

sibility, but its very nature. What is the nature of individual responsibility—
and of evil—in a totalitarian system?

This was the point on which Arendt's critics focused when they charged
that her conclusions served to exonerate individuals like Eichmann. Gideon
Hausner, who led the state prosecution in the Eichmann trial, passionately
disagreed with Arendt's analysis.[20] The trial, he stated, had established that
Eichmann the man was every bit as evil as his deeds. Some of Arendt's
most vehement critics were those who had suffered directly under Nazi
brutality. They believed that Arendt had the luxury of exile (she had left
Nazi Germany in 1933). Because she had not suffered the brutality of the
Nazis firsthand, they contended, she was able to perceive "ordinariness" in
these people. But—as Jean Améry wrote in a haunting account of his own
torture by the Gestapo—the experience of the victims was radically different. They had witnessed firsthand how

the plain, ordinary faces finally become Gestapo faces after all, and how evil over-
lays and exceeds banality. For there is no "banality of evil," and Hannah Arendt,
who wrote about it in her Eichmann book, knew the enemy of mankind only from
hearsay, saw him only through the glass cage. When an event places the most
extreme demands on us, one ought not to speak of banality.[21]

By the early 1960s, then, there were already differences between those
who saw the Holocaust as the product of radical human evil and others
who viewed it as a symbol of profound moral impotence. The early insights
of people like Frankl and Adorno had reflected a worldview that still emphasized the power of free will in individual decisions between good and
evil. That worldview was beginning to shatter. A central aspect of the Holocaust was that individual free will had seemed to count for so little under
Nazism—among victims, bystanders, or perpetrators. The experience of
most victims was that they had been so stripped of their humanity, so
brutalized and degraded, that any "vestige of spiritual freedom" was impossible. And, in varying degrees, the behavior of bystanders and perpetrators suggested that behavior was not so much governed by ethical ideals
of decency or good as by the powerful sway of mass society and state
authority. The human experience under Nazism raised profound questions
about free will and human nature itself.

The research of Yale sociologist Stanley Milgram substantiated this new
terrifying view of human nature. For three years in the early 1960s, Milgram conducted a series of experiments, involving over 1,000 participants,
designed to study obedience to authority. Milgram disguised the real purpose of his study by telling subjects that they were participating in a study
about "memory and learning." Each individual subject was instructed to
"teach" a "learner" (actually an accomplice). The teacher was to read a

list of word pairs and then repeat only the first word of each pair; the learner had to complete the word pair by recalling the correct association and pressing a button to signal the response to the teacher. The teacher was told to respond to incorrect answers by giving the learner an electric shock. With each consecutive incorrect response, the teacher was to increase the intensity of the shock.

Teachers were seated facing a "shock generator" with a row of thirty levers, ranging in 15-volt increments from 15 to 450 volts. Certain voltage levels were labeled, signaling "slight shock," "extreme intensity," "danger: severe shock," and, above the 450-voltage lever, "XXX." The teacher was given a slight shock at the beginning of the experiment to prove that the shock generator was genuine. Also present was an authority figure, played by an experimenter dressed in a white lab coat. Using a standard series of four commands, the authority figure's role was to urge hesitant teachers to continue the experiment. These commands increased the pressure on the teachers. The initial command was "Please continue" or "Please go on." The final command was "You have no other choice, you must go on."

The entire scenario, however, was staged: the shock generator was not real, the "learner" was an accomplice, and the sound effects that accompanied learners' reactions to the electric shocks they received (gasps, cries of pain, mention of a heart problem) were tape recorded.

The results of Milgram's initial experiment were startling: 65 percent of the subjects followed the orders to continue applying shocks to the learners, all the way to 450 volts. They continued despite cries of pain or pleading from learners. More significantly, they continued despite their evident anguish at what they were doing. Milgram described the behavior of one participant:

I observed a mature and initially poised businessman enter the laboratory smiling and confident. Within 20 minutes he was reduced to a twitching, stuttering wreck, who was rapidly approaching a point of nervous collapse. He constantly pulled on his earlobe, and twisted his hands. At one point he pushed his fist into his forehead and muttered: "Oh God, let's stop it." And yet he continued to respond to every word of the experimenter, and obeyed to the end.[22]

Milgram's findings led him to conclude that "obedience to authority" was a powerful motive in human behavior, one so powerful that it could overcome moral misgivings. In later variations of his experiment, he studied the degree to which this obedience could be influenced by situational factors. In one variation, for example, the teachers were placed in a room with several experimenters who disagreed openly about continuing the experiment. In another, there were four teachers (three of whom were accomplices). At various points, the three accomplices refused to continue the experiment; this led to a significant drop in the obedience shown by the fourth teacher (the actual subject). In several other variations, the learner who was receiving the shocks was placed in varying degrees of proximity to the teacher administering the shocks—in an adjoining room, in the same room, and in one variation, the teacher had to physically place the learner's hand on a shock plate. With each increase in physical proximity, rates of obedience decreased.

The outcome of the various experiments clearly indicated the crucial role of authority. The variations that resulted in the smallest degrees of obedience were those where the experiment had been constructed to undermine the authority of the experimenter: e.g., in the variation in which several "experimenters" argued about whether to continue or not.

In 1973, Philip Zimbardo's Stanford prison experiment generated attention (and controversy) similar to the response to the Milgram experiments. Zimbardo took a group of male college-aged volunteers and randomly divided them into "guards" and "prisoners" in a simulated prison situation. The prisoners were held in a mock prison in the basement of the Stanford psychology building. Both groups were given the list of rules for prisoners—times when they could eat, move about, and so forth. The guards were given almost absolute power over what prisoners could do.

In the Stanford experiment, there was no central authority figure in a white lab coat; after being assigned their respective roles, the volunteers were placed in the simulated prison and then observed. Zimbardo hoped to determine whether the behavior of prisoners and guards in real prisons was based more upon their situation or upon their personality traits. The subjects at Stanford had been given personality tests before the experiment to eliminate any participants with obvious personality disturbances.

The patterns of behavior that developed arose spontaneously and quickly, the apparent product of the situation in which they found themselves. The guards became progressively brutal. After initially rebelling, the prisoners became increasingly passive; several even began to act emotionally disturbed. Zimbardo's findings were so surprising—and potentially harmful to the individuals in his experiment—that the experiment, which had been scheduled to run for two weeks, was halted after six days.

Zimbardo's disturbing finding was that his "ordinary" subjects, given absolute power over others, abused it. The Stanford experiment seemed to uncover that the "sleeper" potential for sadism (studied in J. M. Steiner's work on the *Waffen-SS*) can exist in anyone.[23] The clear implication was that these tendencies exist in all of us and can be "awakened" in certain circumstances—particularly when we are members of a group that has strong power over another group.

Combined with Milgram's findings, some disturbing insights emerge. Milgram was looking at obedience, not cruelty (although it could be argued that this plays a subliminal role in his experiments). In fact, one of his findings—the "inverse ratio of readiness to cruelty and proximity to its victim"—seemed to contradict Zimbardo's findings.[24] Both experiments, however, illustrated the power of outside influences over individual behavior and "morality." A designated role, the presence of an authority figure, and the behavior of others all proved to be powerful influences on individual behavior.

The findings of Milgram and Zimbardo challenged many of the assumptions that had shaped Adorno's and Frankl's work. Adorno and Frankl believed that factors like upbringing, emotional health, or a personal commitment to spiritual ideals enabled individuals to transcend the evil reality around them. Milgram's and Zimbardo's work suggested that such factors were irrelevant. The behavior of the subjects in both experiments was not linked to their personalities, but to the situations in which they were placed. Like Zimbardo, Milgram found little correlation between cruelty and personal traits, but a strong connection between cruelty and "a relationship of authority and subordination."[25] He concluded that "inhumanity is a matter of social relationships."[26]

These findings offered some new and unsettling insights into why people behaved as they did during the Holocaust. Was the horrible sadism of SS guards and the deep passivity of bystanders simply the product of their power over those who had been designated as outsiders and victims? And, if their behavior was based upon their designated role in society, can we conclude that anyone is capable of responding this way?

Milgram's and Zimbardo's findings also highlighted aspects of human behavior we find in the Holocaust that confounded traditional theories about human behavior. One was the troubling insight that many individuals, especially perpetrators, seemed to be leading two lives. In one part, they were kind fathers, decent husbands, and model citizens; in the other, they were mass murderers. Milgram posited that the individuals in his experiments developed a "substitute conscience," by which they adopted a different persona to deal with the situation.[27] This concept is similar to the "doubling" theory devised by Robert Jay Lifton in his study of the Nazi doctors. Lifton's book described how these doctors put hundreds of patients to death and conducted cruel experiments, although they continued to lead exemplary private lives. His explanation was that they did so by "doubling"—by compartmentalizing their private and public lives.

Like Arendt's "banality of evil," Lifton's theory of doubling has been criticized. Ervin Staub notes that it "suggests that the killers acted independently of or contrary to their ordinary selves. But SS doctors sent to Auschwitz were not innocent, uninvolved persons . . . They were ideologically committed Nazis who had undergone substantial resocialization."[28]

The critique is similar to the attacks on Arendt's interpretation, and it focuses on the same issues of intentionality and accountability. Whatever its origins, Staub contends, at some point such behavior became intentional. While doubling may have enabled perpetrators to function, most of them finally conformed their motives and beliefs to fit their role.[29]

Staub describes the moral effects of this process as one of "equilibration." Confronted by a discrepancy between motives and values, he says, individuals tend to "shift to a different moral value or principle": "the moral principles that prohibit killing or harming other human beings are replaced by the principles of 'social good,' defined as protection of the German nation from internal subversion and genetic contamination by Jews."[30] People can still feel moral conflict; Staub notes that some Nazis felt revulsion when they witnessed killings directly. But by then, their commitment to the larger "moral principles" espoused by Nazism "made a renewal of moral conflict or change in its modes of resolution unlikely."[31]

Staub and Lifton, of course, were referring to active perpetrators, but some of their insights may help us understand the behavior of bystanders. Whether we agree with Lifton that a psychological break occurred, or with Staub's thesis of a shift in moral values that conforms to the dominant ideology, the patterns of behavior, influences and psychological processes that emerge among bystanders and perpetrators are similar. Staub suspects that individual traits ultimately determined the difference between a bystander or perpetrator: "Perpetrators probably differed from bystanders in personality and initial values."[32] Or, of course, the lack of more active involvement among bystanders may have simply reflected coincidence or the lack of opportunity. For all too many people, history defined their options. Still, it is easy to see how either "moral equilibration" or "doubling" may have occurred among bystanders as well as perpetrators. Both mechanisms may be parts of the process by which bystanders move along the spectrum toward active involvement in the genocide.

Thus, to understand the perpetrators as "ordinary people" is to view them as individuals who did not start out as convinced fanatics or disturbed, potentially violent people, but as bystanders. This understanding is connected to Arendt's "banality of evil." Even at the height of the genocide, perpetrators perceived most aspects of their lives as "normal" (even if this "normalcy" had been redefined). Even the worst among them used the mechanism of "normalcy" to foster the illusion that they were bystanders, not perpetrators. This illusion was a form of denial—a very widespread characteristic of human behavior, on all levels, both during and after the Holocaust. And yet it was effective precisely because it was so widespread. The illusion of "normalcy" was crucial to ensuring that bystanders not question their own passivity.

The issue among perpetrators, of course, was not passivity, but active complicity, or approval, of what was going on. As Lawrence Langer has written, "The widespread absence of remorse among the accused in postwar trials indicates that we may need to discard familiar categories like doubling and to accept the possibility of a regimen of behavior that simply dismisses conscience as an operative moral factor."[33]

It is indeed threatening, as Langer notes, to imagine that both the power to kill and actually killing might be both "personally fulfilling" to some people and "not necessarily a pathological condition, but an expression of impulses as native to our selves as love and compassion."[34]

Denial, moral equilibration, and doubling are all mechanisms by which individuals conformed to Nazi society. As we will see in the next chapter, these mechanisms characterized the response of institutions and the international community as well. Still, there is a difference between confronting a situation directly and reading about it in the newspaper, between having it occur in my neighborhood or thousands of miles away. Physical distance determines the options for intervention, and creates an emotional buffer that offers psychological distance from the consequences of our actions.

Whether they witness something personally or from a distance, however, it is clear that individuals employ certain mechanisms that make their complicity "acceptable." According to Ervin Staub, some of the major mechanisms are (1) *just world thinking*, in which bystanders justify the exclusion of victims through the conviction that the inherent order of things (and thereby the exclusion of victims) is just; (2) *self-distancing* (developing a distance to the situation, the victims, and thereby to the consequences of their actions or passivity); and, finally, (3) *resocialization*: the process by which individuals and institutions are reshaped by the social circumstances around them, so that their attitudes, both toward the victims and toward their own behavior, are altered.[35]

These are all mechanisms by which bystanders (and perpetrators) adjust to their situation and come to accept it. Still, there are traits that enable individuals to withstand these socializing forces—even leading some people to resist the course followed by their fellow citizens and their leaders. In their research on rescuers, Samuel and Pearl Oliner found that the most consistent characteristic was a firm commitment to certain ethical principles:

While other feelings—such as hatred of Nazis, religion, and patriotism, or even deference to an accepted authority whose values the rescuer shared—influenced them, most rescuers explain their actions as responses to a challenge to their fundamental ethical principles.[36]

This finding is supported by Ervin Staub, who emphasizes the importance of the individual's "moral orientation" in determining a response to the plight of others: "A *prosocial value orientation* involves concern about others and the desire to benefit them . . . A *moral rule orientation* embodies the desire to maintain or fulfill moral principles, norms, and rules."[37] In their study of rescuers, the Oliners discovered that basic ethical orientations were more significant than factors like emotional empathy in motivating someone to rescue another.[38]

As Staub and the Oliners remind us, no discussion of human behavior during the Holocaust is complete without a look at the phenomena of rescue and resistance. While the history of the Holocaust offers a great deal of evidence to support the findings of Milgram and others, there are also heroic examples of individuals who did not follow patterns of conformity and complicity. People did not have to remain bystanders or become active perpetrators; there were other options. The real mystery is what made some people capable of resistance. While this will be examined in the latter part of this book, several general observations can be made about rescue and resistance on the level of individual behavior.

The first is that, to a striking degree, acts of rescue were carried out by individuals, not by groups. Jan Karski, a Polish courier who carried news of the genocide to Allied leaders, said: "Six million Jews died and no one offered them effective help. Not any nation, not any government, not any church. The help they did receive, heroic help, was provided only by individuals."[39] Even among the few examples of institutional aid to the victims, the decisive factor seems to have been the role of certain individuals within those institutions.

What moved these people? Here, too, scholars have arrived at different insights about human behavior by looking at rescuers during the Nazi era. The most comprehensive study of rescuers, conducted by Samuel and Pearl Oliner, has already been mentioned. In their book, *The Altruistic Personality*, the Oliners explored the factors that facilitated altruistic behavior. They found that rescuers often came from homes in which they were taught to think independently, or had parents with strong moral concerns; as personalities, rescuers tended to exhibit more independence and adventurousness. They were often (though not always) outsiders, already marginal in some way: either through membership in a banned political or religious organization, or through gender (a disproportionate number of rescuers were women). They seemed to feel a strong sense of connection with the victims.

Many of these factors would seem predictable. What surprises in the Oliners' study (and other books on rescuers)[40] is that no single factor consistently predicts whether someone became a rescuer or not. Strong religious conviction, for example, was not always a motivation; while some rescuers were moved by their religious faith, others were not. While a general "moral orientation," as mentioned previously, was a frequent factor, the roots of this moral orientation varied. To some extent, the phenomenon of rescue is a mystery, and rescuers themselves had difficulty explaining why they acted as they did. It is just as difficult to uncover the true motivations of rescuers as it is to determine conclusively what motivated bystanders. And, as Staub observes, the "evolution of commitment" among rescuers was usually incremental and gradual—just as the Nazis took incremental steps toward genocide, and bystanders moved gradually in the direction of passivity or active complicity.[41]

Individual behavior is indeed shaped by outside factors. The fascinating thing is how this gradual process—whether it is an evolution of commitment or complicity—creates an atmosphere that affects the course of the entire society. "In conditions of extreme danger," Staub writes, "people need support to evolve and maintain the motivation to help. As they begin to help, they also begin to create their own environment, their own context. They build connections to a community that supports them."[42] This was the fabric of rescue and resistance; as we will see in the second section of this book, a similar process created the fabric of complicity.

Zygmunt Bauman has described the Holocaust as a "window" through which we "can catch a rare glimpse of many things otherwise invisible."[43] Within the historical context of the Holocaust, we discover aspects of human behavior that might appear mundane in other circumstances. Despite their different conclusions, there are insights to be gained from the work of Milgram, Zimbardo, Adorno, and Arendt. The work of each of these scholars increases our awareness of the potential in each human being for good or evil.

What does emerge from all these studies is a motif we will confront throughout this book: the ambiguity and complexity of human behavior. To acknowledge this ambiguity does not mean we have to abandon ethical judgment. More importantly, to describe bystanders (or perpetrators) as "ordinary people" does not mean we are looking at "ordinary behavior." As George Kateb observes,

Such ordinariness may not be depravity or inhuman blackness of heart. It may not be radical evil in the Kantian understanding: a Satanic disposition "to adopt evil as evil." It may not be Milton's Satan saying, "Evil be thou my Good," or Claggart in Billy Budd tormented by an innocence he must torment. But it may be something altogether more strange: a nonhuman blankness.[44]

This "nonhuman blankness" describes the puzzle of the bystander during the Holocaust, the disturbing mystery that the sociological and psychological insights can only illuminate but not completely dispel. It echoes the question that permeates every study of the Holocaust: How could this happen? It is inevitable that all attempts to answer this question will fall short, for what we are really seeking to understand is where the roots of human morality lie.

The American theologian Reinhold Niebuhr explored this ethical dilemma in his 1932 classic, Moral Man and Immoral Society. Reflecting on the widespread moral shortcomings of human society, he concluded that ethics and morality were viable concepts on the level of individual behavior, but not on the collective level. The vision of "perpetual peace and brotherhood," wrote Niebuhr, "is a vision prompted by the conscience and insight of individual man, but incapable of fulfillment by collective man."[45] The "social validity" of any moral ideal, he wrote, becomes "progressively weakened" on the indirect and collective levels.

Moral Man and Immoral Society was a warning against the danger (in Niebuhr's view, the impossibility) of declaring absolute moral ideals on the collective level. When Niebuhr wrote it in the early 1930s, he was clearly concerned about the phenomenon of mass behavior and the growing threat posed by ideological movements. The purpose of human society, he argued, could not be to impose moral standards on the masses or permit "the masses" to create an ideology, but to allow morality to flourish among individual citizens—a distinction between ideology and democracy that he elaborated on in a later book, *The Children of Light and the Children of Darkness* (1944).

In the early 1930s, then, Niebuhr was wrestling with the same issue that confronted ethicists and others after 1945. His ideas were echoed by German philosopher Karl Jaspers, in his famous 1947 essay on German guilt. Jaspers reflected on the role of the individual in the collective deeds of a nation:

The self-analysis of a people in historical reflection and the personal self-analysis of the individual are two different things. But the first can happen only by way of the second. What individuals accomplish jointly in communication may, if true, become the spreading consciousness of many and then is called national consciousness.

Again we must reject collective thinking, as fictitious thinking. Any real metamorphosis occurs through individuals—in the individual, in many individuals independent of or mutually inspiring one another.[46]

Much of this book will explore the interaction between individuals and the greater historical forces that culminated in the Holocaust. But individuals—however powerless they may feel—are not utterly at the mercy of history. Just as sociological, historical, and political factors affect individual ethical behavior, the ethical convictions and behavior of individuals can have an effect upon the course taken by communities, institutions, and even nations. "Bystanders often encourage perpetrators, and they themselves are changed as they passively face the suffering of victims," Staub writes. "However, bystanders also have great potential power to inhibit the evolution of increasing destructiveness."[47]

NOTES

1. For a helpful discussion of this with respect to the Holocaust, see Bauman, *Modernity*, 177–79.

2. Ibid., 179.

3. Staub, *The Roots of Evil*, 104.

4. Bauman, *Modernity*, 87.

5. Staub, *The Roots of Evil*, 36.

6. For a more specific exploration of the gender-related issues here, see Claudia Koonz, *Mothers in the Fatherland: Women, Family, and Nazi Politics* (New York: St. Martin's Press, 1987); Renate Bridenthal, Atina Grossmann, and Marion Kaplan, eds., *When Biology Became Destiny: women in Weimar and Nazi Germany* (New York: Monthly Review Press, 1984).

7. Bauman, *Modernity*, 177.

8. See especially Bettelheim's 1943 essay, "Individual and Mass Behavior in Extreme Situations," reprinted in his *Surviving and Other Essays* (New York: Knopf, 1979).

9. In Viktor E. Frankl, *Man's Search for Meaning*, 76.

10. Ibid., 78.

11. Ibid., 74–75.

12. Langer, *Admitting the Holocaust*, 181.

13. Bauman, *Modernity*, 153.

14. Arendt, *Eichmann in Jerusalem*, 93.

15. Ibid., 26–27.

16. Staub, *The Roots of Evil*, 91.

17. Kateb, *Hannah Arendt*, 35.

18. Ibid., 95.

19. Ibid., 78.

20. For his account of the trial and response to Arendt, see Gideon Hausner, *Justice in Jerusalem*.

21. Jean Améry, "Torture," in Roth and Berenbaum, *Holocaust*, 174.

22. Stanley Milgram, "Behavioral Study of Obedience," in *Journal of Abnormal Social Psychology* 67: 377, 1967.

23. See Staub, *The Roots of Evil*, 133; and John M. Steiner, "The SS Yesterday and Today: A Sociopsychological View," in Dimsdale, *Survivors, Victims, and Perpetrators: Essays on the Nazi Holocaust*.

24. Bauman, *Modernity*, 155.

25. Ibid., 153.

26. Ibid., 154.

27. See the discussion of this in Bauman, *Modernity*, 160–161.

28. Staub, *The Roots of Evil*, 143–44.

29. Ibid., 146.

30. Ibid., 148.

31. Ibid.

32. Ibid., 151.

33. Langer, *Admitting the Holocaust*, 182.

34. Ibid.

35. See Ervin Staub, "Moral Exclusion, Personal Goal Theory, and Extreme Destructiveness."

36. Oliner and Oliner, *The Altruistic Personality*, 170.

37. Staub, *The Root of Evil*, 35.

38. See Oliner and Oliner, *The Altruistic Personality*, 174–175.

39. In Maciej Koslowski, "The Mission that Failed" (interview with Jan Karski), in Polonsky, *My Brother's Keeper?*, 95.

40. See, for example, Eva Fogelman, *Conscience and Courage: The Rescuers of the Jews during the Holocaust* (New York: Anchor Books, 1994); Nechama Tec, *When Light Pierced the Darkness: Christian Rescuers of Jews in Nazi-Occupied Poland* (New York: Oxford University Press, 1986); David Gushee, *The Righteous Gentiles of the Holocaust: A Christian Interpretation*.

41. Staub, *The Roots of Evil*, 167.

42. Ibid., 169.

43. Bauman, *Modernity*, viii.

44. Kateb, *Hannah Arendt*, 74.

45. Niebuhr, *Moral Man and Immoral Society*, 21–22.

46. Karl Jaspers, *The Question of German Guilt*, 102.

47. Staub, "Moral Exclusion, Personal Goal Theory, and Extreme Destructiveness," 47.

CHAPTER 3

Collective Forms of Behavior

INSTITUTIONS

It is indeed possible for individuals to shape the course taken by their communities and its institutions. Yet, as anyone involved in an institution knows, institutional priorities tend to acquire a life of their own. That life often seems independent of the convictions, or even the control, of individual members.

Perhaps this is one reason why, in reflecting on the connections between individual ethics and social morality, Niebuhr and Jaspers were dubious about the viability of any "collective" ethic. Both men recognized that any form of collective behavior limits the options of individual members and reinforces central authority. "Membership in a group changes people," as Staub puts it. "The change is greater in groups that exert more control over members and require more total commitment, more extreme actions, or greater sacrifice."[1] In a process he terms "empathic joining," individuals not only conform, but actually define themselves according to the attitudes and goals of the group; this, in turn, shapes their perceptions of reality and their behavior.[2]

These changes can be for the good or bad. Membership in a group can give deeper meaning to individual life; it is an important means by which individuals participate in their societies and shape a social identity. By identifying themselves with a group—an ethnic or national group, the institution they work for or the religious body of which they are a member—people not only adopt that group's principles and ideologies, but may even come to view their private lives in the context of the greater whole. In the positive sense, this may lead them to deeper commitments and a stronger sense of responsibility to act for the sake of a greater good.

Negatively, however, group pressures on individual members may reduce their capacity to understand or accept differing perspectives. The influence of a group can overpower even strong ethical misgivings and emotional discomfort. The term "mass behavior" is often used pejoratively, suggesting the rule of the mob—a group driven by emotion or ideology, in which individuals lose the capacity and the desire to think or act independently.

Because they play such a vital role in any society, social, religious, and political institutions are more than just an organized form of "mass behavior." Just as individual members accommodate themselves to the goals and policies of the group, most institutions conform to the political, social, and economic values of their societies. An intrinsic priority of most institutions is self-preservation, which requires some degree of accommodation to the status quo.

This kind of accommodation was striking among all institutions in Germany, including churches, universities, and governmental bureaucracies like the judiciary and civil service. We have already seen how the *Gleichschaltung* mentioned in the previous chapter was deliberate Nazi policy, but it was not simply imposed and enforced by the state. The case studies of Sonderburg and Mauthausen are only two of many examples that illustrate how individual citizens conformed voluntarily to Nazi policies. Most institutions conformed readily as well. Disturbed by the new Nazi regulations, some individual representatives of institutions did resign their posts in the early months of 1933, but such resignations were the exception. In the public and private sectors, most Germans kept their jobs and quickly adjusted to the new regime. Between January and April 1933, the number of Nazi party members in Germany almost doubled, from 849,000 to 1,644,884.[3] Whether due to enthusiasm or careerism, the increase was one of the first signs of how profoundly Nazism would change German society.

Studies that focus on specific groups illustrate the degree to which *Gleichschaltung* permeated German institutions. Robert Gellately's study of the Gestapo, *The Gestapo and German Society*, shows how local police forces merged almost seamlessly into the new police state, becoming an extension of the Gestapo. The Nazi regime, he notes, did not have to purge police departments of nonparty members and install its own people. On the contrary, throughout German society, there was "widespread social co-operation, collaboration, accommodation, and adjustment. Without social co-operation of various kinds, irrespective of motives, the anti-Semitic policies would have remained so many idle fantasies."[4]

Similar patterns of behavior can be found even among the few institutions that came into conflict with the Nazi regime. The most prominent example of this was the German Evangelical Church (the main Protestant church in Germany), whose record shows resistance and opposition to certain Nazi policies, as well as conspicuous examples of accommodation to the regime.

This ambiguity is particularly intriguing in the Confessing Church, a group within the German Evangelical Church committed to preserving church independence under Nazism. The Confessing Church emerged in opposition to the "German Christians," an extremist group of Protestants who attempted to create a "Reich Church" and enact an Aryan clause in church law that would exclude "non-Aryans" from the clergy. Most Protestants rejected such measures, correctly seeing them as an attempt to conform Christian tradition to Nazi ideological standards. The bitter debate that ensued threatened to split the Protestant Church in some parts of Germany.

It also brought some Confessing Christians into conflict with the Nazi regime on various issues, including the "euthanasia" of institutionalized patients and, in some cases, the persecution of the Jews. In many regions, the Gestapo placed the Confessing Church on its list of state enemies, and harassed and arrested more outspoken Confessing Christians. Some Confessing Christians eventually criticized Nazi policies in public or joined the political resistance against the state. Werner Sylten, Paul Schneider, Ludwig Steil, and Dietrich Bonhoeffer are some of the prominent Confessing Christians who gave their lives in the fight against Nazism.

Even within the Confessing Church, however, the majority of church leaders never protested the state racial laws—and a number of them even publicly supported state measures against the Jews like the April 1, 1933 boycott of Jewish businesses.[5] Others, while not approving the persecution, advised the church against criticizing such a central aspect of Nazi policy.[6] Although they fought the Nazification of their own institutions, both the Catholic and Protestant churches cooperated when it came to nonreligious issues. They offered neither protest nor resistance, for example, when millions of Germans had to obtain proof of their "Aryan" heritage from church records.

There are a number of reasons for the behavior of the institutional churches in Germany. One, of course, was the history of Christian anti-Semitism throughout Europe—a history marked by the Inquisition, church-ordered burnings and destructions of Talmuds and temple relics during the Middle Ages, and the numerous Christian proclamations that forbade intermarriage between Christians and Jews, barred Jews from various professions, and created compulsory ghettoes.[7]

Such attitudes toward Jews merged with Christian teachings about Judaism, which emphasized Jesus of Nazareth as the fulfillment of the Hebrew scriptures and preached that the people of Israel would inevitably acknowledge Jesus as Messiah. Even among Christians whose personal attitudes toward Jews were socially and politically tolerant, the widespread assumption was "that Judaism was a *religio licita*, a legally permissible religion, even though a deluded one; that it worshiped the true God, although inadequately; that it was a primary faith, although one humiliated and superseded."[8] All too many Christians agreed with the German minister in 1933 who said, "Anti-Semitism is justified, but this anti-Semitism must remain within the biblically set limits."[9] He didn't approve of political violence, but essentially agreed with the Nazi slogan that "the Jews were our misfortune."

Confessing Christians' objections to a church Aryan law was that it contradicted Christian teachings on baptism and conversion, and set political and racial guidelines for who could belong to the church. This did not mean, however, that they questioned the legitimacy of the Nazi government. Nationalism and anti-Semitism were widespread in the German Evangelical Church, even among those who disagreed with the regime on other issues. The battles that the churches fought with the Nazi leadership essentially concerned church independence. Even those church leaders troubled by Nazism genuinely believed that they could best protect their members by preserving the institutional freedom of their church. Church policies were cautious, and church leaders tried to avoid taking positions that might bring their institution into conflict with the Nazi regime.

The more radical members of the Confessing Church condemned this caution at the time. There were courageous Christians who, in publicly opposing Nazism, failed to win the public support of their church. A striking example comes from the ranks of the Confessing Church in Bavaria in 1943. The Lempp Circle, a small group of Protestants, had written a statement protesting the deportations of the Jews. They sent a copy to the bishop of Bavaria, Hans Meiser, asking for his signature and support. Meiser responded that, as a bishop, he could not take a public position; his priorities were to protect his institution. He noted that he

regretted, to be sure, the terrible things taking place in Poland and the concentration camps. But if he were to do something officially, he would only be arrested, and the Jews wouldn't have been helped; the persecution would become even more severe. In addition, he, Meiser, was responsible for a large regional church. If persecution broke loose, suffering and unhappiness would come over thousands of families.[10]

The bishop's caution was partly based on anti-Jewish prejudice (Meiser, in fact, consistently opposed any church statement on behalf of the Jews[11]), but it also reflected his strategic concerns as an institutional leader. He was joined by many colleagues, not all of them anti-Semites, who feared that open opposition to the Nazi regime would lead to the persecution and deaths of church members, and perhaps the forced dissolution of the church itself.

This fear was not unreasonable. In the early years of the regime, Nazi prison camps were filled with Communists and Social Democrats who had publicly opposed the regime; several leading Nazis, including Hitler himself, alluded ominously to plans to eradicate the churches.[12]

Yet the church's silence undermined the resistance of its more radical members,[13] and it probably hindered the development of more widespread opposition to Nazism among the German population. While not monolithically supportive of Nazism, the institutional Protestant church ultimately functioned in a way that reinforced Nazi power—a fact that the German Evangelical Church itself acknowledged in the Stuttgart Declaration of Guilt in 1945, when it apologized to the international Christian community and noted that it found itself "in a solidarity of guilt" with its nation.[14]

The example of the Evangelical Church in Nazi Germany illustrates how an institution can function as a "bystander." In its efforts to preserve its autonomy and its very existence, the institutional church effectively sided with state authority. This, in turn, enabled the regime to tighten its hold on the entire society. The church's institutional conformity and its compromises with Nazi leaders clearly influenced the viability of protest by individual Christians.

More critically, the church's behavior under Nazism undermined its own moral credibility, as it acknowledged in the Stuttgart Declaration. One question is to what degree this was the product of the political circumstances that confronted the church after 1933, and to what extent it was based upon traditional teachings and the church's understanding of its role. In any case, the course followed by most church leaders during the Nazi era was consistent with their own understanding of individual and institutional ethics. Shaped by a long tradition of obedience to state authorities, the German Evangelical Church viewed conformity and obedience to authority as virtues. In his encounter with the Lempp Circle, Bishop Meiser clearly believed that these virtues were necessary to preserve the church's options in Nazi Germany.

Meiser's understanding of the proper relationship between individual ethics, institutional responsibility, and obedience to authority was shared by many leaders of other German institutions, and is characteristic of modern institutional bureaucracy in general. The pioneering work of the German sociologist Max Weber (1864–1920) described the dynamics of this long before the advent of Nazism, and gives us some insight into how institutions functioned during the Nazi period.[15] Weber recognized that a new form of organization had emerged, one whose governing principle was rationality, not the wishes or convictions of its individual members: "The objective discharge of business," Weber noted, "primarily means a discharge of business according to calculable rules and without regard for persons."[16]

Weber believed that "rationality" had taken over; the way in which modern society was structured and functioned left little room for individual conscience in the public sphere. He saw a relationship between the values expounded by Protestantism and those that served as the foundation of modern capitalism. In particular, he felt that the distinction between public and private, between conscience and "rationality" revealed the strong imprint of Protestant teachings, particularly the Lutheran doctrine of two kingdoms, which distinguished between the worldly realm, represented by state authority, and the heavenly kingdom. The question was "whether the intrinsic value of ethical conduct—the 'pure will' or the 'conscience' as it used to be called—is sufficient for its justification, following the maxim of the Christian moralists: 'the Christian acts rightly and leaves the consequences of his action to God.' "[17] Similarly, the individual members of modern society believed they had only to fulfill their designated roles; the greater consequences would take care of themselves.

Through unquestioning loyalty to the dictates of authority, the modern bureaucrat functions in much the same way. As Weber observed:

The honor of the civil servant is vested in his ability to execute conscientiously the order of superior authorities, exactly as if the order agreed with his own conviction. This holds even if the order seems wrong to him and if, despite the civil servant's remonstrances, the authority insists on the order.[18]

Weber's observation has ominous significance when we consider the ways in which authority—in the guise of institutional power—can generate and legitimize violence against a designated group. In an extreme case like Nazi Germany, individual members of social and political institutions essentially abdicated the *right* of conscience to their leaders, who, in the name of the institution or the state, determined the correct course of action for all.

This had important ethical consequences. Individuals, even those who worked in institutions or were members of the bureaucracy, felt absolved of any kind of moral authority for what was happening. Many Germans defended themselves after 1945 by claiming that they had maintained an "inner resistance" to Nazism, even when they were compelled to obey Nazi laws. In *Eichmann in Jerusalem*, Arendt noted the inherent contradiction here, reflected by the number of Germans, including some on trial for war crimes, who claimed to be "inwardly opposed" to what they had done.[19] Yet they had hardly lived as outcasts in Nazi Germany; they had remained active as citizens and members of leading German institutions. At the same time, they behaved as though their own consciences had become irrelevant when they "had" to obey Nazi orders. This distinction enabled them to believe that they had continued to have a conscience and to understand the difference between right and wrong—to live in "inner resistance" even while they publicly obeyed Nazi laws.

This kind of ethical distinction, of course, gives social and political institutions great power. In an essay entitled "Violence without Moral Restraint," sociologist Herbert Kelman lists three prerequisites for the erosion of moral inhibitions against violent atrocities: (1) the *authorization* of violence; (2) the *routinization* of violent actions; and (3) the *dehumanization* of victims.[20] The very nature of Kelman's prerequisites is institutional—it is institutions, or their representatives, who authorize and create the routines that dehumanize the selected victims; thus, their power over the moral inhibitions of individuals is devastating. The will and conscience of the individual is relegated to the private realm, an arrangement legitimated by the modern state. Such are the mechanisms by which institutions foster individual complicity and passivity.

It is possible for an institution to function this way even if its own behavior is essentially passive. By not protesting Nazi measures against the Jews, and by allowing church records to be used as proof of "racial purity," the churches tacitly authorized state violence against the Jews. In other German bureaucracies—such as the educational system and the civil service—additional routines of exclusion and discrimination were established early. "Non-Aryans" lost their jobs, "Aryans" had to fill out forms of racial purity, school curricula and bureaucratic regulations were rewritten to meet racial criteria.

The lack of protest against these routines only laid the foundation for subsequent, more murderous routines like compiling death lists and sending people to the gas chambers. As Ervin Staub has observed, institutional cooperation is necessary for widespread discrimination and mistreatment of a specific group to occur, and institutions thus play a powerful role in creating a society in which prejudice is part of its very fabric.[21] Sanctioned by government and society, the impact of prejudice extends far beyond the realm of individual conviction—even while the pretense is maintained that prejudice is an individual, not a social, sin. In this context, it becomes increasingly difficult for individual bystanders to remain passive spectators. Through their connections to social and political institutions, they are involved in numerous ways.

Institutional accommodation to Nazism helped Hitler strengthen his hold on German society at a very early stage. But it did more; as we've already noted, institutional accommodation to injustice reduces the viability of individual resistance to that injustice. The conformity of major German institutions created a veneer of legitimacy for the Nazi regime. Like Weber's obedient civil servant, individuals in all walks of German life found themselves following orders in the name of the national cause, which was supported by the acquiescence of the institutions of which they were members. Zygmunt Bauman has noted "the easiness with which most people slip into the role requiring cruelty or at least moral blindness—if only the role has been fortified and legitimized by superior authority."[22] The position taken by an institution can be crucial in either undermining or supporting the power of the state.

As one example illustrates, the possibilities for individual resistance were limited. In July 1940, Judge Lothar Kreyssig, a member of the Confessing Church, protested the Nazi euthanasia program. The court over which Kreyssig presided served as legal guardian for a number of institutionalized patients. After receiving the official notices of their deaths, he concluded that they had been murdered, and wrote to Nazi Justice Minister Franz Gürtner that "as a Christian he must object. Moreover, he stated that these killings violated existing law and that as legal guardian he must act to protect his wards. Before doing so, however, he considered it his duty 'to obtain information and advice from my superiors.' "[23] Gürtner told him that the euthanasia program was a secret state matter, but Kreyssig continued to press for answers. In August 1940, Kreyssig finally notified the hospitals and the justice ministry that none of his wards could be transferred without his explicit approval. As a result, he was forced into early retirement by Justice Minister Gürtner.

As Kreyssig's case shows, any kind of resistance or opposition within the civil service had little chance of succeeding. He opposed the state euthanasia measures (in addition, he was deeply troubled by the persecution of the Jews). Still, as a judge in Nazi Germany, he believed he had no other option than to work through the proper channels. Once he abandoned this conviction and offered serious resistance—using his position to block the transfer of patients—he lost his job.

Kreyssig's case, though rare, was not unique; there are records of other civil servants who attempted to block various Nazi policies.[24] Their objections brought them into conflict with their previous understanding of their professional and ethical responsibilities. Such examples poignantly illustrate the slight effectiveness of individual conscience within the bureaucracy of a system like Nazism.

They also highlight the very specific problems that arose within the realm of "professional ethics" under Nazism. Kreyssig's sense of professionalism led him to work through the proper channels and seek "information and advice from my superiors." And yet those like Kreyssig who sought to render more than lip service to professional ethics were quickly removed. Although "professional ethics" usually describes a point of intersection between individual and institutional behavior, under Nazism, it became a trap.

The way in which the medical profession confronted this issue is instructive, first during the widespread sterilization programs of the early 1930s, then in the Nazi euthanasia measures, and, finally, in the medical "experiments" and selections that were performed in the concentration camps. One might assume that the doctors involved would have been torn between their own ethical or religious principles (including, of course, their Hippocratic oath) and the demands placed on them as members of medical institutions in Nazi Germany.

Yet the historical record shows widespread conformity among doctors. Some doctors, of course, agreed with Nazi ideology that depicted institutionalized patients, Jews, and gypsies as social burdens and genetic hazards. Other doctors did not agree, yet they identified so strongly with their professional role that this negated any personal misgivings they might have had. The euthanasia program became an instructive case study in how "professional ethics" can be adapted to state or institutional dictates.[25]

The issues that arose in the sphere of professional ethics during the Third Reich exemplified Weber's observations about individual conformity to institutional bureaucracy. The compartmentalization of ethics into the private and public spheres is characteristic of how modern bureaucratic institutions are organized and function. The compartmentalized roles of its individual members make it easier for an institution to function; and this arrangement removes individual members from the immediate consequences of their actions. It was easier for individuals to conform to their institutional role if they could see this as purely part of their job, as something distinct from the private realm in which they were good spouses, churchgoers, and so forth. "The essentially private person, anxious to make a good life for his family and totally lacking in any attachment to the idea of citizenship, is the perfect cog," as George Kateb writes.[26]

The ethical outcome of such compartmentalization was that it preserved the illusion of normality for everyone involved. A society can only function normally if its institutions do and, in Nazi Germany, they did. Just as individual perpetrators of the genocide were psychologically normal, "the institutions responsible for the Holocaust, even if found criminal, were in no legitimate sociological sense pathological or abnormal."[27] Churches, hospitals, universities, the civil service, and other institutions operated under Nazism as they had before. Even those institutions directly involved in mass murder—the SS and the concentration camp bureaucracies, for example—functioned "normally." In their structure and operations, they were indistinguishable from other institutions; that is part of the horror.

More than anything else, institutional conformity wove the web of "normality" and cemented the impact of Nazi *Gleichschaltung*. The compliance of social and political institutions is crucial to the success of a totalitarian government. To the extent that any major institution refuses to cooperate, or defends values that contradict those of the state, the image of a stable society is undermined. Similarly, the normal life of individual citizens depends upon the illusion, at least, that everything around them is normal. If the schools shut down, the civil service stops functioning, the banks collapse, or the courts try to undermine the government with their decisions, dissident voices gain more impact, and bystanders are confronted with a different alternative. On the other hand, when things are "normal"—i.e., when institutions and government are aligned—any protest or resistance that does emerge will be marginalized.

This is why the early months of the Nazi regime were marked simultaneously by the brutal elimination of all potentially dissident voices and by the *Gleichschaltung* that ensured that life would go on as usual. The cooperation of German institutions was crucial, since numerous aspects of German life after 1933 were—in reality—extremely abnormal. New rules and restrictions had appeared, changing German life at all levels. Neighbors and colleagues lost their jobs, people were arrested, signs appeared that prohibited Jews from park benches and swimming pools, homes and businesses were vandalized.

In fact, German life had changed so radically that many Germans spoke of a "revolution" having occurred. Yet, throughout Germany, organizations and institutions adapted; things continued to run normally. Normality, of course, was an illusion—a Nazified view of what was normal. What enabled it to become "normality" was that most Germans, by accommodating themselves to it, were able to conduct their lives pretty much as before.

This was the first step in the fundamental corruption of the institutions involved—even those like the churches, which believed that they could preserve their institutional integrity by retaining some degree of independence. In reality, they had come down on the side of "normality," of the Nazi state. German institutions (and their individual members) became progressively corrupt and complicit.

In the process, it was not only (or even always) the case that German institutions found themselves in fundamental agreement with Nazi aims. The institutional traditions that preceded Nazism also played a role. As Zygmunt Bauman notes, the problem is not just that there were aspects of modernity that led to certain forms of institutional behavior we saw during the Holocaust. The underlying crisis is that there was apparently no mechanism or set of values within those institutions to *prevent* what happened.[28] As theologian Franklin Littell writes, "The death camps were not planned and built . . . by ignorant and unschooled savages. The killing centres were, like their inventors, products of what had been for generations one of the best university systems in the world."[29]

Had the churches preached differently, the courts operated differently, and the schools taught tolerance, not prejudice—history might have taken a different course. In looking at the role of institutions in the Holocaust, then, we must examine the ethical systems and presumptions operating within general society and enforced by that society's institutions. In the words of philosopher Peter Haas, we must study "ethics as a force that gives character to the institutions and people living under its influence."[30]

One reason for institutional complicity under Nazism was certainly the conviction of many institutional leaders that they must work for the collective good and remain otherwise "neutral," leaving major decisions about society's direction up to the state. But these leaders and their institutions were not blank slates; their judgments were shaped by prejudice, nationalism, and their own sense of privilege. Because they were not Nazism's intended victims, they could continue as before and even benefit from the changes that had swept their society. The moral indifference of bystanders—their "nonhuman blankness," as Kateb put it—was sustained by the institutions that shaped their society.

The history of Nazi Germany offers countless examples of how institutions served as bystanders: by supporting state policies and carrying out state orders, by facilitating complicity and blocking effective resistance by individuals. The work of Allport, Milgram, Zimbardo, and Staub gives some insight into the role of institutions. Milgram and Zimbardo were observing individuals, but their findings clearly revealed the links between collective influence, authority, and the individual's inhibitions against violent behavior. These inhibitions are diminished when people are given a certain role in a group (Zimbardo) and by the tendency of most people to obey authority (Milgram). Thus, the factors that reduce individual inhibitions against violence are implicitly related to the course followed by the institutions of which they are part.

Above all, this has a devastating effect on the likelihood and viability of protest and resistance. "Perhaps the most profound effect of a successful totalitarian system," notes Staub, "is the lack of dissenting voices that offer a perspective different from that cultivated by authorities or engender inner conflict or sympathy with victims."[31] When major institutions side silently with state authority, it becomes even more difficult for dissenting voices—and for solidarity with the victims—to emerge.

THE INTERNATIONAL COMMUNITY

In 1941, the International Committee of the Red Cross began to receive reports that Nazi concentration camps—which the international community had previously viewed as brutal labor camps or prisons for political dissidents—were killing factories for hundreds of thousands of European Jews. By the end of 1942, some Red Cross officials in Geneva felt that the organization should make a public statement on the matter. Others urged caution, citing the importance of the Red Cross's neutral status for its humanitarian work. As a result, the Red Cross never issued any public statement during the Holocaust, although it shared the information it received about the genocide with other international organizations and officials.

After the war ended, the Red Cross was criticized for its silence. In 1948, the organization defended its record:

Public protest and denunciation would have been of no avail . . . For the Committee to protest publicly would have been not only to outstep its functions, but also to lose thereby all chance of pursuing them, by creating an immediate breach with the government concerned. The Committee would thus have abandoned to their fate the very people whom it wished to save . . . The prestige of the Red Cross idea lives not by words, but by deeds—by deeds which are, after all, the most eloquent of all protests.[32]

The Red Cross statement echoed many of the arguments made by institutions in Nazi Germany or the Nazi-occupied countries: it emphasized its institutional mandate, the necessity of working through proper channels, and the constraints imposed by the political circumstances of the time. Like Bavarian Bishop Meiser and countless others, the leaders of the Red Cross decided that the importance of their organization's role outweighed any possible benefits of taking a public position against Nazi authorities.

But, while some of the issues faced by international institutions were similar to those that confronted institutions under Nazi occupation, international groups had other options open to them. In Nazi Germany and the occupied countries, the fear that an open confrontation with Nazi authorities might lead to repercussions against an organization and its members was not unreasonable. Most international organizations did not have to fear such direct consequences. While the International Red Cross had to tread carefully to retain a certain freedom for its activities (for example, to gain Nazi permission to visit the camps), it was in the unique position of being able to publicize the truth about the "Final Solution" to the rest of the world. Its silence made its humanitarian missions (such as its visit to Theresienstadt, which the Nazis used for their own propaganda purposes) a bitter success at best. The lingering question was whether, given its power and prestige, the Red Cross might have accomplished its humanitarian mandate better had it been a more forceful advocate on behalf of Nazism's victims, even at the cost of its own activities.

The same question confronts the international community as a whole. Its reaction to the genocide of the Jews was, as Raul Hilberg puts it, "dilatory"—piecemeal, often halfhearted, and characterized throughout by pragmatism and caution, rather than a fervent effort to save human lives.[33] Despite occasional public protests and quiet diplomatic efforts, the international community failed to stop the persecution and genocide of the Jews.

Could it have done otherwise? Although the verdict of posterity is understandably harsh on this point, the question deserves consideration.

Closer examination shows that the international community was not entirely silent or passive; throughout the period, there were protests and actions on behalf of the victims of Nazism. The failure of these actions was partly due to the relatively small number of people involved; but it was also due to the fact that certain factors made effective international intervention difficult, if not impossible.

An account by Gerhard Riegner, head of the World Jewish Congress in Geneva at the time, reveals how difficult it was for outrage to be transformed into effective action. At the end of 1941, recalls Riegner, knowledge of the genocide was beginning to spread. In Switzerland, the public learned that refugees were being turned away at the Swiss border, and that some refugees who had entered Switzerland were even being deported:

A wave of protest struck the country and those who lived through this period remember with emotion this unique and exhilarating experience. The newspapers from right to left violently criticized the attitude of the government. There was a near unanimous outcry to uphold the principle of the right of asylum and many political, civic, and religious bodies voiced their vehement protest.

A very stormy meeting of the *Zentralstelle fur Fluchtlingshilfe* [Central Office for Refugee Aid], which was held on August 24, asked at least for certain changes and corrections in the regulations.[34]

The outcome, Riegner recalls, was that the Swiss police minister ordered an end to the expulsions "in special cases." The Swiss parliament held a debate and eased some restrictions, especially for women, children, and elderly refugees. Church refugee aid organizations compiled lists of refugees to serve as guidelines for the border police. ("This procedure, however, was distasteful," Riegner notes. "Every name that was put on the list condemned others who were omitted or forgotten."[35]) Nothing happened beyond these initial actions. The outburst of sympathy for the refugees was genuine but short-lived. Some additional lives were saved, but, in the end, the Swiss government did not alter its policies fundamentally.

A similar incident occurred in the United States, where a March 1943 Madison Square Garden rally organized by religious groups, labor unions, and others "indicated the depth of public concern for the European Jews."[36] Historian Henry Feingold writes that 22,000 people attended the Madison Square Garden rally "and at least 15,000 more waited outside to hear the impassioned speeches of the leaders of American Jewry."[37]

What factors prevented such outcries from leading to a stronger and more extensive international response to the genocide? If we are to explore the possibilities for a different kind of response in the future, we must first understand the specific issues that arise on the international level.

Especially in the early years after the Holocaust, it was argued that knowledge of what was happening behind Nazi borders—particularly concerning the scale of the genocide—reached the international community and its leaders too late. Subsequent scholarship has laid this contention to rest. Throughout the 1930s, knowledge about events in Nazi Germany was fairly extensive.[38] Information about the actual genocide spread more slowly, initially in the form of rumors about atrocities on the eastern front. Because similar reports during World War I had proven to be unfounded, these new accounts were treated with caution, especially in the press. Still, as Riegner's account above illustrates, detailed information about the death camps and the scope of the genocide was beginning to reach the Allied countries by late 1941.

Walter Laquer's *The Terrible Secret*, Deborah Lipstadt's *Beyond Belief*, Robert Ross's *So It was True*, and David Wyman's *The Abandonment of the Jews* are only several of the many works that portray the extent to which information about the persecution of the Jews was available throughout the Nazi era. Ross, for example, thoroughly documents the coverage of Nazi Germany in the U.S. religious press. Because of ties between U.S. and German churches, religious coverage here focused on the issues facing the German churches, but Ross counted several hundred articles about the Nazi measures against the Jews that were both detailed and accurate.[39] Articles about the repressive measures of the new Nazi regime began to appear in the secular press as well.[40]

In response, there were protests. News of the April 1, 1933 boycott in Berlin of Jewish businesses led to a protest rally in Madison Square Garden and threats of a boycott of German goods in this country, as well as letters of protest from U.S. church leaders to their German colleagues. A total of 1,200 American clergymen from twenty-six different denominations sponsored advertisements in the *New York Times* on May 26 and 29, 1933, condemning the anti-Jewish actions.[41] After German church leaders responded by defending the Nazi measures, their U.S. colleagues reacted bluntly. In a November 1933 letter to Berlin church councilman August Schreiber, Federal Council of Churches official S. Parkes Cadman observed:

[C]olleagues of mine were assured this summer in Berlin by official representatives of the churches that the (German) policy could be described as one of "humane extermination" . . . Frankly speaking, the Christians of America cannot conceive of any extermination of human beings as "humane." They find it even more difficult to understand how churchmen in any land at any time can deliberately lend their influence to the carrying on of such policy . . . Yet we have been forced to observe that, even before the revolution, when freedom of speech was still a reality in Germany, there were no protests that reached us from churchmen in Germany against the violent anti-Semitism of the National Socialists. Since then we have had a great number of apologies for the situation, but no official and few personal statements which seem to recognize the moral factors involved.[42]

Leaders from U.S. trade unions and Christian and Jewish organizations criticized the Nazi measures against the Jews and the general dismantling of civil liberties under the new regime. The emigration of the first refugees from Nazi Germany, including such prominent figures as Albert Einstein and Thomas Mann, sparked additional protests and solidarity rallies with those who had been imprisoned in Germany. The international Christian community issued statements specifically condemning the Nazi persecution of the Jews. In September 1933, at the international conference of the World Alliance for Peace and Friendship among the Churches in Sofia, Bulgaria, the delegates passed a resolution stating: "We especially deplore the fact that the State measures against the Jews in Germany have had such an effect on public opinion that in some circles the Jewish race is considered a race of inferior status."[43] After the November 1938 pogrom, Christian ecumenical organizations in Geneva sent a joint letter to all member churches, stating the duty of the church "to remind ourselves of the stand which we have taken as an ecumenical movement against anti-Semitism in all its forms."[44]

The letter urged churches to press their governments to take in more Jewish refugees. These efforts intensified in the United States and Great Britain in 1942, after Gerhard Riegner convinced Christian ecumenical leaders that the Nazis had begun the full-scale genocide of the European Jews.

On December 11, 1942, the U.S. Federal Council of Churches announced:

It is impossible to avoid the conclusion that something like a policy of deliberate extermination of the Jews in Europe is being carried out. The violence and inhumanity which Nazi leaders have publicly avowed towards all Jews are apparently now coming to a climax in a virtual massacre. We are resolved to do our full part in establishing conditions in which such treatment of the Jews shall end.[45]

Only five days later, the newly formed British Council of Christians and Jews started a public campaign that called for various measures to facilitate the emigration and resettlement of European Jews, including additional Allied aid to any country offering Jews refuge.

Thus, the international community was not completely passive to the plight of Jews and others suffering under Nazism.[46] The historical record shows a wide spectrum of responses, ranging from callous indifference to fervent attempts to intervene. As Robert Ross notes, U.S. Christian leaders

gave money; held rallies or participated in rallies; wrote, approved and signed statements of protests; sent representatives to Germany, some of whom met with Hitler and other leading Nazis; petitioned President Roosevelt, the United States State Department and the United States Congress; formed committees within denominations and interdenominationally; cooperated from time to time with concerned Jewish organizations and Jewish leaders; and offered petitions of prayer.[47]

Yet—as was the case in Riegner's account about Switzerland—these initial protests flared, sputtered, and died down. In the United States, Christian leaders who tried to mobilize their churches against Nazism were in a minority; they found virtually no support among their congregational constituencies.[48] The Federal Council of Churches designated May 2, 1943, as a "Day of Compassion for the Jews of Europe," hoping that churches throughout the United States would observe it in their services; the response was minimal.[49] As early as November 1934, the American Christian Committee for German Refugees was forced to acknowledge the lack of interest and commitment among its member churches:

[T]he response of Christians has everywhere, certainly in the United States, been most meager . . .

The United Jewish Appeal reports that of the $1,800,000 thus far raised by it, the actual money received from the efforts of the American Christian Committee did not exceed five or six thousand dollars . . . To this amount should be added the $2,131.25 which our Treasurer's report shows to have been received directly by the committee, making a total of, we will say, $8,000.[50]

The international religious community knew the details of what was happening to the Jews under Nazism, and at least some of its leaders were passionate opponents of anti-Semitism. What, then, explains the general indifference among church members? Anti-Semitism remained a factor. Despite the eloquent statements condemning anti-Semitism that were issued by church leaders, their convictions found little resonance among churchgoers in general.[51] This anti-Semitic prejudice shaped international reactions in a number of ways. Throughout the world, the plight of refugees was viewed as a "Jewish problem."

Other factors played a role as well. In the United States, the response to events in Europe was shaped by the general atmosphere of isolationism and the domestic concerns brought about by the Depression. In the Protestant churches, the era was marked by what historian Robert Handy has called "a religious depression"; charitable giving went down in Protestant congregations and the focus turned inward.[52] In general,

though some leaders were willing to speak out about the growing refugee crises in Europe and the Middle East, the Protestant rank and file was still almost as remote from the issues as they were in 1910. International Protestant relief was still on the whole far too disorganized to mount unified efforts. Perhaps equally important, few of the refugees of the 1920s and 1930s were Protestants.[53]

The attitude that the refugees were "a Jewish problem" was widespread; throughout the 1930s, Americans focused on other issues as more important. During the late 1930s, for example, the one to three million refugees produced by the Spanish Civil War obscured the plight of the European Jews in many newspapers.[54]

Thus, despite occasional outbursts of emotion provoked by news reports or newsreels of Nazi brutality, the early protests failed to generate the will to take in and help the refugees from Nazi Europe and, ultimately, to stop the "Final Solution." This failure was not due to a lack of knowledge or information; nor was it always due to a lack of sympathy.

The question was not knowledge—as noted above, those who wanted to know, could—but what significance they attached to that information. Perhaps some of the limitations were emotional. Throughout the world, the predominant reaction to reports from Europe was disbelief, indifference, passivity, and a sense of powerlessness. Michael Marrus notes that these reactions occurred even among the Palestinian Jews, 80 percent of whom had emigrated from eastern Europe.[55] The early news about the genocide, writes historian Jacob Katz, "seemed absolutely unbelievable—impossible." "Yet once it became evident that the unbelievable had indeed occurred, it began to seem altogether necessary and inevitable."[56]

This is illustrated by the response of U.S. Supreme Court Justice Felix Frankfurter to Polish emissary Jan Karski. Karski, a courageous member of the Polish underground, escaped Nazi Europe to bring firsthand reports of the genocide to the Allied countries. In 1943, he met with Roosevelt, Frankfurter, and others in Washington. After listening to Karski, Judge Frankfurter announced that he couldn't believe what he had just heard. A Polish diplomat attending the discussion expressed outrage that Frankfurter could suggest Karski was lying. Frankfurter's reply was revealing: "I am not saying that he is lying. I only said that I cannot believe him, and there is a difference."[57] Karski's own comment on the encounter was that he "met with disbelief many times." News about the genocide, he recalled, was "rejected, even subconsciously . . . There are things which minds and hearts refuse to accept."[58]

Such responses are typical of bystanders inside and outside Nazi Germany. In a sense, they were a form of denial—not the denial of those people today who claim that the Holocaust never happened, but a form of denial that came to characterize bystanders everywhere: *the denial that it was possible to do anything to stop what was happening.* Paralyzed by the sense of helplessness and powerlessness, people became convinced that what was happening was inevitable. It is impossible to know how much such underlying denial shaped the response of the international community. Yet this phenomenon suggests that we are looking at something other than simple indifference or even prejudice. As Lawrence Langer has written, "We still can't grasp the inner workings of what I call the 'aversion-to-crisis faculty,' which kept both potential victims and the nations that might have given them refuge from acknowledging the fatal threat to European Jewry that was expanding almost daily."[59]

The clearest example of this was the international response to the refugee crisis. It was the one issue that clearly demanded an international, non-military response from the very beginning.[60] International leaders were forced to review the refugee and emigration policies of their own nations, and determine how this would affect their relations with Nazi Germany.

The historical evidence reveals two conflicting reactions. One is the spontaneous waves of sympathy that occasionally swept various countries following press reports about the Jews' plight. Riegner's account of the public reaction in Switzerland and the 1943 rally in Madison Square Garden are two examples.

Such public displays put pressure on the respective governments to respond. The response of governmental leaders, however, consisted more of piecemeal measures, designed to assuage public opinion, than concrete plans to help the refugees. The two international meetings of Allied governments to deal with the refugee crisis, Evian in 1938 and Bermuda in 1943, yielded no results. Those present at both meetings, especially the United States, made clear from the beginning that they were unwilling to accept more refugees. Observers at both meetings accused the official delegates of deliberate window dressing. A U.S. observer called Evian "a facade behind which the civilized governments could hide their inability to act."[61] His remark was echoed by a British delegate to the Bermuda conference in 1943: that it was "self-justification, a facade for inaction . . . there were no results that I can recall."[62]

As the international response shows, the question of "what people knew" concerns much more than mere knowledge of the genocide. Writing about the silence of the U.S. Christian community, for example, Robert Ross notes that it "was not a silence of ignorance or of lack of information."[63] The American religious press had reported many of the details about the persecution of Jews and even details about the concentration camps. In many cases, "silence," far from representing lack of knowledge, indicated that the foreign community was not prepared to seriously intervene.[64]

The issue, then, is not just what people knew, but what they were prepared to know—the significance they attached to that knowledge. As Karski's account of his discussion with Felix Frankfurter suggests, the readiness to know is absent when there is no fundamental readiness to act. In other words, a basic ethical stance of "preparedness" is necessary for people to become engaged even on the level of simply acknowledging that something is happening. What Langer terms the "aversion-to-crisis faculty" simply means that people whose fundamental stance toward the world around them is passive will tune out what they don't want to know.

This is one reason for the passivity of the international community. To a striking degree, it parallels the behavior we find among bystanders in Germany. Most Germans knew what was happening to the Jews. Yet, as Lawrence Stokes notes, Germans "saw and heard enough to be intimidated, but were sufficiently undisturbed in their own security to remain overwhelmingly passive spectators to the most terrible outrage of their era."[65]

This does not rule out anti-Semitism as a factor; it only suggests that there were other reasons for the passivity of the international community toward the plight of the Jews. To understand more completely why the international community failed as it did, we must consider not only the specific dynamics that shape international institutions, but the issues that confront nations and their representatives when confronted by a crisis occurring behind the borders of another nation.

Nations and Intervention

Certainly some of the international community's failures stemmed from issues similar to those that we find among institutions. Even conscientious representatives of international organizations who wanted to help European Jews were constrained, not just by the lack of support by their members, but by institutional policies. David Wyman cites the example of the International Red Cross, which was asked by the U.S. War Refugee Board in 1942 to convince German authorities to allow the Jews confined in the ghettos and camps to be "assimilated" under the 1929 Geneva Convention. This would have given Jews in the camps prisoner-of-war status, permitting the Red Cross to make regular visits and send food to them. As Wyman writes, "The IRC refused, explaining that such a move would 'go far beyond the limits' of its traditional work and expose it to charges of intervening in Germany's internal affairs."[66] Such a request, argued the IRC, would only antagonize Nazi leaders and undermine its chance to visit the camps at all.

The Red Cross's response was based on pragmatism; in one form or another, most international institutions hedged their bets. The Red Cross did so to protect its ability to carry out its own activities. But there were numerous nongovernmental, noncharitable institutions—such as banks and other businesses—who, far from using their connections to pressure German colleagues to change what was happening in their country, actually sought to profit from the situation. Decades after the end of the Holocaust, the details of such international complicity are still emerging. The record of the Swiss banking community, which laundered Nazi money and froze the accounts of the Jewish victims, is one example; the number of artistic works owned by Jewish victims that ended up in major art collections and prominent museums is another.

The Red Cross's response, however, raises a serious issue that confronted all international organizations: the principle of national sovereignty. As long as other nations recognized Adolf Hitler as the legitimate German head of state, international organizations that opposed Nazi measures found little open support from their respective government leaders. Like their governments, they had to respect the integrity of national boundaries (a key argument made by the Red Cross throughout the period). And, after war began in 1939, the activities of international organizations were secondary to the military priorities set by their governments. Religious refugee work became a "political orphan" during World War II; "once America entered the war, religious groups were expected to conform to Allied military policy."[67]

Even before the war, international organizations respected the boundaries of German national sovereignty. While viewed with alarm and abhorrence outside of Germany, the Nazis' repressive measures against German citizens—Jews, political dissidents, some sectors of the churches—were seen as grounds for protest, not intervention. In its postwar review of its behavior, the Red Cross stated this explicitly:

The right to humanitarian actions was, however, [the] only authority for trespassing in a field which States considered to be exclusively their domestic concern, in which no international treaty provisions could run. Some measure of prudence was therefore essential, and the Committee refrained from steps that held no hope of success; these would merely have resulted in compromising, to no one's advantage, those of the Committee's activities that rested on tradition or on the Conventions.[68]

Related to the issue of national sovereignty is the fact, as Ervin Staub notes, "that states have traditionally not regarded themselves as having moral responsibilities."[69] International organizations like the Red Cross believed that their responsibility was to carry out their institutional purpose. For the modern nation-state, objective self-interest is its primary responsibility. This imposes clear restrictions on what outside states and organizations will even attempt on moral grounds. As historian Henry Feingold says, "It is more dangerous than ever to be powerless in the secular world because the modern nation state is not capable of making human responses, and the moral force, which perhaps once permitted monarchs to do so, no longer exists."[70]

Feingold is not denying the existence of compassion and concern. His point is that the case for intervention in the affairs of another country is no longer based upon a king's moral convictions or pragmatic alliances, but only where a nation's self-interest gives it a stake in what happens elsewhere. In the case of Nazi Germany, the perception of other nations was that their interests were endangered only after their territorial borders were threatened. The 1938 Munich agreement, and British prime minister Neville Chamberlain's famous statement that the treaty had achieved "peace in our time," have become metaphors for the dangers of compliance with the terms set by dictators. In retrospect, it is easy to see that Nazi Germany posed a threat to Europe long before it attacked Poland on September 1, 1939.

But the development of international intervention during the Holocaust is largely a tale of how different countries became involved in World War II. For the nations of Europe, of course, this was not a matter of choice. The German attack on Poland forced the international community to confront the Nazi threat to Europe, at least militarily. The lesson many people derived from this history was that a nation like Nazi Germany can only be defeated, and its victims rescued, by military force.

What else might have been possible? When Jan Karski visited Allied leaders in 1943, he asked them to give Nazi leaders a list of ultimatums that had been compiled by eastern European Jewish leaders. The ultimatums were explicit and practical, calling upon the Allies to "inform the German nation through radio, leaflets, and other means about the government's crimes against the Jews" and warn the Germans of the military steps that would be taken if the genocide were not stopped.[71]

It is impossible to know, of course, whether such ultimatums might have saved more lives. The experience with Nazi Germany taught other countries a great deal about the dangers of acquiescence to dictators, but did not result in clear international principles on how to respond to such threats in the future. Where military action is ruled out, most nations limit intervention in other countries to humanitarian aid and diplomatic initiatives. Even when United Nations troops are deployed, their mission is often explicitly nonmilitary (e.g., they are deployed to protect aid officials or refugees). Establishing the rationale and terms for such involvement is difficult. Diplomacy and other forms of nonmilitary leverage have successfully averted war and improved political circumstances in some cases, but they appear ineffective when confronted by the Holocaust and other cases of modern genocide.

This reality has led historian Henry Feingold to make a sober assessment. In an article about the response of the American Jewish community to the Holocaust, Feingold calls for a new look "to make sense, if sense can be made, of their indifference. We may discover that the assigning of humanitarian mission, to states, agencies and communities like American Jewry, is an exercise in futility."[72]

Should the persecution and genocide of the Jews have been grounds for international intervention? Should similar criteria for intervention exist today? How should a nation address a conflict in which it has no direct stake? At what point is intervention called for? Are there situations that demand our response on moral and humanitarian grounds, even where no pragmatic grounds for involvement exist (and where, perhaps, there is good reason *not* to get involved)? Various forums have wrestled with these questions since 1945. The only criteria that emerged in the wake of the Holocaust was for establishing international tribunals that could bring the offending nation and its leaders to justice—which, in the case of Nazi Germany, only became possible after its military defeat.

Even in Nuremburg, the limitations of international law in dealing with the issues raised by genocide became evident. Those limitations arose at the dividing line between individual and collective responsibility. Lyal Sunga, author of a study of international law and human rights, succinctly states the problem:

Most human rights instruments in international law are designed to restrain the State rather than the individual human being from violating human rights . . . Accordingly, many human rights, especially civil and political rights, whether guaranteed nationally or internationally, are directed against the power of the State and formulated in the negative. They oblige the State rather than other entities, not to interfere unduly with the rights and freedoms of individuals . . .

Where the State is oblivious to international pressure and fails to undertake or honour human rights obligations, individuals who actually carry out human rights violations are not likely to be punished.

An effective way to deter human rights violations in these types of cases may be to expose the individual responsible for committing the violation to risk of international legal sanction in a personal capacity. Almost all existing rules of international responsibility bind States only; the individual is bound only in exceptional circumstances.[73]

Conversely, Sunga continues, states are responsible under international law for such violations

only . . . if the act committed by the individual offense could be imputed to the State. In other words, no responsibility of the State and hence no reparation, would be possible unless the State was responsible for the act committed by the agent. Accordingly, the general thrust of State responsibility in classic international law is the establishment of imputability of the State for certain wrongs committed by its agents or organs.[74]

Sunga's analysis pinpoints the problem: in cases of genocide, where are individuals responsible, and where does a collective responsibility exist? In Nuremberg, only individual Nazi leaders were tried, not the German nation itself; nothing else would have been possible under international law. Where the postwar German state did assume a kind of collective national responsibility (notably through the reparations Germany paid to the state of Israel and to individual concentration camp survivors), its policies were based on political considerations, not established legal principle.

These distinctions—between what is legally, morally, or politically pos-

sible in administering justice—have often been used to excuse moral evasion or cowardice. Yet it may be necessary to recognize their importance,
if we are ever to discover the possibilities for moral advocacy on the international level. It is a question that continues to haunt us today. Decades
after the end of the Third Reich, the international community still has not
discovered a way to determine the grounds for intervention in response to
persecution or genocide. If anything, the phenomenon of genocide and the
terrible examples of totalitarian regimes during this century have reminded
us both of the horrific control wielded by modern totalitarianism and of
the widespread powerlessness—not just among citizens of those societies,
but of the outside world as well—to combat such brutality.

Yet despite our despair over the moral failures of individuals—and our
fear that, as Feingold puts it, "greater values" may not exist—there are
possibilities contained within the dry concepts of international law. In the
wake of the Eichmann trial, Hannah Arendt reflected on this, citing Nuremberg prosecutor Telford Taylor:

Criminal proceedings, since they are mandatory and thus initiated even if the victim
would prefer to forgive and forget, rest on laws whose "essence"—to quote Telford
Taylor, writing in the *New York Times Magazine*—"is that a crime is not committed only against the victim but primarily against the community whose law is
violated." The wrongdoer is brought to justice because his act has disturbed and
gravely endangered the community as a whole, and not because, as in civil suits,
damage has been done to individuals who are entitled to reparation. The reparation
effected in criminal cases is of an altogether different nature; it is the body politic
itself that stands in need of being "repaired," and it is the general public order that
has been thrown out of gear and must be restored, as it were. It is, in other words,
the law, not the plaintiff, that must prevail.[75]

Taylor (and Arendt) recognized that the significance of the Nazi crimes
went far beyond the injuries done to individual victims. A crime had been
committed against the human community, and this required some response
from the human community. Taylor was speaking of morality, of course,
but in a very different sense than Niebuhr had. The morality of the greater
human community is what law, or justice based upon law, is all about.
Indeed, we could argue that the kind of morality of law that Taylor defends
can be enacted *only* on the collective or communal level. During the Holocaust, individuals were far more effective than institutions in offering
compassion and rescue to the victims. But they could not stop the Nazi
machinery of murder. J. Nichols's summary of the situation depicts its complexity:

No credible international organization had been formed to coordinate governmental efforts; the Roosevelt administration spoke eloquently of the plight of European Jews, but its actions indicated a desire to distance itself from politically

unpopular efforts to liberalize immigration law or otherwise to increase the number
of Jews reaching America. International diplomats considered schemes to purchase
the lives of refugees; political leaders dreamed of impractical colonization plans;
religious leaders argued for their favored approaches; and the public was left divided between the appeals of refugee advocates and the shrill denunciations of
immigration restrictionists and America Firsters.[76]

The complexity of this situation may help us to understand why the
occasional public outbursts of compassion like those in Switzerland and
the United States did not lead anywhere. When Niebuhr argued that a
"collective ethics" was impossible, perhaps he was trying to say the same
thing as Feingold—that it is unrealistic to expect a "collective spirit" of
morality to emerge from thousands of individuals joining together. Such
collective outbursts may express emotion, but that is not the same thing as
morality. The only thing that could have helped was a deliberate and consistent international response to the genocide—something that governments
were unwilling or unable to develop. Aside from military solutions, the
collective refusal of humanity to tolerate genocide, as exemplified in the
legal sensibility of justice described by Taylor, may be the *only* force that
can stop genocide.

This failure brings us back to the gap described earlier: between empathy
and action, between true knowledge and denial. In considering this gap,
the deeper issue is the ineffectiveness—some would say the nonexistence—
of greater values. Henry Feingold poignantly writes that many people believed "that there exists such a spirit of civilization, a sense of humanitarian
concern in the world, which could have been mobilized to save Jewish lives
during the Holocaust." But such a spirit, says Feingold, "did not in fact
exist."[77]

Is this true? As some of the illustrations offered above show, it would
seem that in some cases, such a spirit did exist. The historical record shows
a far greater range of responses to the plight of the European Jews than is
often conceded. Whether this adds up to "a spirit of civilization," however,
is another question.

The dichotomy between the failure of such a spirit, and the few instances
where it emerged, is worth exploring if we are truly to understand what
happened to international bystanders during the Holocaust. If their passivity was based upon prejudice or lack of compassion, we can draw certain
ethical conclusions from that. If, however, bystanders actually tried or
wanted to do something but failed—which, as the record shows, is what
happened in some cases—then we must draw a more nuanced conclusion
about the ethical standards and failures of these bystanders.

In any case, it is evident that various factors converged to create what
we could call the "moral world" of the bystanders. As Telford Taylor realized, the moral foundation of individual responsibility is based upon a

sense of connection and responsibility to a greater whole. There are numerous links between the role of individuals and the collective power of institutions and the international community. In the next section, we will explore how these links created a world in which genocide was possible.

NOTES

1. Staub, *The Roots of Evil*, 237.
2. Ibid., 238.
3. Heinz Bergschicker, ed., *Deutsche Chronik 1933–1945: Alltag im Faschismus* (Berlin: Elefanten Press, 1983), 52.
4. Gellately, *The Gestapo and German Society*, 184.
5. See Gerlach, *Als die Zeugen schwiegen*, 37–40. The English translation of Gerlach's book is being published by the University of Nebraska Press.
6. Ibid.
7. For a more detailed history, see Rosemary Radford Ruether, *Faith and Fratricide: The Theological Roots of Anti-Semitism* (Minneapolis: Seabury, 1974).
8. Cohen, *The Tremendum*, 12–13.
9. Gerlach, *Als die Zeugen schwiegen*, 120.
10. Ibid., 370.
11. Ibid., 153–154, 158.
12. See John S. Conway, *The Nazi Persecution of the Churches 1933–1945* (New York: Basic Books, 1968), 76–77, 101–103, and chapter 8 for the comments of other Nazi leaders, especially Martin Bormann.
13. For details on how this occurred with regard to specific issues like the anti-Jewish policies and euthanasia, see Victoria Barnett, *For the Soul of the People: Protestant Protest against Hitler* (New York: Oxford University Press, 1992), 110–121, 152–154.
14. Quoted in Barnett, *For the Soul of the People*, 209.
15. Max Weber, *The Protestant Ethic and the Spirit of Capitalism*, translated by Talcott Parsons (Los Angeles: Roxbury Publishing Company, 1996).
16. From *Max Weber: Essays in Sociology*, trans. Hans Gerth and C. Wright Mills (New York: Oxford University Press, 1946), 215.
17. Weber, "The Meaning of Ethical Neutrality," in *The Methodology of the Social Sciences*, trans. and ed. by Edward A. Shils and Henry A. Finsch (New York: Free Press of Glencoe, Inc., 1949), 16.
18. In Bauman, *Modernity*, 22.
19. Arendt, *Eichmann in Jerusalem*, 127.
20. Kelman, "Violence without Moral Restraint," 25–49.
21. Staub, *Roots of Evil*, 66.
22. Bauman, *Modernity*, 168.
23. Friedländer, The *Origins of Nazi Genocide*, 119.
24. Ibid., 119–123.
25. See Ernst Klee, *Euthanasie im NS-Staat* (Frankfurt: Fischer Verlag, 1983).
26. Kateb, *Hannah Arendt*, 73.
27. Ibid., 19.
28. Ibid., 18.

29. Ibid., 126.

30. Haas, *Morality after Auschwitz*, 111.

31. Staub, *Roots of Evil*, 122–125.

32. William Shawcross, *The Quality of Mercy. Cambodia, Holocaust and Modern Conscience* (New York: Simon & Schuster, 1984), 47–48.

33. Hilberg, *Perpetrators, Victims, Bystanders*, 255.

34. Gerhard Riegner, "Switzerland and the Leadership of Its Jewish Community during the Second World War," in Randolph L. Braham, ed., *Jewish Leadership during the Nazi Era*. Social Science Monographs and Institute for Holocaust Studies of the City University of New York (New York: Columbia University Press, 1985), 80.

35. Ibid., 81.

36. J. Bruce Nichols, *The Uneasy Alliance: Religion, Refugee Work, and U.S. Foreign Policy* (New York: Oxford University Press, 1988), 60.

37. Feingold, *The Politics of Rescue*, 175.

38. See especially "Part one: Perceptions of the Holocaust," in Marrus, ed. *The Nazi Holocaust: 8. Bystanders to the Holocaust*, Vol. 1, 3–121.

39. Ross, *So It Was True*, 271.

40. See Lipstadt, *Beyond Belief*.

41. Gerlach, *Als die Zeugen schwiegen*, Note 71, 112.

42. Ibid., 112.

43. Eberhard Bethge, *Dietrich Bonhoeffer: Man of Vision, Man of Courage*, ed. by Edwin Robertson (New York: Harper & Row, 1970), 369.

44. Willem A. Visser't Hooft, *Memoirs* (Philadelphia: Westminster Press, 1973), 91.

45. Ibid., 167.

46. For a nuanced overview of how different nations responded, see Yehuda Bauer, "Jew and Gentile: The Holocaust and After," in Michael R. Marrus, *The Nazi Holocaust: Historical Articles on the Destruction of European Jews* (Westport, CT: Meckler, 1989), Volume 4.1, *The "Final Solution" Outside Germany*, 19–63.

47. Ross, *So It Was True*, 287–288.

48. For a comprehensive account of the ecumenical response in the United States, see Genizi, *American Apathy: The Plight of Christian Refugees from Nazism*.

49. See Wyman, *The Abandonment of the Jews*, 102–104.

50. Minutes, Nov. 5 1934. Federal Council of Churches papers, *RG18 Box 3 F 12 "American Committee for Christian Refugees Jan 34–Dec 1937,"* Presbyterian Church (USA) Department of History and Records Management Services, Philadelphia.

51. See Wyman, *The Abandonment of the Jews*, 14–15; Lipstadt, *Beyond Belief*, 127.

52. Nichols, *The Uneasy Alliance*, 41.

53. Ibid.

54. Ibid., 46.

55. Marrus, *The Holocaust in History*, 169–170.

56. Ibid., 158.

57. Maciej Koslowski, "The Mission that Failed" (interview with Jan Karski), in Polonsky, *My Brother's Keeper?*, 87–88.

58. Ibid., 95.

59. Langer, "What More Can Be Said about the Holocaust?" in *Admitting the Holocaust*, 179.

60. See Feingold, *The Politics of Rescue*; and also Genizi, *American Apathy: The Plight of Christian Refugees from Nazism*.

61. Feingold, *The Politics of Rescue*, 33.

62. Nichols, *The Uneasy Alliance*, 61.

63. Ross, *So It Was True*, 286.

64. Ibid., 289.

65. Lawrence D. Stokes, "The German People and the Destruction of the European Jews," in Marrus, *The Nazi Holocaust*, Vol. 5.1: *Public Opinion and Relations to the Jews in Nazi Europe*, 85.

66. Wyman, *The Abandonment of the Jews*, 283–284.

67. Nichols, *The Uneasy Alliance*, 53, 55.

68. *Report of the International Committee of the Red Cross on Its Activities during the Second World War*, Vol. III, "Relief Activities" (Geneva: ICRC, May 1948).

69. Staub, *The Roots of Evil*, 158.

70. Feingold, "The Witness Role of American Jewry: A Second Look," in Ryan, *Human Responses to the Holocaust*, 91.

71. From Koslowski, "The Mission that Failed," in Polonsky, *My Brother's Keeper?*, 83–84.

72. Henry Feingold, "The Witness Role of American Jewry: A Second Look," in Ryan, *Human Responses to the Holocaust*, 83.

73. Sunga, *Individual Responsibility in International Law*, 1–2.

74. Ibid., 20.

75. Arendt, *Eichmann in Jerusalem*, 261.

76. Nichols, *The Uneasy Alliance*, 50–51.

77. Feingold, "Who Shall Bear Guilt for the Holocaust: The Human Dilemma," in Marrus, *The Nazi Holocaust*, Vol. 8.2: *Bystanders to the Holocaust*, 141–142.

CHAPTER 4

Interpreting the Holocaust

As we have seen, studies of human behavior—whether in small villages like Sonderburg and Mauthausen, in institutions like hospitals, or internationally—offer a complex picture of how ordinary people behaved during the Holocaust. The vast majority of people, in Germany and elsewhere, became "bystanders." What factors combined to make them so?

To understand the behavior of bystanders, we must interpret the Holocaust. In essence, we must answer the question: "What happened?" The question may seem absurd. We know what happened to the European Jews and the other victims of Nazism, in painful detail. Yet neither the question nor our responses to it are purely historical. Every study of the Holocaust is an interpretation of what the writer thinks happened. The premise of this book, for example, is that the behavior of bystanders has both historical and ethical significance for any understanding of the Holocaust. Another scholar might focus on another issue, such as economic or political developments, religious prejudice, or German cultural dynamics.

In fact, there are a number of very different, and often conflicting, interpretations of the Holocaust. One of the most interesting recent intellectual controversies concerned Harvard scholar Daniel Goldhagen's book, *Hitler's Willing Executioners*, published in 1996. Goldhagen contends that the majority of Germans had voluntarily and enthusiastically carried out the genocide of the Jews. Goldhagen argues that German culture was so thoroughly anti-Semitic that genocide was virtually inevitable, and concludes that a uniquely German "exterminationist" anti-Semitism was the sole cause of the Holocaust.

A number of scholars vehemently disagree with Goldhagen's thesis. As the ensuing debate illustrates, Holocaust scholars hold a variety of historical and political views; it is possible to interpret the same historical material quite differently. Psychiatrist Bruno Bettelheim viewed the Holocaust as not "the latest chapter in anti-Semitism but rather one among the first chapters in modern totalitarianism."[1] Philosopher Hannah Arendt made a similar argument, focusing on the historical and political emergence of totalitarianism in Nazi Germany; she attributed the passivity of bystanders to fear and perceived powerlessness. Sociologist Zygmunt Bauman has analyzed the Holocaust in the context of modernity—not as the product of uniquely German circumstances, but as an inherent possibility in any modern society. "We live in a type of society that made the Holocaust possible," he writes, "and that contained nothing which could stop the Holocaust from happening."[2] Ervin Staub in contrast, emphasizes the psychological and cultural roots of genocide.

In other words, historical clarity about *what* happened doesn't mean unanimity about *how* or *why* it happened, or even about what significance the Holocaust has for the rest of the world, decades later. Anti-Semitism, psychological factors, modernity, German cultural traits, and compartmentalized bureaucracies have all been cited as primary causes of the Holocaust.

Virtually all these interpretations are linked to how their proponents judge and understand human behavior during the Holocaust. Invariably, judgments about bystander behavior are connected not only to our interpretation of what happened, but to the ethical conclusions we draw as a result. In turn, our ethical and historical conclusions determine our understanding of the bystanders. If we agree with Goldhagen that almost all Germans had been inculcated with a virulent hatred of the Jews, we are making some very clear assumptions about the role of bystanders. We would conclude, for example, that the apathy or passivity of bystanders who were not directly involved in the genocide reflected their approval of it. If, on the other hand, we accept Bauman's thesis that the Holocaust emerged from the structures of modernity, we might interpret the passive indifference of bystanders as an expression of individual powerlessness, a characteristic we find in many modern societies. Accordingly, Bauman argues that a Holocaust-like situation is possible anywhere; Goldhagen believes that it could only have happened in Germany.

The task of Holocaust interpretation entails more than taking a historical standpoint and defending it. The study of the Holocaust compels us to examine the deepest levels of historical consciousness and ethical significance. Saul Friedländer once wrote that, as the *Shoah* becomes part of history, its memory would become "ritualized" for some and "historicized" for most.[3] For most scholars of the Holocaust, however, these two aspects are interwoven. In a sense, we seek to ritualize what really happened—to make our historical analysis both accurate and ethically responsible. In this sense, much Holocaust scholarship itself is a response to the event. As we do our research, many of us hear Rabbi Irving Greenberg's warning to write nothing that could not be said in the presence of burning children.

In other words, the task of interpreting the Holocaust historically operates under a unique burden, and many of the controversies are based not only on historical differences of opinion, but on their ethical implications. During the 1980s, for example, the so-called German revisionist historians, led by Ernst Nolte, contended that the death camps were an accidental side effect of Germany's war against the Soviet Union. Most scholars found Nolte's revisionist arguments both historically untenable and ethically offensive.

In analyzing the ethical consequences of Holocaust interpretations, Zygmunt Bauman has noted that the narrowest interpretations (e.g., seeing it as a uniquely German development) tend to let the rest of humanity off the hook. In other words, if the Holocaust is the singular outcome of German history or culture, it poses no fundamental questions for the rest of us. Yet, interpretations on the other extreme—which view the Holocaust as just one more case of human evil—ignore those aspects that are unique to the Holocaust. "One way or another," writes Bauman, "the bomb is defused; no major revision of our social theory is really necessary."[4]

The recognition that the task of understanding the Holocaust is twofold—historical and ethical—is one reason why the process of interpreting the Holocaust has gradually changed in the decades since 1945. Theologian Arthur Cohen has outlined four stages in the development of Holocaust studies, each one marked by a different level of knowledge and interpretation. The decade that followed 1945, for example, "was the time of the statistical accounting . . . and dealing of judgment to the accused, culminating in the Eichmann trial of 1961."[5] The second decade was marked by the emergence of Holocaust literature like the early writings of Elie Wiesel, whose "vivifying witness" elaborated on the statistics. In the third decade, says Cohen, " 'the question of meaning' became central."[6] The fourth decade (during which Cohen wrote his book on the Holocaust as *tremendum*) was one in which "the distance between ourselves and *the event* . . . has grown," leading to a more comprehensive vantage point from which to examine the Holocaust.[7] The gradual descent to the depths of the history of the Holocaust, says Cohen, also reflected a movement from one level of consciousness to another—from "thinking about the historical" to "thinking about the meaning of the historical."[8]

As Cohen's four stages suggest, history, ritual, and ethics influence one another. There are few studies of the Holocaust that do not touch on all three levels of understanding. How we interpret an event renders an ethical judgement, which in turn shapes how we ritualize the event—whether through the act of memory or ritual itself.

How do we go about interpreting the behavior of bystanders in the historical context of the Holocaust—bringing these figures out of the shadows and examining their actions, motivations, and beliefs? The task is not an easy one. Although bystanders had a great deal to do with the Holocaust, most of our reliable information is about the perpetrators and victims. The bystanders are the silent figures that populate the background; many of their motives are unreadable and therefore much more open to interpretation.

In the following chapters, we will review how scholars from various disciplines have interpreted the Holocaust, in the hope of gaining some ethical insights about the significance of bystanders.

HISTORICAL INTERPRETATIONS OF THE HOLOCAUST

History, to paraphrase Shakespeare, is a stage on which major dramas are played out, involving nations and often lasting years. Each of the millions of people who cross this stage has a role, however small or great. Through the lens of history, we can see where individuals, institutions, and nations stand in relation to one another. Drawing closer to examine the details of the historical drama, we learn more about who these people are, how and why they stand where they do, and how they affect one another.

The historical outline of the drama is based on the dates, numbers, and statistics that tell us what happened and who was involved. Sometimes the historical facts offer clear explanations for how and why something happened: the assassination of a king leads to chaos or a shift in power; a war results in a number of dead and the realignment of boundaries; growing industrialization lures workers in from rural areas and leads to the rise of large urban centers.

But even the facts take us only so far. They do not entirely explain why Nazism arose in Germany, why it took the forms it did, and why the Germans under Nazism eventually tried to murder all the Jews in Europe. To form any conclusions, we must wrestle with more complicated issues that are not always immediately visible on the historical stage. While a detailed history of Nazi Germany or the Holocaust is beyond the scope of this book, an overview of the basic facts is necessary before we can focus on their possible significance for bystander behavior.

Even here, there are a number of possible starting points. We can go as far back as the beginning of humankind to observe the bloody history of collective human behavior against people or groups deemed to be "outsiders." We can examine the history of Christianity and the centuries of church-condoned persecution of the Jews throughout Europe. We can analyze the effect of the Enlightenment and the emergence of secularism, tolerance, and civil liberties in many European countries, including Germany, reflected by the Jewish emancipation that occurred in the 19th century.

Looking specifically at Germany, we see a region whose people first began to wrestle with the concept of nationhood during the late 19th century, under the leadership of Otto von Bismarck. In the process, the question of what it meant to be German took on political, cultural, and ethnic connotations; not surprisingly, this led an increasingly ideologized definition about who was "not" German. This coincided with a resurgence of nationalist and racialized thinking throughout late 19th-century Europe.[9]

After its defeat in 1918, Germany embarked on a fifteen-year experiment in parliamentary democracy for which it was not prepared, and which it endured with great resentment and bitterness. On all levels of society, things fell apart. The Weimar Republic was governed by a series of coalitions whose members fought bitterly with one another. The period was marked by economic insecurity, high unemployment, and the growth of extremist groups on the right and the left. By the end of the 1920s, both the Nazi and the Communist parties were drawing enough votes in popular elections to make them a significant political factor. Part of Adolf Hitler's appeal to the German mainstream, in fact, was that he seemed to offer a viable political alternative to Communism. In a political landscape noticeably bereft of strong leadership, he appeared to be a decisive and charismatic political leader.

As a result, most Germans welcomed the emergence of the Nazi party as a strong partner in the government coalition established after the 1933 elections. That coalition was short-lived. The Nazi leadership consolidated its power rapidly and totally, and Hitler's first moves were to dismantle the power of his coalition partners. Real and potential political enemies were murdered, imprisoned, or exiled; opposing political parties were banned. The civil service gradually became an extension of the Nazi party. A steady progression of laws systematically excluded the Jews from German society, beginning with the civil service and the universities, escalating with the 1935 Nuremberg laws, and culminating in the laws requiring Jews to wear the yellow star and, finally, in the deportations to the death camps. Nazi Germany also sought to dominate Europe, beginning with the diplomatic intimidation of neighboring countries and, eventually, waging a war of conquest that laid waste to Europe. Wherever they went, the Nazis sought to eradicate the Jewish population as well.

From 1933 to 1939, the response of the rest of Europe, and the world, was overwhelmingly passive. There were tentative foreign protests against the anti-Jewish measures in Germany, but other nations continued to maintain diplomatic relations with Germany. When Hitler directly challenged the international community—by leaving the League of Nations in 1933, rearming the German military in 1935, annexing Austria and the Sudetenland in 1938—international leaders retreated. Indeed, historian Gordon Craig writes,

the Western Powers seemed to believe the economic appeasement would persuade Hitler to become a peaceful and satisfied member of the international community, and they not only did not insist that the German Government make good its deficits in trading accounts and pay its debts to their citizens, but redoubled their efforts to confer economic advantage upon Hitler whenever he committed an outrageous action.[10]

Nor did the international community take the plight of the growing number of refugees seriously, either by opening foreign borders to them or by exerting pressure on Germany.[11] The few attempts to deal with the refugee issue—notably the international conference at Evian, Switzerland in 1938—failed. Viewing the Jews as a "problem," the countries represented at Evian had no desire to absorb thousands of Jewish emigrants. Only with the German attack on Poland and the war's rapid spread throughout Europe did the international community stand up to Nazi Germany—a response motivated by self-defense and national self-interest, not on behalf of the victims of Nazism.

Throughout this period, the historical evidence shows a wide range of behavior among Germans, from enthusiastic support for Nazism to silent "indifference" to active resistance. Already, we can see that the historical record does not answer all our questions. Was German enthusiasm for the new regime based on anti-Semitism, or nationalism? Did it express a combination of factors, such as relief at the end of the economic depression, and hope for renewed national pride? Was "indifference"—inside and outside Nazi Germany—merely a mask for anti-Semitism? To what extent did it reflect other emotions, such as fear, political conformity, or, outside Nazi Germany, uncertainty about how to respond effectively to the refugee crisis? Where resistance arose, was it really on behalf of the victims of Nazism, or was it motivated more by internal political considerations? What are the roots of bystander complicity, whether it was expressed as passivity or as active support for the regime? Can the tangled threads of complicity be traced back to a single source?

Despite the scope of detailed scholarship on the Holocaust, there is no conclusive answer to these questions, and scholars confront several problems in analyzing them. The historical record reveals a broad spectrum of behavior, among both Germans and people outside Germany, and a number of details must be taken into consideration. Yehuda Bauer observes

that motivations and actions differed; that one must differentiate between different national traditions, between different political and economic circumstances, between nations conquered by the Nazis and those on the outside, between people and their leaders . . . generalizations are easy to utter and much more difficult to defend.[12]

In the case of the Holocaust or any genocide, religious or ethnic hatred would appear to be the obvious motive. Why else would an entire population be targeted, and why else would there be so little resistance to the genocide among the nonvictim population? The underlying question, however, is whether this reason is sufficient in itself, or whether other factors played a decisive role in "activating" this hatred. What combination of factors enables prejudice to culminate in the genocide of an entire people? And is prejudice really the central factor, or do other causes play an even more important role in unleashing the violence against the victims?

To answer these questions, we need to have a clear picture of how people actually did respond to the Nazi persecution of the Jews and the other victims, from the early beginnings of that persecution in 1933 to its final form in the death camps. The studies of individual, institutional, and international behavior reviewed in the previous chapters offer some insights into what happened. Three specific historical issues are crucial to understanding the role of bystanders during the Holocasut: the dynamics of totalitarianism; the development and role of prejudice; and the underlying dynamics of the widespread "indifference" that existed. Subsequent chapters will deal with these three points in detail. First, however, there are two general issues that form the background of any historical overview: the incremental development of Nazi policies; and how cultural, social, and political dynamics shape individual and collective behavior in any society.

THE INCREMENTAL DEVELOPMENT OF NAZI POLICIES

In January 1933, no one, inside or outside Germany, realized that the newly established Third Reich would culminate in the annihilation of the European Jews. While the brutal and totalitarian nature of Nazi rule was evident within days of Hitler's rise to power, it was not at all clear where Nazi policies would lead. Historians have long debated whether Hitler planned from the beginning to murder the Jews (as the "intentionalists" claim) or whether the genocide evolved from Nazi policies initially intended only to drive Jews out of German territory (this is the "functionalist" position). It is safe to say that, although the genocide of Jews was certainly one possible outcome of Nazi policies from the beginning, it hardly seemed inevitable to observers at the time.

This incremental development is a factor that distinguishes the Holocaust from other genocides in history, most of which have occurred in the course of bitter civil wars or clearly delineated political struggles. Genocide is usually preceded by a long history of political, territorial, and ethnic animosity, which, provoked by a political crisis, spirals out of control into an orgy of mass murder. These genocides are in some sense historically and politically "explicable" (although the term should be used cautiously).

There are parallels in the events that led up to the Holocaust. There was a long history of the persecution of Jews in Christian Europe, and the evidence shows that anti-Semitism certainly shaped the reaction of bystanders in Nazi Germany and abroad. Yet historians do not unanimously support the notion that anti-Semitism, in and of itself, led to the catastrophic measures against the Jewish people.[13] They note other historical developments—such as the Enlightenment, the growth of parliamentary democracy, and the Jewish emancipation in many regions of Europe—that actually seemed to indicate a greater tolerance, and a departure from the "ghettoization" of Jews.

Nowhere, in fact, did these liberalizing trends appear stronger than in Germany. After the pogroms in eastern Europe in the early 20th century, many of the Jewish refugees from those countries went to Germany.[14] Even then, the Jewish percentage of the German population dwindled steadily after 1880 and comprised less than 2 percent of the population in 1933.[15] There were no territorial disputes (a source of ethnic animosity in other situations) between Jewish and non-Jewish Germans.[16]

Of all the Jewish populations in Europe, the Jews who lived in Germany believed themselves to be the most assimilated. Nonetheless, the few in-depth portraits we have of German villages at the beginning of the Nazi era (such as Henry's study of Sonderburg) illustrate the limits of this assimilation, revealing how Jews and non-Jews existed as separate communities, despite the increased opportunities for Jews in the public sphere (a result of the emancipation laws).[17]

The first signals of potential genocide in Germany were not the eruption of civil war or the resurrection of long-standing animosities between different ethnic groups, but state measures that many ordinary Germans shrugged off as esoteric civil liberties questions. We now know where the dismantling of civil liberties can lead; one of the legacies of the Holocaust, particularly in Germany, is an appreciation of their importance. In 1933, however, Nazi racial laws were only part of a number of policies restructuring every aspect of German life, banning certain organizations and absorbing others into party-led organizations. Most Germans were concerned only about the regulations that applied to them. Even those directly affected by the racial laws failed to grasp the larger issues at stake. Initially, people who were partly "non-Aryan" under the new racial laws, Jews who had converted to Christianity, and Jews who had served in the German military in World War I mistakenly believed that they would be safer than "full Jews." They responded to the new racial laws not with public protests, but with private attempts to seek exemption.

Nazi racial policy and the persecution of the Jews developed gradually—

a fact that should be considered independently of the degree to which anti-Semitism shaped the actions and beliefs of non-Jewish Germans. Lawrence Stokes observes that "just as Nazi social policy, for example, was very different in 1933 from what it became in 1939, so too the regime's racial program underwent a steady evolution after 1933, almost invariably in the direction of increasing radicalization."[18] Public awareness of the ominous consequences of these policies grew incrementally as well. The realization that it was urgently necessary to resist such policies came far too late. A few Jews and non-Jews had the foresight to leave Germany when Hitler became chancellor. Most did not, and it is poignant to trace, in the diaries and letters that remain, how long it took victims and bystanders alike to realize the full implications of Hitler's policies.

It is easy to overlook this factor, since, in retrospect, the persecution and genocide of the Jews appears to be the definitive aspect of Nazi political and social culture. Yet six years passed between Hitler's ascent to power and the first mass killings of Jews in Poland in 1939; the first deportations of German Jews began in 1941. During the early Nazi period, even Jewish Germans did not imagine that Nazi policies would culminate in genocide. While a wave of Jewish emigrants left Nazi Germany after the enactment of the civil service laws in 1933, annual levels of Jewish emigration actually dropped in subsequent years, rising again only after the November pogrom in 1938.[19] Some who had initially emigrated in 1933 even returned in 1934 and 1935.[20]

The gradual intensification of the Nazi persecution of the Jews had two clear historical consequences. Because genocidal policies evolved gradually, there was time to create a extensive bureaucracy, to build the death camps and develop ever more precise methods of "extermination." The well-organized, smoothly running bureaucracy of death that resulted was one development that distinguishes the Holocaust from other genocides.

Indeed, we can argue that the incremental movement toward genocide was one factor that shaped the specific nature of the Holocaust, allowing for interaction between the technology of genocide and "the dehumanization of the victims."[21]

Second, and more importantly, this incremental development allowed genocidal policies to become an integral part of Nazi German culture and society. Despite apologists' claims, this was not something that occurred outside German borders during the war; the ground was laid thoroughly, beginning in 1933. In the process, Germans in all walks of life became implicated as the genocidal bureaucracy began to affect them.

This historical fact is a crucial one when we examine the behavior of bystanders between 1933 and 1945. The fact that it took years for people to grasp the significance of Nazi racial policies influenced the behavior of bystanders in two respects. The first is that people at all levels of society grasped the serious implications of what was happening to the Jews too late. This was true outside Germany as well. Despite the sporadic foreign protests against measures like the 1933 boycotts of Jewish businesses and the 1938 November pogrom, no one realized that the desperate situation of the Jews under Nazism would culminate in genocide and end only with Germany's military defeat.

The second consequence of the incremental severity of Nazi racial policies is that very few Germans remained unaffected by the growing pressures on ordinary citizens. A few courageous individuals stood in clear political opposition to the new Nazi regime in 1933; most of them had soon been killed, imprisoned, or exiled.[22] The rest of the populace was ensnared in an ever-tightening web of complicity. Laws that seemed innocuous in 1933 had more ominous significance by 1935—but, by 1935, Germans had lived for two years under Nazism, and become enmeshed in certain patterns of behavior that made them less free and able to resist. It is easier to leave a ship when it is still in the harbor than when it has reached the open seas.

This dynamic was examined in the studies of human behavior cited earlier. Sociologists Herbert Kelman and Stanley Milgram have both cited "sequential action" as a factor that helps to "lock" people into a situation. A significant aspect of the Milgram experiments, in fact, was that the increases in voltage were in small increments.[23] By the time Milgram's subjects were applying supposedly painful shocks to the "learners," they had already complied with the notion that their role in the experiment was to apply shocks. As Kelman notes, once an individual "has taken the initial step, he is in a new psychological and social situation in which the pressures to continue are quite powerful."[24] In his book *Ordinary People*, Fred Katz cites two cases (an SS guard in Auschwitz and a soldier in My Lai) where individuals successfully avoided such pressures by taking a clear stand against the action from the beginning. This suggests "that one can extricate oneself from a horrendous situation by acting immediately, while one's 'outside' perspective is still intact," and it is why the values with which people *enter* a situation are crucial.[25]

The power of sequential actions makes continued involvement easier and disengagement increasingly difficult. Ervin Staub described the significance of this during the early years of Nazism:

Protest, resistance and noncompliance at an early stage might have been highly effective . . . The monolithic culture and totalitarian system eliminated public discussion and protest that would have called attention to anti-Nazi values and conceptions of reality. A breakdown of uniformity and the expression of contrary views might have influenced bystanders not committed to Nazi ideology.[26]

But this breakdown did not occur. To the extent that they did not consciously resist the process, ordinary Germans became part of the Nazi society and, accordingly, less able to oppose and stop it. Step by step, they became more involved.[27] Eventually, bystanders blamed the victims "as the simplest way of easing their own consciences."[28]

To summarize: there are clearly a number of factors that shaped the behavior of bystanders during the Nazi era. Yet the way in which these factors emerged—and the gradual development of Nazi policies—may in itself have been a key factor in keeping people "bystanders."

CULTURAL, SOCIAL, AND POLITICAL DYNAMICS

This incremental process was influenced by the cultural, social, and political dynamics that shape individual and collective behavior in any society. These dynamics are especially crucial in understanding the development of an unprecedented case of intentional, organized evil like the Holocaust.

What factors in Germany were precursors for what happened, and which ones were the result, not the cause, of Nazi totalitarianism? To what extent, for example, was a genocidal mentality introduced and enforced by the Nazi regime; to what extent did genocidal tendencies already exist within the population? Was this "genocidal mentality" the product of numerous factors—not just anti-Semitism, but nationalism, widespread resentment against the victors of World War I, and the tradition of obedience to state authority?

In Germany, the significance of certain patterns of obedience to the state became clear only in retrospect. In his study of the Gestapo, for example, historian Robert Gellately notes that the policing of private citizens' political activity began during the 19th century in Prussia. As a result, certain developments during the 1930s (such as the requirement that all citizens register their racial ancestry with the local police) that might have served as warning signals in other countries were not unprecedented in Germany— although the Gestapo, of course, would eventually have far broader powers than the political police of earlier times. Gellately also writes that public willingness to grant broader powers to the police increased during the chaotic years of the Weimar Republic, paving the way for the widespread approval of the Nazi "Führer Principle," which centralized all authority in one person.

Any study of historical factors must also take into account the existence of other cultural tendencies within German society before the rise of Nazism. Here, too, scholars disagree about the significance of these tendencies. Historian Stanley Payne contends that the period before 1914 showed the emergence of a strong political and cultural liberalism, and an actual decline in the influence of extremist anti-Semitic parties: "although there existed certain strong influences of ultranationalism, ethnocentrism, and authoritarianism, the general movement of most of German political, social, and cultural life took an opposite direction during the two generations before 1914."[29] British scholar Peter Pulzer disagrees, arguing that a resurgence of anti-Semitism occurred during the Bismarck era and that the situation for German Jews improved only during the Weimar Republic.[30]

It is clear, however, that the status of German Jews between 1848 and 1933 underwent many changes, as did attitudes toward them among the non-Jewish population. These attitudes were shaped by the political mood of the country. In the minds of many Germans, cultural trends, such as the growth of secularism, feminism, the social democratic movement, and the rise of avant-garde art, theater and literature, became identified with the social and political chaos of the Weimar years. Weimar culture did not develop during a period of stability, but in the devastating aftermath of World War I. The political tone of the Weimar era was shaped by widespread German resentment of the Versailles Treaty, the uncertainties of the early postwar period (marked in many places by street battles and local communist and workers' uprisings), and the economic hardships of the depression, including extreme inflation and high unemployment.

The Nazis brilliantly attacked on both fronts: against political instability and the "degeneration" of cultural life. Politically, they promised that a strong Führer would end the uncertainty; culturally, they called for a return to old traditional values. Upon assuming power, they immediately followed through—burning books, banning all kinds of cultural expression, imprisoning cultural and political "enemies" (Communists, Social Democrats, homosexuals, etc.), and driving over 2,000 intellectuals and creative artists into exile in 1933 alone.[31] Thomas Mann, Albert Einstein, Paul Tillich, and Bertolt Brecht were only a few of those who left shortly after the Nazis took power.

These developments were tolerated by many Germans because they seemed to offer a coherent vision for Germany—a national "self-concept" that would end the chaos and resentment left in the wake of the 1918 defeat. As Ervin Staub observes, the notion of a singular national "self-concept" is problematic, particularly when the diverse political tendencies cited above are taken into consideration.[32] Still, the Nazi vision of a German identity held widespread appeal. It incorporated various ideological principles, such as the notion of a triumphant "Third Reich" (the second, created under Chancellor Otto von Bismarck in 1871, ended with Kaiser Wilhelm II's abdication in 1918) and the need for *Lebensraum* (room to live) for "Aryans." These were not just political slogans that shaped German attitudes; they had devastating consequences for all of Europe.

At the heart of the Nazi self-concept, however, was its vision of a culturally and ethnically pure nation. Inherent in the notion of what was truly German—ethnically, politically, and culturally—was the determination to eradicate that which was "not" German. That which was not German was not only viewed with disdain, but as an active danger to the healthy "Aryan" German nation. Many artists and writers were targeted because their work represented "degenerate" ideals that might undermine traditional values and thus destroy German society from within. Homosexuals were persecuted for the same reason. In the Nazi quest to create a genetically pure and healthy populace, the mentally ill and disabled were sterilized, and eventually murdered.

But the persecution of the Jews falls into a distinct category for several reasons. The first is that anti-Semitism was not merely a Nazi or a German phenomenon; it had existed for centuries, throughout the world. The persecution and genocide of the Jews under Nazism—and the reaction of the rest of the world to that genocide—raises several questions. In what ways, for example, was it unique to Nazism or Germany, and to what extent must we search for its roots in other factors (such as certain Christian teachings) that predisposed both Germans and others to view Jewish suffering with indifference? How did Nazi ideology foster and manipulate certain anti-Semitic notions? Is there, as Zygmunt Bauman argues, a "discontinuity between the traditional, pre-modern Jew-hatred and the modern exterminatory design indispensable for the perpetration of the Holocaust"?[33] Is there a significant tension between bystanders' support for the persecution of Jews and their revulsion at the actual genocide? Or is it the case, as Ian Kershaw writes, that Nazi propaganda was obviously most effective when "it was building upon, not countering, already existing values and mentalities"?[34] These questions will be examined more closely in a subsequent chapter.

SUMMARY

Historians are properly cautious about making assumptions beyond what can be documented as fact. But in studying the Holocaust, there is a limit to what can be understood solely on the basis of the historical data. Even a basic knowledge of the historical developments that culminated in the Holocaust does not give us the full picture.

In his introduction to *Voices from the Holocaust*, a collection of survivor testimonies, Elie Wiesel wrote, "In this book historical facts are less important than the manner in which the witness remembers and communicates them. The errors themselves—of memory or of perception—deserve a place in the dossier."[35]

Wiesel's comment may strike us as odd. It would seem that including errors of memory or perception does a disservice, both to those who survived the Holocaust and to those who wish to understand its history. His point, however, is that accounts that include errors may still convey an emotional (perhaps even an ethical) truth about what happened. More importantly, we cannot comprehend the Holocaust's legacy today if we do not acknowledge the validity of this other level of truth. The accounts of witnesses—particularly the victims and survivors—amplify the documents and facts, enabling us to understand what they meant to people then, and what they mean for us today.

For that reason, interpretations of the Holocaust must take into account the historical facts, the perceptions and emotions of those who lived through it, and the ethical conclusions that can be legitimately drawn from it. All these facets shape our interpretations of history. As historian Charles Maier once wrote, "The Nazi experience does test the limits of what history can 'explain.' "[36] There are historical explanations for the developments that led to Nazism and the dynamics that arose within Nazi Germany—but the emotional truth conveyed by the survivors of that terror reminds us that the Holocaust is ultimately inexplicable.

Indeed, one of the most intriguing responses to Maier's remark comes from a theologian and philosopher, Gil Baillie. In his incisive study of René Girard's work on violence, Baillie noted: "If 'the Nazi experience tests the limits of what history can explain,' it is because the explanatory power of 'history' begins and ends with its ability to explain away the victims and the violence vented against them."[37]

In the very process of seeking historical explanations for the gas chambers and the burning children, says Baillie, we discover that it is impossible to explain them in any way that makes sense, intellectually or morally. To the extent that they suggest a "reason" for the Holocaust, the explanations themselves become problematic. We are confronting issues that extend beyond the realm of history into religious and ethical territory: questions about human behavior and the forces that shape it, and about the deeper significance of history.

Thus, we have already begun to look behind the stage of our drama to see what hidden aspects of this history are relevant for understanding "bystander behavior" during the Holocaust.

NOTES

1. In Staub, *The Roots of Evil*, 126.
2. Bauman, *Modernity*, 87.
3. Saul Friedländer, "On the Representation of the *Shoah* in Present-Day Western Culture," in Bauer et al., eds., *Remembering for the Future*, Vol. II (London: Oxford University Press, 1989), 3094.
4. Bauman, *Modernity*, 2.
5. Cohen, *The Tremendum*, 2.
6. Ibid., 3.
7. Ibid., 4.
8. Ibid.
9. For a good discussion of why the "Jewish question" was different in Germany than elsewhere in Europe, see Peter Pulzer, *Jews and the German State: The Political History of a Minority 1848–1933* (Cambridge, Mass.: Blackwell Publishers, 1992), 28–44.

10. Gordon A. Craig, *Germany 1866–1945* (New York: Oxford University Press, 1978), 616.

11. See Wyman, *The Abandonment of the Jews*; also Richard Breitman and Alan Kraut, *American Refugee Policy and European Jewry, 1933–1945* (Bloomington: Indiana University Press, 1987).

12. Yehuda Bauer, "Jew and Gentile: The Holocaust and After," in Marrus, *The Nazi Holocaust: Historical Articles on the Destruction of European Jews*, Vol. 4.1, *The "Final Solution" Outside Germany*, 60.

13. See Franklin H. Littell, ed., *Hyping the Holocaust: Scholars Answer Goldhagen* (East Rockaway, NY: Cummings and Hathaway, 1997).

14. See Herbert A. Strauss, "Jewish Emigration from Germany: Nazi Policies and Jewish Responses," in Marrus, *The Nazi Holocaust*, Vol. 8.1, *Bystanders to the Holocaust*, 170.

15. Gellately, *The Gestapo and German Society*, 84.

16. See Richarz, *Jewish Life in Germany*, and Gordon, *Hitler, Germans and the Jewish Question*, especially 41–49.

17. See Henry, *Victims and Neighbors*, and Allen, *The Nazi Seizure of Power*.

18. Lawrence D. Stokes, "The German People and the Destruction of the European Jews," 61–86, in Marrus, *The Nazi Holocaust*, Vol. 1, *Public Opinion and Relations to the Jews in Nazi Europe*, 65.

19. See Werner Rosenstock, "Exodus 1933–1939: A Survey of Jewish Emigration from Germany," 145–146, and Strauss, "Jewish Emigration," especially 178–185, both in Marrus, *The Nazi Holocaust*, Vol. 8.1, *Bystanders to the Holocaust*. As both Strauss and Rosenstock note, the reduction in emigration in 1934–1937 may have been due both to immigration restrictions by foreign governments and to the fact that subsequent waves of Jewish emigrants had fewer means to do so. Those in a position to leave Nazi Germany, professionally and financially, were the first to do so, in 1933.

Several scholars note the lull in violence (compared with 1933) against individuals in 1934 and early 1935 as one reason that some Jews opted to remain in Germany. (See Karl Schleunes, *The Twisted Road to Auschwitz* (Chicago: University of Illinois Press, 1990), 199. One factor was the altered situation after the Röhm putsch in June 1934. Prior to that, persecution was more widespread and violent, carried out by local groups of storm troopers, who were not under central command. By 1935, Heinrich Himmler consolidated the Gestapo and political police forces, ending the independent actions of local SA leaders. The result, as Gellately notes, was that people thought there would be more law and order. (Gellately, *The Gestapo and German Society*, 41.)

20. Schleunes, *The Twisted Road to Auschwitz*, 188–199.

21. See Michael Marrus's analysis, *The Holocaust in History*, 46–51.

22. For an overview, see Hoffmann, *The History of the German Resistance*, 3–17. Between 1933 and 1945, notes Hoffmann, three million Germans were imprisoned on political grounds, 800,000 of them for active resistance. (Ibid., 16.)

23. See Bauman, *Modernity*, 157–159; Katz, *Ordinary People*, 29–31, and 188; Kelman, "Violence without Moral Restraint."

24. Kelman, Ibid., 46.

25. Katz, *Ordinary People*, 118.

26. Staub, *The Roots of Evil*, 152.

27. Bauman, *Modernity*, 128.

28. Ibid.

29. Payne, *A History of Fascism*, 148.

30. Pulzer, *Jews and the German State*, 36–40 and 342–343.

31. Berenbaum, *The World Must Know* (Boston: Little, Brown, 1995), 24.

32. See Staub, *The Roots of Evil*, 54–55.

33. Bauman, *Modernity*, 185.

34. Kershaw, *The 'Hitler Myth,'* 4.

35. Sylvia Rothchild, *Voices from the Holocaust* (Toronto: New American Library, 1981), 3.

36. Maier, *The Unmasterable Past*, 100.

37. Gil Baillie, *Violence Unveiled: Humanity at the Crossroads*, 14.

CHAPTER 5

The Role of Totalitarianism

The inhabitants of a totalitarian country are thrown into and caught in the process of nature or history for the sake of accelerating its movement; as such, they can only be executioners or victims of its inherent law.

—Hannah Arendt[1]

Dissecting the ways in which the totalitarian nature of Nazi society affected Germans' behavior raises some extraordinarily difficult questions. Hitler's party came to power in popular elections (albeit by a minority of the vote), and his ascent to the German leadership occurred legally within the German parliamentary electoral process. This process, of course, was one of the first things Hitler dismantled. Once he was in office, his first steps were to centralize power and take measures against his political opposition. Only days after Hitler took the oath of office, the totalitarian nature of Nazism had been revealed.

Nonetheless, the Nazi regime had widespread popular support; even many of those Germans who eventually resisted were enthusiastic at the beginning. There was only token resistance to the *Gleichschaltung* of German society that had brought most major institutions of German life under Nazi control by 1935. As we have seen in the case of the churches, even this resistance usually did not signify opposition to Nazi policies, but was more an attempt to preserve institutional independence. Similarly, some scholars argue that the serious resistance that later emerged from

German diplomatic and military circles was based more on opposition to Hitler's leadership of the war than outrage over the Holocaust.

In any case, Nazi Germany is not a straightforward history of an absolute dictator who brutally subjugated an unwilling population. Hitler's consolidation of power was facilitated by popular support. The quickness with which many Germans conformed to Nazi regulations, joined party organizations, and turned against their neighbors and colleagues who had been singled out as "enemies" is striking.

Still, historians have argued for years about how much popular support Hitler really had for his policies in the years that followed, particularly once the war began in 1939. It is also difficult to discern how much of this support was based on popular enthusiasm for the racial laws and how much can be traced to other motives. After studying the "morale reports" gathered by the Nazi party, as well as the underground information compiled by opposition political groups, historian Ian Kershaw contends that the documents portray "a regime which throughout has only minimal popular support."[2] Among the general population between 1935 and 1939, says Kershaw, there was growing anger at Nazi party corruption, increasing awareness of the extent of the regime's repression, and, as the war loomed, a pervasive sense of insecurity.[3]

Kershaw's conclusions are not shared by all historians,[4] and he acknowledges that

middle class disillusionment with economic reality under Nazism was no barrier to its remaining politically and ideologically the backbone of the regime's support, even if this support was for the most part passive and resigned rather than active and enthusiastic. Complaint and compliance were related characteristics of middle-class life in the Third Reich.[5]

His findings raise important questions, however, as they are based on one of the few comprehensive studies of an entire region. Many of the documents he uncovered in Bavaria revealed indifference and reluctance to comply with Nazi policies, including the racial laws. Thus, Kershaw offers a complex picture of how totalitarianism looked on the local level, suggesting that there may be a number of motives for the complicity and indifference of bystanders.

While scholars differ about the significance of these motives, Kershaw's point—that behavior that *appears* indifferent or passive may mask other feelings and motivations—is an important one when we are looking at bystanders. In another study of public opinion in Nazi Germany, Otto Kulka and A. Rodrigue observed that "under the surface of the outwardly uniform totalitarian *Gleichschaltung*, the basic diversity of opinions on individual, social, political, religious and other grounds, did not disappear."[6] Kulka and Rodrigue disagree with some of Kershaw's conclusions, yet they are noting the same phenomenon: that the German public appeared "indifferent," not wholeheartedly enthusiastic, particularly over the course of time. This suggests that, underneath this indifference, not all Germans thought alike about Nazi policies.

If, as Kulka and Rodrigue suggest, ordinary Germans held a variety of opinions—including critical ones about the regime—what were their ethical responsibilities? Do we judge those who were passively critical differently than we would Germans who were convinced and enthusiastic Nazis? The question of the *accountability* of bystanders in a dictatorship or totalitarian society is complex. Although there are some factors that are unique to Nazism, any totalitarian state seeks to control the behavior of ordinary citizens, using certain mechanisms that affect ethics in the public and the private spheres. Ultimately, these mechanisms help to create an atmosphere that gives implicit moral permission for state aims—what Robert Gellately calls the "social reinforcement of the terror system."[7] Citing William Allen's study of a German town, for example, Gellately observes how German schoolteachers "began, without ever having been ordered to do so, to encourage changes in students' behavior more appropriate to the new state of affairs."[8] We find similar examples in the studies of Sonderburg and Mauthausen. They illustrate how, in a totalitarian society, the state's power over individual behavior makes resistance or public opposition even more difficult. At the same time, individuals often conform so readily that "coercion" may be the wrong word.

The real puzzle, then, is to discern precisely where coercion begins and free will ends. To what extent is the conformity of individuals based on ideological agreement with the state—in the case of Nazi Germany, with Nazi anti-Semitism and nationalism? To what extent is it the product of a totalitarian system that manipulates factors like fear, conformity, nationalism, peer pressure, or traditions of obedience to authority? Did pressure on individuals in Nazi Germany change over time, as the regime tightened its hold on various spheres of German life? To what extent, even in a totalitarian society, are individual citizens able to maintain some independence of opinion, at least privately? What is the ethical relevance of such independence of thought, and, conversely, of "indifference" or passivity?

As these questions show, to cite totalitarianism as a factor in bystander behavior in Nazi Germany does not mean to absolve individuals of all responsibility or to accept the premise that they were utterly powerless to behave otherwise. It does mean that we must explore the various means by which the behavior of ordinary citizens, whatever their underlying motivations, helped to create a political system in which the genocide of the Jews became possible.

THE DYNAMICS OF TOTALITARIANISM

Historian Stanley Payne defines totalitarianism as "a state system that attempts to exercise direct control over all significant aspects of all major national institutions, from the economy and the armed forces to the judicial system, the churches, and culture."[9]

Payne's definition focuses on the macrocosmic nature of totalitarianism, especially its effects on the institutional and state levels. But totalitarianism is not just defined by its peculiar patterns of power and authority over institutions, but by the effects these patterns have on the lives of individuals. The strength and survival of a totalitarian system depends not only upon centralized power, but upon the widespread accommodation of individuals to this power. Ultimately, what characterizes totalitarianism most is the power it achieves over the most mundane or intimate levels of human life. "If Nazi leaders had had their way," writes Claudia Koonz, "nothing would have remained private; everything, including the illusion of loving families and apolitical women, had its political use ... Hitler needed women who would convey an illusion of clean-cut decency that masked a murderous state."[10]

As Koonz's remark indicates, an examination of Nazism's attitudes toward the role of women can give some important insights into how totalitarianism functions.[11] Nazi propaganda used rigid gender stereotypes to convey political messages ("Aryan" women were characterized as strong or Madonna-like, and the role of motherhood was glorified; Jewish women were portrayed as whores). The counterpart of such stereotypes among males was the portrayal of Nazism, and the emerging Nazi nation, as an explicitly "manly" culture: militaristic, strong, unwilling to tolerate any weakness.[12]

As an expression of totalitarianism, the main relevance of Nazism's use of gendered stereotypes is the way in which such stereotypes epitomized the state's power over the public and private spheres. Teachings about women and their "place" helped maintain the clear division between the political sphere and the private realm of family and home. The cooperation of women in upholding this distinction between the public and private worlds—in particular, their role in preserving the illusion of the private realm as a viable, humanized "retreat" from the explicit brutality of Nazism—was crucial.[13]

The definitive aspect of a totalitarian society is its concept and use of power. Totalitarian regimes, as Arendt wrote in her study of totalitarianism, are based upon "a new and unprecedented concept of power."[14] This concept is not just unprecedented because it attempts to reach into all spheres of human life; the use of power by such regimes is often irrational and even self-destructive. The fanatical pursuit of ideological goals, for example, is often marked by a "supreme disregard for immediate consequences" and "contempt for utilitarian motives."[15] This irrationality is what makes such regimes so dangerous. Ideology becomes all; rational self-interest is secondary. Among other things, this introduces "into international politics a new and more disturbing factor than mere aggressiveness would have been able to do."[16]

Yet in a totalitarian system, power is not merely imposed and enforced from above. As both Gellately and Koonz observe, it operates much more insidiously. Gellately shows that the Gestapo's powerful hold over German society was possible only through the cooperation of ordinary citizens, thus affecting a "far broader range of behavior" throughout society.[17] In the long term, Nazism was powerful not just because of the numbers of party stalwarts, but because millions of Germans were prepared to inform on one another, obey orders, and remain passive while others became victims. In 1929, Hitler observed that the "great thing" about the Nazi movement was that its members

have outwardly become almost a unit, that actually these members are uniform not only in ideas, but that even the facial expression is almost the same. Look at these laughing eyes, this fanatical enthusiasm and you will discover . . . how a hundred thousand men in a movement become a single type.[18]

In his study of the Gestapo, Gellately convincingly illustrates how quickly and thoroughly ordinary Germans—bystanders—became an intrinsic part of Nazi society. Not only did they tacitly approve of Hitler's policies; they actually participated. Contrary to earlier studies that assumed that German police officers were gradually replaced by Nazi party members, Gellately discovered that most of those who eventually served in the Gestapo, local police, and the criminal and secret police forces had been at their jobs long before 1933. They were neither party loyalists nor fanatics. As noted earlier, their willingness to intimidate, persecute, and spy upon the opposition was not just due to ideological agreement with the aims of Nazism; it was facilitated by the existence of political police forces in Germany long before 1933.[19] Exerting pressure on the population to conform politically had been an accepted part of police work even before Hitler came to power—a factor that shaped public attitudes toward the Gestapo.

There were other ways in which attitudes among the German population in 1933 were shaped by the preceding period. The very way in which Weimar democracy disintegrated had crucial consequences for what followed. Democracy is undermined, writes Zygmunt Bauman, when political instability "succeeds in paralysing old seats of social power without as yet replacing them with new ones—and create for this reason a state of affairs in which political and military forces are neither counterbalanced nor restrained by resourceful and influential social ones."[20]

In Germany, this process had consequences for both victims and bystanders. Just as the emancipation of the Jews was one aspect of the larger political processes of liberalization and a growing democratic sensibility, the reversal of these processes placed the newly assimilated minority at considerable risk. "Jewish prosperity and survival in modern conditions needed liberal institutions and an open civil society," Pulzer writes.[21]

Ordinary non-Jewish citizens were also affected by the wide-scale dislocation of values that occurred in the aftermath of World War I. Unlike the Jews, they were not at risk of losing recently won political or social gains. Still, it appeared to many Germans that society itself had lost its bearings. Bauman uses Viktor Frankl's term "existential vacuum" to describe the result: the loss of viable traditions that set clear public and private parameters for individual behavior. Seeking such parameters, citizens flee into conformity or totalitarianism.[22]

The main difference between this process in premodern times and modernity, says Bauman, is that in premodern societies such upheavals "left the primeval, communal controls of order intact or at least still viable" and that "they weakened, rather than strengthened the possibility of organized action on a supracommunal level."[23] In contrast, Nazism and Stalinism were characterized by the displacement of old elites and power centers by "new, centrally supervised forms emanating from, and legitimized by, the state."[24] This, in turn, was reinforced by the complicity of citizens who welcomed both the emergence of strong leadership and their own role as members of a united German *Volk*—the "single type" described by Hitler.

The picture that emerges at the grass roots level is similar to what has been observed in other repressive societies, such as Stalinism, Rumania under Ceausescu, and some of the Latin American dictatorships. Publicly, people became involved in the "bread and circuses" that characterize all dictatorships—the party organizations, parades, and festivals. Propaganda, with its images of the Aryan family, the German *Volk*, and the Führer, encouraged individual citizens to identify with such images; it also singled out scapegoats (Jews, the mentally ill and disabled, gypsies) that offered the public a clear picture of their "enemy." Such propaganda encouraged citizens to participate in more insidious developments like the emergence of a secret police that relied heavily on citizens' denunciations.

To some extent, this development in Nazi Germany seems to have been driven by the voluntary compliance of ordinary citizens. The descriptions of daily life in the books of Frances Henry or William Allen, for example, reveal the chilling drive toward political conformity that began to build immediately after the Nazis assumed power. Still, the aspect of coercion cannot be ignored. In the political atmosphere that immediately developed after Hitler's rise to power, it would have been easy for any German to see which way the wind was blowing. It was an atmosphere marked by "the significance of 'mutual suspicion' which came to permeate all social relationships," as Hannah Arendt put it.[25] The early months of the Third Reich were marked by mass arrests and sporadic political violence. While the Nazi leaders were consolidating their political power, local SA groups carried out a chaotic reign of terror against perceived political enemies. Not infrequently, they used their new power to settle personal disputes. By autumn of 1933, almost 100,000 people had been arrested at some point, and between 500 and 600 killed. Many of these arrests, notes Gellately, were not made by the police, but by renegade SA groups; they were essentially acts of "simple kidnapping by unauthorized persons."[26] Local SA units also operated independent "camps," which were an early "characteristic feature of the Nazi "revolution." During the course of 1934, these camps were either closed or put under the centralized control of Himmler and the SS. But they were a significant factor in creating an atmosphere of terror during the early Nazi period. For example, the Nazis arrested over 5,000 people in Bavaria alone in the spring of 1933. By August 1933, over 4,000 were still imprisoned:

The object of the exercise was to influence public opinion in Bavaria. In the absence of enthusiasm, silence, compliance, or apathetic accommodation was to be preferred to opposition or dissent. The arrests were orchestrated in such a way that "in each village and each city at least several people were touched by them." These "disappeared" into custody and were usually "depressed and terrified" upon their release; their reappearance contributed to the intimidation and climate of fear.[27]

One effect of this early "arbitrariness and brutality" was that it enabled the Nazi regime to consolidate power very quickly.[28] Ironically, there was even widespread relief when the independently operated prison camps became concentration camps under centralized SS leadership during the course of 1934; many Germans believed that the brutal abuses of power would now end.

The point was not so much the threat of Nazi retaliation against protesters; actual retaliation was random and incalculable. Some people refused to comply with Nazi measures without suffering any consequences; as Goldhagen notes, there are even records of a few individuals who successfully requested transfers out of the death camps and the police battalions without suffering any consequences.[29] Yet there are enough examples of brutal Nazi retaliation against critics—as well as measures like the numerous arrests cited by Gellately—that totalitarian pressure is a credible explanation for some bystander behavior.

There are certain differences between these developments as they emerged in the Soviet Union under Stalin and in Nazi Germany. The fundamental difference between the two regimes, according to historian Charles Maier, was that German terror enforced "an iron law of predictable consequence . . . The principle of Soviet terror was to enforce the arbitrary discipline of nonpredictability."[30] While the early months of Nazism were marked by the random violence described above, this phase soon ended. There were no major realignments of factions within the Nazi party after the Röhm purge in 1934. In contrast, Stalin consistently used such purges to control the Communist party and eliminate his opponents.

Another important distinction, Maier notes, was the racial foundation of Nazi terror. The Jews had been singled out for persecution and extinction; the studies of Mauthausen and Sonderburg make clear that ordinary people were conscious of this fact. In contrast, the victims of Stalin's reign of terror were targeted arbitrarily; perhaps more importantly, the purpose of such terror was to consolidate power and enforce Stalin's hold on the population. In Nazi Germany, however, the "rules remained consistent" for those to whom the racial laws did not apply.[31] The persecution of the Jews was not just a totalitarian act of intimidation. The reason was ideological; according to Nazi racist doctrine, the Jews had to be eliminated.

There are some striking similarities, however, between Nazism and Stalinism. Both were brutal regimes that governed by terror and viciously attacked their "enemies." Both regimes shared another characteristic of modern totalitarianism that relates specifically to the phenomenon of genocide. In modern genocide, writes Bauman, "the end itself is a grand vision of a better, and radically different, society."[32] The Nazis murdered millions of victims mechanically, in the name of "an objectively better human world" that was defined along ideological lines.[33] Although the Soviet purges under Stalin do not, strictly speaking, constitute genocide, the mass murders there—like the genocide of the Jews under Nazism—were carried out as part of an ideological agenda. This aspect is also evident in the Cambodian genocide.

The primary parallels between Nazism and regimes like Stalinism, then, are based upon the ideological and totalitarian nature of those regimes. Still, there are differences between the dynamics of terror in each case that have important consequences for how we understand the role of bystanders. In Nazi Germany, as Maier noted, "the loyal or passive non-Jewish subject did not have to live with terror as did the Russian intelligentsia, party members, functionaries, or factory managers."[34] Throughout Germany, people could thrive under the new system as long as they conformed. In part because of such dynamics, Hannah Arendt contended that Nazi Germany was only in the process of becoming a totalitarian regime, never actually reaching the full status that Soviet totalitarianism did under Stalin—although she believed that it would have done so, had Hitler won World War II.

It can be argued that this is what placed the citizens of Nazi Germany in a different ethical situation, giving them other possibilities and responsibilities. To a degree that was impossible in Stalinist Russia, Germans could conform, stay by the sidelines, and thus remain witnesses or bystanders to what was happening to others. In the case of Nazi Germany, an element of moral volition must be juxtaposed with any discussion of "powerlessness" among Germans and Nazism.

The dilemma is that, in any dictatorship, the individual's perception of powerlessness does reflect an actual reality. Nonconformity in a totalitarian state is viewed as resistance, by the state and citizens alike. It is not possible for individuals to simply refuse to comply with state regulations (such as sending their children to required state activities) without fearing the consequences. Even small acts of resistance require a willingness to take what may be significant risks.

This makes the behavior of most people almost predictable. Faced with potential consequences for themselves and their families, they do indeed feel powerless—even when, within the confines of their private lives, they are able to lead "normal" lives. This powerlessness is linked to a related factor that helps to incapacitate individuals morally—what Bauman terms the phenomenon of "free-floating responsibility."[35] Under totalitarian rule, individuals soon find that they have been relieved of any real authority or autonomy, since the state's power is so pervasive that it affects even individual decisions about where to live and what jobs people can have. As Arendt wrote, "it is in the very nature of totalitarian regimes to demand unlimited power. Such power can only be secured if literally all men, without a single exception, are reliably dominated in every aspect of their life."[36] The government has control not just over the larger issues that affect people, but over their own personal fates. As a result, the individual's "moral authority as such" is "incapacitated without having been openly challenged or denied."[37]

In his famous experiments, for example, Stanley Milgram discovered that his subjects were able to renounce their own responsibility for their actions in the experiment only when an authority figure was present who "directed" the experiment. When Milgram restaged his experiment, using several experimenters who openly disagreed with one another, the obedience observed in the other experiments completely disappeared. The significance of this is that "the readiness to act against one's own better judgment, and against the voice of one's conscience, is not just the function of authoritative command, but the result of exposure to a single-minded, unequivocal and monopolistic source of authority."[38]

For this reason, as Ervin Staub notes, "perhaps the most profound effect of a successful totalitarian system is the lack of dissenting voices that offer a perspective different from that cultivated by authorities or engender inner conflict or sympathy with victims."[39] When no outcry emerges to offer differing opinions or protests to the policies of the central authority, the perception is reinforced that individuals are powerless.

This puts bystanders in a different position, since it creates the alibi for "powerlessness." Indeed, it does more, for their acceptance of their own "powerlessness" (and of the legitimacy of state power) is precisely what enables them to lead "normal" lives and remain "upstanding" citizens. The research of Gellately and others shows that this kind of pervasive state power was made possible only by the cooperation of ordinary citizens, which intersected with social and political mechanisms that operated coercively.

This phenomenon has led some scholars to conclude that this kind of powerlessness (and its corresponding complicity) is a symptom not so much of totalitarianism as of modernity. Sociologist Rainer Baum, for example, attributes the "moral indifference" of bystanders to "a temptation built into the fabric of our modern Western division of labor."[40] German Protestant bishop Wolfgang Huber agrees: "The organization of the Holocaust is a dreadful example of how bureaucratic processes function without reference to morality—from selection in the home town through to the end in the gas chambers of Auschwitz . . . Wherever modern bureaucracies function without reference to moral principles and without effective checks, the possibility of Holocaust-type situations exists."[41]

To an extent, however, these arguments confuse the symptoms of the Nazi genocidal system with the factors that created it. By citing "modernity" as the factor that creates powerlessness, Bauman and others focus primarily on the systematic and bureaucratically organized nature of the Nazi genocide.

Other scholars contend that the technological nature of the Nazi genocide, while certainly an expression of modern culture, was only a tool. They argue that the Jews were not slaughtered just because the technology to do so had been developed, but because the "moral" permission had been given at another level of society. A comparative look at other genocides (e.g. Armenia, Cambodia, Rwanda, or Bosnia) shows that technology is not a necessary factor in genocide. The Nazi genocidal apparatus did indeed function to some extent like a "machine." Yet, on another level, the brutality and violence that drove it were as primitive as such motives were centuries ago. More significantly, the actual deaths of the victims of Nazism were brutal and bloody—and were witnessed by other human beings.

Thus, the assumption that the genocide of the Jews was principally the *outcome* of technology or totalitarian bureaucracy is problematic. It is true that one key difference between the Nazi genocide of Jews and other historical genocides is the degree to which it was institutionalized and bureaucratized. This is one reason that Arendt, historian Peter Hoffmann and others contend that, had Nazism prevailed, other sectors of the population would have been targeted. The selection of victims is not accidental, says Arendt, but a never-ending process, an intrinsic part of the way totalitarian systems operate. "If it were only a matter of hating Jews or bourgeois, the totalitarian regimes could, after the commission of one gigantic crime, return, as it were, to the rules of normal life and government. As we know, the opposite is the case."[42] "Modernity" as such is not the cause of the Holocaust. Its real significance is that the social expressions of modernity— the division between the public and private realms, the compartmentalization of institutions—have a particularly ominous and important role within a totalitarian system. Historian Charles Maier writes,

The problem is not that genocidal decisions were implemented and escalated at lower levels. It is that bureaucratic momentum can be murderous only within certain contexts . . . only where the central legitimating norms have been perverted and made criminal can the average functionary's zeal lead to genocide.[43]

This is true not only for individual behavior in a totalitarian system, but for its social institutions as well—since they, too, are controlled by the state. For the sake of maintaining institutional viability, they conform—often under the illusion that by conforming, they have retained some freedom. This mixture of state control and institutional conformity is often deadly. Even the ordinary routines of institutions acquire "a criminal dimension."[44] Hospitals, for example, continue to function as they had before, even when part of their routine becomes the "elimination" of patients with disabilities. In the very act of continuing to function normally, they help legitimate state power. Such institutional behavior plays an important role in preventing individual opposition to it.[45]

The effects of this ripple throughout all levels of society: through either coercion or free will, individuals retreat from difficult (or dangerous) moral choices by acquiescing to the will of a larger group. Institutional leaders may see resistance as an option for individuals, but not for institutions. Lacking the support of their institutions, individuals conform. The moral reservations of people on both levels are deliberately subsumed to the perceived national interest. Reflecting on Max Weber's civil servant, who believed that honor consisted of serving state authority even when in personal disagreement with state policies, Bauman notes: "Through honor, discipline is substituted for moral responsibility."[46] Or, as the credo of the SS was, "My honor is my loyalty" (*"Meine Ehre heisst Treue"*).[47] Thus, the "mass man" so glorified in Nazi ideology (or the socialist "new man" under Stalinism) emerges.

THE ROLE OF PREJUDICE

The mechanisms of exclusion, prejudice, and "psychological distance" are precisely what keep the system running. Factors like anti-Semitism or ethnic hatred do not inevitably lead to totalitarianism; such behaviors can and do exist in all kinds of political systems. In a totalitarian society, however, these prejudices have considerable significance in determining what will happen. It can even be said that totalitarian societies are strengthened by such dynamics and weakened by their absence. The traditional tools of a dictator include the fostering of hatred and division among different groups within the population. These dynamics do not so much create totalitarianism as reinforce it.

At the same time, this gives individuals and groups within the society a seductive sense of power over others. As "insiders," their relative power (contrasted with the complete disenfranchisement of the "other," the "outsider") gives them a sense of enfranchisement—although, as citizens of a totalitarian system, they have no rights that they can depend on. This is the context in which we must understand the examples of "ordinary" people who become enthusiastic murderers of Jews. Among bystanders, the process of excluding people from society becomes a circular one; the very act of defining people as objects of prejudice serves to reinforce the prejudice. Eventually, as Miroslav Volf has observed, these processes (exclusion, devaluation, and indifference) form an entire system of behavior in which individual members no longer feel responsible (and may even argue that they are "powerless") for what is done to others:

A "system"—a political, economic, or cultural system—insinuates itself between myself and the other. If the other is excluded, it is the system that is doing the excluding, a system in which I participate because I must survive and against which I do not rebel because it cannot be changed . . . I start to view horror and my implication in it as normalcy.[48]

At this point, the citizens of a totalitarian society have become "locked in" at so many levels that it is virtually impossible to step outside of this framework. As Karl Jaspers wrote, "Once a dictatorship has been established, no liberation from within is possible."[49] This is a bleak view, but it recognizes the extent to which the "normalcy" described by Volf becomes an important factor in cementing the state's hold on its citizens.

Ironically, one of the primary manifestations of normality—which has been observed in a number of totalitarian regimes—is the tendency of individuals to retreat into the private realm.

NORMALITY: THE INDIVIDUAL UNDER TOTALITARIAN RULE

Scholars have different perspectives on what "normality" in a totalitarian situation really represents. Jacob Talmon views totalitarian society as a homogeneous, ideologically integrated union of the state and the enthusiastic masses.[50] Hannah Arendt believed that this union was the product of state terror.[51] Talmon's view interprets "normality" as a voluntary creation that enables individuals to pursue their lives unhindered; Arendt sees it as a new reality, enforced by state terror, which gives people no option but to comply.

But, as Kulka and Rodrigue note, both perspectives recognize that one can't research social attitudes independently of an analysis of totalitarianism.[52] In a work that appeared soon after the fall of Nazi Germany, Eva Reichmann even argued that the totalitarian nature of Nazism was so pervasive that it made documentation and oral statements after January 30, 1933 unreliable.[53]

The unique nature of a dictatorship like Nazism means that, although many "normal" behavioral options are eliminated, people still follow familiar routines. This fosters the illusion that their behavior continues to be "normal" and "rational" under the circumstances, although it is clear to any outsider that many of the behaviors involved are neither normal nor rational.[54] Is it "normal" to take your children to the park when you have seen Jews being deported? Is it "rational" to fill out forms that determine who will die in gas chambers, simply because your job consists of filling out forms?

For some people, there was a stark discrepancy between what had become normal under Nazism and what they were willing to tolerate. Franz Kaufmann, a Berlin lawyer, wrote of watching the Gestapo round up Jews and asked, "Should we go on as if nothing happened?" Kaufmann's response was to work with several friends to find hiding places for Jews, collect food rationing cards for them, and to help some escape to Switzerland; he was arrested and murdered in 1943 by the Gestapo.[55]

Yet the majority of people did "go on as if nothing had happened," aided to a great extent by the Nazi success in fostering what Bauman calls "the illusion of rationality." The genocide of the Jews depended above all on "persuading all involved, both victims and bystanders, that it was more sensible to cooperate than to resist."[56] The Nazis had created a society in which "the rationality of survival would render all other motives of human action irrational . . . reason was the enemy of morality. Logic required consent to crime. Rational defence of one's survival called for non-resistance to the other's destruction . . . This rationality robbed human life of humanity."[57]

"Normality," in fact, was a terrible illusion, as the memoirs, fiction, and poetry written by survivors of the Holocaust illustrate. This literature strips normality of its illusions, or juxtaposes it with images of horror that reveal normality as the madness it is. Some of the most haunting figures in Wiesel's work, in fact, are his madmen, whose madness "challenge the assumptions of the lucid."[58] The fact that bystanders continue to lead normal lives seems "normal." The "madmen" are those who protest, raise their voices, refusing to stay on the sidelines. And yet it is Wiesel's madmen, observes Robert McAfee Brown, who "communicate the real truth about the human situation."[59]

This dynamic extended even into the world of the victims. In the ghettos, the Gestapo insidiously gave Jewish leaders responsibility but no power. The Nazi death machine continued to hold the real power; for Jewish leaders ordered to compile lists of people's belongings, apartments, and (eventually) of victims, "there was no solution within the range of their options that did not serve German objectives."[60] As Bauman notes, the strategy of the Jewish Councils to rescue who they could was not their own strategy, but an "extension" of the Nazi "strategy of destruction, worked out and administered by forces bent on annihilation . . . the rationality of the rules is always the weapon of the rulers."[61] As elsewhere, Nazi strategy was gradual and incremental. At the beginning, recalled one rabbi, the Jewish Councils were asked to concede "relatively unimportant" things: money, apartments, etc. But, "finally, the Nazis asked for the life itself."[62]

Outside the ghetto, the streetcars still operated, children played in the parks, and throughout Nazi Germany, people could perform most of their tasks as normal. When this changed in wartime, as bombs rained upon German cities, the Nazi measures were given a new context in which they appeared as explicable, "rational" wartime measures (and, indeed, this was one rationalization for them after 1945). The Nazi version of "normality" imposed a bizarre world of terror on its victims, who were forced either to opt for the madness that saw reality clearly or preserve some kind of normality that included the very destruction of their world.

Within the victims' world, the parameters of normality and madness differ from those that delineate the world of the bystanders. One of the aspects that characterizes the world of the bystanders is the misuse of language—the "total dissonance," in the words of Saul Friedlander, "between the apocalypse that was and the normality that is," which makes "adequate representation elusive."[63] Friedlander cites Himmler's famous speech of October 1943, in which he told SS troops that one of their greatest achievements was "We have killed the Jewish people but we have remained decent."[64] Himmler's words, like Nazism in general, stood traditional morality on its head.

The corruption of morality in a totalitarian system is mirrored by the corruption and manipulation of language that constructed the new "normality." Language, as Alvin Rosenfeld observes, became a multifaceted weapon of ideology, an important tool for Nazism's "theologized politics and secularized ideology." Michael Hamburger notes that the function of Nazified language

is to telescope a great number of individuals into a corporate abstraction. Elsewhere these individuals become "*the* German student" and all the universities become "*the* German university." Heidegger's vocabulary alone accomplishes a *Gleichschaltung* which excludes the very possibility that any one student might have a will of his own . . . [Heidegger] adds his own existential halo . . . to such established phantom words as *Geist, Schicksal*, and *Wesen*; and the whole performance serves to convince the young scholars of Germany that their freedom consists in conformity, their will in obeying the new laws. What Heidegger was providing here is not philosophy, as we understand it, but secularized theology; and the religion it expounds is the religion of nationalism.[65]

This process was also evident in the euphemisms that dominated the language of Nazi leaders and ordinary citizens alike. Words like "deportation," "selection," and "extermination" do not really disguise the truth about what is happening; far more insidiously, they give a tone of "rationality" to the process of genocide. As Arendt wrote, "The net effect of this language system was not to keep these people ignorant of what they were doing, but to prevent them from equating it with their old 'normal' knowledge of murder and lies."[66] Language itself is used to ensure passivity.

What is the role of individual responsibility and judgment in this context? Staub reflects on this in terms of the individual's relation to the group, noting the tension between the socialization of individual mores (e.g., an emphasis upon obedience) and the individual's capacity to make independent moral judgments.

Many groups . . . teach their members individual moral responsibility. To the extent that socialization clearly teaches this, it is reasonable to hold people responsible for their moral decisions and actions. However, there is usually ambiguous and conflicting instruction. Loyalty to the group is required and often defined as obedience to its standards and leaders. Loyalty and obedience are even taught as moral values . . . Even in a society that fosters individual moral responsibility, there is no guarantee that individuals will oppose the group. Resisting is extremely difficult.[67]

In totalitarian societies, individuals often deliberately withdraw from the public sphere. This phenomenon (and its legacy after a dictatorship has fallen) has only begun to be studied.[68] In the attempt to maintain "normality," individuals' lives become increasingly divided into separate spheres, the public and the private. Publicly, the individual conforms where necessary to political dictates. But the individual distinguishes this sphere from the private world of home, family, and friends, and seeks refuge in this private world.

More significantly, this private world is the realm of morality where the individual still feels responsible for his or her actions. Particularly in eastern Europe during the Communist era, this phenomenon was often described as a positive development—as a way of maintaining "inner freedom" or as an expression of "internal opposition" or resistance. (This juxtaposition, of course, mirrors the ethical division between the public and private realms that some Christian thinkers have made.)

Yet such withdrawal does not necessarily express opposition; any number of motives, including unconscious ones, may lead to such withdrawal. What it does represent, however, is a strong break between an individual sense of identity and the identity enforced by the state. This break may be necessary for psychological and creative survival in a dictatorship. Karl Jaspers argued that people can survive physically and psychologically in a dictatorship only by *withdrawing*—i.e., by creating a private sphere within which some part of life seems intact, where they feel they still operate as moral beings. Thus, some degree of withdrawal is a prerequisite for resistance. By attaching greater importance to private values that are different from those supported by the state authorities, the private realm creates the "free space" in which underground opposition can grow. It signifies "an implicit recognition of individual obligations transcending the demands of the national community."[69]

For some individuals in Nazi Germany, this private sphere became the realm of resistance:

holding oneself aloof from this national community was a gesture of spiritual self-preservation. The greater the pressures to conform, the greater was the need to distance oneself from the "magical influence" of mass consent. Intellectual opposition to the regime therefore commonly took the form of studied indifference.[70]

For most people, however, the private sphere was a realm of passivity and pretense. Even some of the most brutal perpetrators described their private lives as exemplary idylls, distinct from their responsibilities as Nazi citizens.[71] Indeed, there is the very real risk that the division between the public and private is not only the refuge of the bystander, but actually creates bystanders. This psychological process of "internal emigration" also helped preserve the illusion of "normality" and, indeed, was utilized by people afterward to rationalize their conformity.[72]

For bystanders, however, the issue raised by "internal emigration" is that, while this process helps preserve individual sanity and even offers a realm for resistance in a dictatorship, it may also sever the sense of connectedness to others—including the relationship to the victims who desperately depend on even small signs of solidarity. All too often, "internal emigration" signifies passivity, not resistance. It is characterized by an inability to feel a connection with the victims.

Krzysztof Konarzewski has observed that empathy and protest are both expressions of altruism, because both (empathy on behalf of something, and protest against something) are expressions of a relationship to what is happening.[73] Passivity—what the diarist Jochen Klepper described as the "retreat into the private"[74]—breaks that relationship, and thus breaks the relationship to the victims as well. This is an important factor to consider with respect to the behavior of individual bystanders, particularly in Nazi Germany.

SUMMARY

The issues that face bystanders in a totalitarian system are complex and numerous. The German philosopher Karl Jaspers recognized this in his famous 1947 speech on German guilt. Even in a totalitarian society, Jaspers wrote,

political conditions are inseparable from a people's whole way of life. There is no absolute division of politics and human existence as long as man is still realizing an existence rather than perishing in eremitical seclusion . . . The way of life affects political events, and the resulting political conditions in turn place their imprint on the way of life. This is why there can be no radical separation of moral and political guilt.[75]

In a totalitarian society, a matrix of complicity is created that is often so complex that individual citizens, both at the time and later, often view themselves as victims, as having been "powerless." From this vantage point, Arendt's quote at the beginning of the chapter—that people are either victims or executioners—may seem too severe.

We do well to remember, however, that part of what defines a totalitarian system is its attempt to draw clear lines between different realms of experience, the identities (and fates) of different groups. By so doing, it does not just preserve the "normality" that enables the perpetrators and bystanders to live in untroubled comfort. It sets the parameters for their identity.

In *Man's Search for Meaning*, Viktor Frankl wrote of the importance for human beings of the necessary tension "between what one is and what one should become."[76] Was one factor in the bystanders' behavior the fact that they found themselves in a totalitarian society that tried to resolve this tension on the societal level? The seduction of normality was that it represented a "tensionless well-being." The Nazis had already decided what everyone should be. And to the extent that the Germans accepted this decision with relief (which many did, after the Weimar years), they abandoned their own personal struggle for meaning and adopted Nazi standards. For those who could or would not adopt the Nazi ideal of what they should be, two options remained: the "inner withdrawal" to a private, passively lived life, or the active decision to protest and resist.

Individual withdrawal and passivity are certainly common patterns in totalitarian societies, but even the most passive individuals are not blank slates imprinted with the dominant value system of their society. This is particularly important when we examine the role of prejudice. As Staub reminds us, the essence of totalitarian violence is not just state power over ordinary citizens, but the brutal distinctions made between those who belong and are defined as productive members, and those who, as "the other," are excluded. In a totalitarian system, prejudice serves numerous functions. It can be an expression of identity and of alignment with authority. It may be disguised as old tradition or new ideology. In any case, it was such a fundamental part of Nazism that it cannot be neglected in any study of bystanders during that period.

NOTES

1. Arendt, *Origins of Totalitarianism*, 468.
2. Kershaw, *Popular Opinion*, 9.

3. Ibid., 148.

4. For a discussion of Kershaw's research and the responses of other historians to it, see Marrus, *Holocaust in History*, 89–94.

5. Ibid., 154–155.

6. Otto Kulka and A. Rodrigue, "The German Population and the Jews in the Third Reich," 46–61, in Marrus, *The Nazi Holocaust*, Vol. 5.1, *Public Opinion and Relations to the Jews in Nazi Europe*, 51.

7. Gellately, *The Gestapo and German Society*, 10.

8. Ibid.

9. Payne, *History of Fascism*, 206.

10. Claudia Koonz, *Mothers in the Fatherland: Women, the Family, and Nazi Politics* (New York: St. Martin's Press, 1986).

11. In addition to Koonz's book, see *When Biology Became Destiny: Women in Weimar and Nazi Germany*, in Renate Bridenthal, Atina Grossmann, and Marion Kaplan, eds. (New York: Monthly Review Press, 1984).

12. With regard to this issue and the "German Christian" movement, see Doris Bergen, *Twisted Cross: The German Christian movement in the Third Reich* (Chapel Hill: University of North Carolina Press, 1996), chapters 4 and 7.

13. Gitta Sereny's interviews with the wife of Franz Stangl illustrate this. Sereny, *Into That Darkness: An Examination of Conscience* (New York: Vintage Books, 1983).

14. Arendt, *Origins of Totalitarianism*, 417.

15. Ibid., 418.

16. Ibid.

17. Gellately, *The Gestapo and German Society*, 70ff.

18. Arendt, *Origins of Totalitarianism*, 418.

19. Gellately, *The Gestapo and German Society*, 70–72.

20. Bauman, *Modernity*, 111.

21. Peter G. J. Pulzer, *The Rise of Political Anti-Semitism in Germany and Austria* (New York: Wiley, 1964), 324.

22. Bauman, *Modernity*, 111.

23. Ibid., 112.

24. Ibid., 114.

25. Cited in Gellately, *The Gestapo and German Society*, 6.

26. Ibid., 40.

27. Ibid., 39.

28. Ibid., 35.

29. See Daniel J. Goldhagen, *Hitler's Willing Executioners: Ordinary Germans and the Holocaust* (New York: Knopf, 1996), 253–255.

30. Maier, *The Unmasterable Past*, 81.

31. Ibid., 80.

32. Bauman, *Modernity*, 91.

33. Ibid., 92.

34. Maier, *The Unmasterable Past*, 82.

35. Bauman, *Modernity*, 162–163.

36. Arendt, *Origins of Totalitarianism*, 456.

37. Bauman, *Modernity*, 163.

38. Ibid., 165.

39. Staub, *The Roots of Evil*, 125.

40. Rainer Baum, "Holocaust: Moral Indifference as the Form of Modern Evil," in Rosenberg and Myers, *Echoes from the Holocaust*, 81.

41. Wolfgang Huber, "Answering for the Past—Shaping the Future," in *Ökumenische Rundschau*, April 1995, Heft 2, 151 (translation by German Language Service, World Council of Churches).

42. Arendt, *Origins of Totalitarianism*, 424.

43. Maier, *The Unmasterable Past*, 97.

44. Bauman, *Modernity*, 115.

45. David Moss, "The Shibboleth of Modernity: Reflections on Theological Thinking after the *Shoah*," in *Literature and Theology*, 6: 63, March 1992.

46. Bauman, *Modernity*, 22.

47. Arendt, *Origins of Totalitarianism*, 324.

48. Volf, *Exclusion and Embrace*, 77.

49. Jaspers, *The Question of German Guilt*, 99.

50. Cited in Kulka and Rodrigue, "The German Population and the Jews in the Third Reich," in Marrus, *The Nazi Holocaust*, Vol. 5.1, *Public Opinion and Relations to the Jews in Nazi Europe*, 47.

51. Ibid.

52. Ibid., 48.

53. Eva Reichmann, *Hostages of Civilization. The Social Sources of National Socialist Anti-Semitism* (Boston: Beacon Press, 1951).

54. Bauman, *Modernity*, 135.

55. Victoria Barnett, *For the Soul of the People: Protestant Protest against Hitler* (New York: Oxford University Press, 1992), 186–187.

56. From Polonsky, *My Brother's Keeper?*, 25.

57. Ibid.

58. Brown, *Elie Wiesel: Messenger to All Humanity*, 208.

59. Ibid.

60. Bauman, *Modernity*, 136.

61. Ibid., 142.

62. Ibid., 143.

63. Saul Friedlander, "On the Representation of the Shoah," in *Remembering for the Future I*, edited by Yehuda Bauer et al. (New York: Pergamon Press, 1989), Vol. III, 3095.

64. Ibid., 3114.

65. Michael Hamburger, *From Prophecy to Exorcism* (London: Longmans, 1965), 22–23, cited in Rosenfeld, *A Double Dying*, 132.

66. Arendt, *Eichmann in Jerusalem*, 86.

67. Staub, *The Roots of Evil*, 148–149.

68. See the discussion of Argentina in Staub, *The Roots of Evil*, 210–231 and Tina Rosenberg's *Children of Cain: Violence and the Violent in Latin America* (New York: Penguin Books, 1991).

69. Wilkinson, *The Intellectual Resistance in Europe*, 114.

70. Ibid.

71. See Gitta Sereny's studies of Franz Stangl, commandant of Treblinka (*Into That Darkness: An Examination of Conscience*, New York: Vintage Books, 1983) and Albert Speer (*Albert Speer: His Battle with Truth*, New York: Knopf, 1995).

72. See Arendt, *Eichmann in Jerusalem*, 127.

73. Krzysztof Konarzewski, "Empathy and Protest: Two Roots of Heroic Altruism," in Oliner et al., *Embracing the Other*.

74. Jochen Klepper, *Unter dem Schatten Deiner Flügel. Aus dem Tagebüchern 1932–1942* (Stuttgart: Deutsche Verlags-Anstalt, 1956), 41.

75. Jaspers, *The Question of German Guilt*, 76–77.

76. Frankl, *Man's Search for Meaning*, 110.

CHAPTER 6

Attitudes toward "The Other": Prejudice and Indifference

Studies of European Jewish life—from the shtetls of eastern Europe to the cities of Berlin, Vienna, and Frankfurt—portray a vibrant and diverse people who made major intellectual and cultural contributions to the countries in which they lived. After their political emancipation during the 19th century, many European Jews concluded that the truest and most permanent form of emancipation was assimilation. This was particularly true in Germany, where many Jews believed that they were such an integral part of that culture that they could not imagine not being part of it. After 1933, they were stunned to realize that they were the targets of the Nazi racial laws—that Hitler's diatribes were directed at them. Convinced that there had been some mistake, World War I veterans pinned on their medals and visited local Nazi officials to emphasize their patriotism.[1] In March 1933, the Jewish congregation of Berlin sent a statement to Hitler affirming "the pledge that we belong to the German people; it is our sacred duty, our right and our deepest wish that we take an active part in its renewal and rise."[2] As late as 1936, the "Reich Association of Jewish Front Soldiers" commemorated their fallen comrades from World War I with a ceremony in Berlin that stressed their loyalty to the Fatherland.[3]

None of it mattered. The Nazis sought to make Germany *Judenfrei* of these people, each and every one of them: veterans, bankers, farmers, housewives, famous musicians, scientists, schoolchildren, infants, Orthodox rabbis, nonobservant Jews, Jews who had converted to Christianity, people who had never thought of themselves as Jewish but had Jewish grandmothers. In many villages of Europe, the Jews formed a distinct subculture;

in the major cities, they considered themselves "assimilated." Under Nazi terrorism, wherever they lived, they were at risk in every kind of neighborhood, from every walk of life.

One of Adolf Hitler's most astonishing and disturbing achievements was his success in dividing German Jews and non-Jews so completely, long before the Jews were taken away to the separate universe of the concentration camps. There was one set of laws for "Aryans," and another for Jews. There were separate schools, shopping hours, park benches—a separate world that grew and eventually became all-encompassing until, when the ghettos vanished, that entire world vanished with them.

Ingeborg Hecht describes the resulting isolation of "non-Aryans" in her memoir, *Invisible Walls*. The Nuremberg laws banned Jews from the most ordinary spheres of everyday life: from attending the theater, from sports clubs, from listening to the radio, from owning a telephone. Describing the withdrawal of the outcasts into an ever-smaller realm, Hecht recalled how it affected her personality and her dealings with others:

You had to bamboozle all the people you encountered into liking you, so as to disarm them in an emergency. You had to work on them surreptitiously so that, whatever happened, their compassion would be primed and ready, for example, to mitigate the lust for hatred ordained by the authorities . . . The outcast's weapon was to be likable.[4]

As Hecht's account shows, the very survival of Jewish Germans depended upon their personal relationships with non-Jews, at a time when they were being excluded from all levels of ordinary human relationship. Throughout Europe, the majority of Jews who were rescued were helped by individuals—people with whom they had some kind of relationship, people for whom they remained friends, neighbors, and colleagues.

The rescue of Jews ultimately depended upon the courage and good will of individuals—and the isolation of Jews, first in Germany and then in the Nazi-occupied countries, was also contingent on the behavior and attitudes of individuals. Nazi laws would have been ineffective without the cooperation of ordinary people. Under Nazi law, bystanders—those unaffected by these measures—continued to live their lives unencumbered; the cost was indifference to what was being done to the victims of Nazism. In Helen Fein's classic phrase, Jews were not included in "the universe of obligation: that circle of persons towards whom obligations are owed, to whom rules apply and whose injured call for expiation by the community."[5]

In approaching the question of "the other," perhaps the dynamics of relationship are a good place to begin. German Jews were stunned by the swiftness with which they were excluded from their society precisely because they had felt so integrated in that culture, personally and professionally.

The studies done by Frances Henry and others illustrate this; they also illustrate the degree to which full integration was an illusion. In her study of Sonderburg, Henry argues that Jews in Germany had achieved "structural integration" in the workplace and schools, but not the social integration that signified true assimilation. Emancipation and assimilation had erased many of the previous boundaries for Jews. But even intermarriage, conversion to Christianity, or secularization could not eradicate the divisions between Jews and non-Jews completely. Despite a degree of assimilation that was historically unprecedented elsewhere in Europe, Jews continued to be viewed as "different."

Thus, an analysis of the historical development of the different levels of anti-Jewish prejudice is important. The real significance of this prejudice was that many people (inside and outside Germany) saw Jews as the perennial outsiders, as "the other," long before the Holocaust. Weimar foreign minister Walther Rathenau, one of the most politically successful German Jews, expressed it poignantly in words that echo the sentiments of minorities in many societies. "In the youth of every German Jew," he wrote, "there is a painful moment that he remembers all his life: when for the first time he becomes fully aware that he came into the world as a second-class citizen, and that no amount of ability and no personal merit can free him from this situation."[6] In 1922, at the height of his career, Rathenau was assassinated by right-wing extremists.

The studies of Mauthausen and Sonderburg illustrate how excluding people from the community—defining them as "outsiders"—profoundly changes the daily relationships between individuals and groups. A gap between the insiders and outsiders opens; as it is reinforced by law and popular opinion, it widens. Consciously or unconsciously, the insiders reshape their own identities in ways that justify the exclusion of the outsiders. The first step is rationalization—what Staub calls "just world thinking." We shape our perceptions to fit the world as it is: somehow, we think, our situation is legitimate and there is a good reason for it. We take steps to secure our own status and position; inevitably, these steps set us more clearly apart from those who do not belong. As the status of "insiders" becomes more secure, that of "outsiders" becomes more precarious.

The final, terrible result of this process is that those defined as "the other" are denied even sympathy. The tendency to justify the existing order and one's place within it leads many bystanders, as Polish sociologist Stanislaw Ossowski notes, to turn against the victims. The victims are not only blamed for their weakness; those who have benefited from the tragedy—the bystanders—"convince themselves . . . that [it] was morally justified."[7] Victims are not just ignored. Eventually, they "become repugnant to others" and are perceived as threats to the community and as burdens on society and on the consciences of those who remain silent.

How does this happen? By what process do individuals or groups become "the other"—suspect, less than equal, undeserving, and, ultimately, a sinister element that needs to be "eliminated"?

PREJUDICE

The most obvious reason is prejudice. By definition, prejudice is the process of defining and devaluating groups and individuals on the basis of some aspect of their identity. Skin color, gender, racial or national background, religion, and culture are used as grounds to define these groups as "the other."

Yet prejudice is more than merely noting the differences among people. It attributes meaning to them; it defines other people on the basis of their differences. It leads people to assume that others are different, not just in superficial or circumstantial ways, but fundamentally. Prejudice emphasizes the differences among peoples, not the characteristics they have in common. For that reason, as Staub observes, the very act of describing someone as "other" is dehumanizing: "Just defining people as 'them' results in devaluating them."[8] The devaluation of other human beings is based upon the collection of beliefs, superstitions, and assumptions that make up prejudice.

French sociologist Pierre-André Taguieff has listed three stages of racism.[9] The first, he says, is the common reaction of caution to an unknown stranger. The more different the stranger is from us, the more cautious we are likely to be. Implicit in our caution is the recognition that the stranger is somehow an outsider: unknown and likely to differ from us; we fear these differences might prove inconvenient, unacceptable, or even dangerous.

On the second level, that of "rationalized racism," we develop theories to justify our caution. Xenophobic and ethnocentric theories, for example, seek to explain why outsiders or people different from us do not belong or fit in. Such theories draw a line between "us" and "them" that defines who can belong in our society.

The third level, "tertiary" racism, uses biological arguments to justify the first two levels. As Zygmunt Bauman observes, the power of "tertiary" racism is not just that it uses biological arguments, but that such arguments are irrevocable. Tertiary racism argues that "the other" is not just different, but that those differences are inborn and immutable. Hence, differences—particularly those we don't like or understand—become the reason for the exclusion or oppression of others. Tertiary racism assumes that, because "the other" can never change, it is necessary to build, not eradicate, the boundaries between different groups. This attitude has profound consequences for civil law, assimilation, and intermarriage.

In looking at the Holocaust, the issue of prejudice would appear to be a very straightforward one. Any study of genocide must acknowledge the role of prejudice against the victims, and examine how individuals and institutions promote and benefit from this prejudice.

Most people, when they think of the victims of Nazism, think of the Jews, whom the Nazis planned to annihilate. The role of prejudice is often cited as the factor that distinguishes the Jews from the other victims of Nazism. Other groups, however, were also categorized as "outsiders" in Nazi society. In some respects, the persecution and exclusion of these groups—gypsies, homosexuals, the mentally ill, physically disabled, and people with hereditary illnesses—was similar to the persecution of the Jews. All of these groups were vilified in Nazi propaganda as representing a social and even biological menace to a healthy "Aryan" society.

But, although members of these groups were ostracized from German society and murdered, the Jews became the central symbol of "the other." "Non-Aryan" was not an all-compassing term for those the Nazis didn't like, but a synonym for "Jewish." The reason for considering the fate of the European Jews separately from that of the other victims of Nazism is the nature of anti-Jewish prejudice and the way in which it functioned.

The way in which the Jews became defined as "other" is historically and culturally complex; a closer study of German history, before and during Nazism, shows how anti-Semitism became interwoven with a number of other factors. Prejudice and persecution of the Jews had existed for centuries throughout Europe. It also proved to be a factor in the response of countries outside Europe, like the United States.[10]

Yet the historical record of anti-Jewish prejudice is actually quite complex, and some of these complexities become important when we try to understand bystander behavior. To grasp the full significance of anti-Semitic prejudice in a study of the Holocaust, we must understand what historical factors converged to enable the Nazis to target the Jews so successfully, and what factors influenced the response of the rest of the world—especially the Christian churches—to the Nazi persecution of the Jews.

Historically, we can identify two clear forms of anti-Jewish prejudice.[11] One, of course, was the racial anti-Semitism that culminated in the Nazi genocide. The second was so-called "Christian" anti-Semitism, perhaps more literally termed anti-Judaism. Both of these forms contributed to the Holocaust and shaped the attitudes of bystanders. The distinction here between them is not to determine which is the lesser evil, but to see how their historically different forms affected bystander behavior.

Historically, Christian anti-Semitism has taken two forms. The first was based upon the theological conviction that Jesus was Messiah for all peoples. This understanding of the universality of Jesus' mission had particular significance for the Christian understanding of Judaism, since Jesus and his early followers came out of the Judaic tradition. The traditional Christian perspective on Judaism was "supersessionist": that is, it held that the Christian New Testament was the fulfillment of the Old Testament scriptures, that Christianity had superseded Judaism, and that the eventual conversion of Jews to Christianity was inevitable. Thus, throughout the history of the Christian church, Judaism was viewed not just as a transitory religion, but as one whose members were condemned as long as they did not accept Jesus as their Messiah. Because of its common roots with Judaism, Christianity's evangelical efforts to convert Jews had particular significance. Indeed, during the Nazi era, we find some Christian groups who rescued Jews precisely because they were the "chosen people," destined for a special purpose in God's revelation. A 1943 letter from one such circle in Geneva stated this attitude succinctly:

The Church knows no racial hatred. She repudiates the ideas of race inculcated by national-socialism. She looks upon the Jewish problem as a question with which Christians are faced by God. In compliance with the will of God, the Church of our Lord Jesus Christ looks forward to the day when the true Messiah will be accepted by the Jews.[12]

Such statements clearly reflected Christian condescension, at the very least, toward the Jews. It is interesting to note, however, that these attitudes led some in the churches to resist Nazism and help its victims. As noted previously, there were several ecumenical statements during the 1930s that condemned the Nazi measures against the Jews and anti-Semitism. In fact, in Germany, the most significant opposition to the Nazi racial interpretation of the Jewish question emerged from within the Christian churches. In one of the earliest statements on the matter, Dietrich Bonhoeffer wrote in April 1933:

Seen from the perspective of the church of Christ, Judaism is never a racial, but a religious concept. It does not signify the biologically questionable order of the Jewish race, but the "people of Israel." The "people" of Israel, however, is constituted by the Law of God; one can thus become a Jew through acceptance of the Law. But one cannot become a racial Jew.[13]

Racism was the core of Nazi ideology; Christian doctrine and scripture explicitly preached the transcending of racial differences. This difference clearly brought Christians into conflict with the Nazi regime, and the battle between mainstream church leaders and the radical "German Christians" was based upon this argument. While most mainstream church leaders supported much of the Nazi political agenda, their understanding of Christian mission still included the conversion of Jews and, hence, their inclusion in the church. In his study of Bavaria, Kershaw discovered a 1936 Gestapo document blaming the churches for the lack of anti-Semitism among Bavarian farmers. "It's often the case," the Gestapo official wrote, "in the rural parishes that the clergy portray the Jews to their parish as the chosen people and practically demand that the population buy from the Jews."[14]

But the church's message and its confrontations with the Nazi state were ambiguous. Even as the churches opposed racial laws, especially within the church itself, they supported other aspects of Nazi dogma. Nor, despite their talk about the "chosen people," were they entirely free of ethnic assumptions and prejudice. Kershaw notes that, while there were few blatantly anti-Semitic sermons, "it was more frequent that, while clergy didn't preach racial hatred, a racist perspective and fundamental acknowledgement of the 'racial problem' was evident."[15] In an Advent sermon in 1933, for example, Bavarian Catholic Cardinal Faulhaber warned that "love of one's own race should never be turned into hatred of another people," but he added that the church did not object to "the urge to keep the characteristics of a people as pure as possible, and by pointing to the blood-community, to deepen a sense of ethnic community."[16]

For most church members, Nazism was not a new religion that replaced Christianity, and Christian teachings—including those about the conversion of Jews—remained valid. Still, church leaders explicitly confined their misgivings about this aspect of Nazism to the realm of the church. Faulhaber's sermon (and the sermons of many other preachers) showed that the churches were willing to concede the legitimacy of racial precepts in the society around them.

Faulhaber's sermon, however, was not just influenced by the pervasive prejudices of his society. It reflected a far more insidious problem for the churches, which theologian Miroslav Volf has called the "sacralization of cultural identity."[17] In any examination of the Christian churches in Nazi Germany, it is sometimes difficult to determine where the churches' positions were motivated by anti-Semitism and where the traditions of nationalism and obedience to the state played a more significant role. But there is a clear pattern of church acquiescence in the form of support for the underlying cultural and nationalistic notions.

The most extreme example of this was the "German Christians," the group within the Protestant church that supported Nazi ideological notions of an ethnic cultural and national identity.[18] But the "sacralization of cultural identity" was a more widespread phenomenon; its roots went back to the very establishment of the Christian church in Europe. European culture since the Middle Ages defined itself as explicitly Christian; this definition even appeared as part of the political constitutions of some countries. Church teachings about the Jews were integrated into general assumptions about European Christian culture. An example of this kind of thinking comes from the German historian Heinrich von Treitschke, who was an influential political thinker during the 19th century:

I am not an adherent of the doctrine of the Christian state. The state is a secular organization and should act with justice and impartiality toward non-Christians also. But without any doubt, we Germans are a Christian nation. To spread our universal religion among the heathen, our ancestors shed their blood; to develop and perfect it, they suffered and battled as martyrs and heroes. At every step, as I progress deeper in understanding the history of our country, it becomes more and more clear to me how deeply Christianity is entwined with every fiber of the German character . . . Christian ideals inspire our arts and sciences. Christian spirit animates all healthy institutions of our state and our society. Judaism, on the other hand, is the national religion of a tribe which was originally alien to us.[19]

As Treitschke's remarks show, Jews were "outsiders" by definition in a "Christian culture." The influence of Christian anti-Judaism extended far beyond the walls of the church; it formed a certain kind of political culture that viewed itself as explicitly Christian. Throughout Europe, the principal route to assimilation was religious conversion.

Such attitudes were not quite the same as the "racial anti-Semitism" that was based upon dubious ethnic theories viewing the Jewish people as a separate, inferior race—although racial anti-Semitism was undergirded by the cultural anti-Semitism described above. In the 19th century, scholars in a number of fields began to explore the cultural differences among peoples and concluded that they were based upon ethnic distinctions. European anthropologists had begun to visit and study other cultures; their work included detailed observations about physiological differences. In many fields, including medicine, anthropology, history, and philosophy, ethnic, racial, and cultural theories converged. Factors like gender, skin color, and skull size were considered to be the determinants of individual ability and collective culture.

These developments occurred outside the churches. But, Volf's critique of the "sacralization of cultural identity" is more than just a warning against church passivity toward racism. His real point is that, to the extent that the church cannot critique the culture of which it is a member, it becomes a part of that culture. The history of the churches under Nazism offers a case study of this. Because of its significant role and influence in Western cultures, the Church has often sanctified the values and norms of that culture, thereby playing a crucial role in ethnic conflicts. For this reason, argues Volf, "religion must be de-ethnicized so that ethnicity can be de-sacralized."[20] The "German Christians" were an extreme example of a group that sought to redefine faith along ethnic lines. But even their opponents in the church, who fought for a faith that would permit the conversion of others, did so within the constraints of their ongoing support for a "Christian" culture. Faulhaber's sermon, with its support for "the ethnic community" that would be kept "as pure as possible," was only one example.

The result was that, even where the churches opposed the extremist racial anti-Semitism of the Nazis, their own teachings and their historical role within European culture led them to view the Jews as "the other." "As Christians," notes Ian Kershaw, "the majority of pastors rejected the excesses of the Nazi regime; as people in an atmosphere characterized by animosity against the Jews, they reflected the latent anti-Semitism of that society."[21]

MODERNITY, ASSIMILATION, AND RACISM

It is intriguing that the rise of ethnocentric thinking in Europe occurred at a time when some of the political and social boundaries between different groups were being erased. Indeed, what happened in Nazi Germany cannot be understood without looking at two historical developments: the cultural and political debate about German identity during the period in which the modern German nation-state emerged; and the general historical development in Western culture of what we call "modernity."

When Chancellor Otto von Bismarck sought to unite the regions of Germany into one nation, it was the beginning of a new period of German discussion about the "national" question. For centuries, Germany had been a federation of principalities headed by various noble families. The regional loyalties that resulted continued to exercise a powerful influence; many citizens thought of themselves more as Prussians or Bavarians than as Germans. The common ground they shared with Germans in other regions was language and culture.

As a result, German identity was understood in ethnic terms long before 1933. People of Germanic descent, whether they lived in Prussia, Austria, the Sudeten region of Czechoslovakia, or Russia, were considered "German." Pan-German nationalists dreamed that all these people would one day be united into one German nation; this dream spread during the 19th century.[22] At the same time, as a result of the emergence of racialized scholarship, public discussion about German cultural and national identity took on a strong ethnic component. Some thinkers argued that to be superior, a culture had to be culturally and ethnically homogeneous. Those who believed that any true culture had to be "ethnically pure" viewed assimilation by other groups as undesirable and impossible. The presuppositions about "Christian" culture and the importance of maintaining the "purity" of language and culture were interwoven into such theories.

It is not a far step from such theories to more pejorative assumptions about "the other." The theory that a culture has to be homogeneous clearly devalues all other groups and influences that don't belong to the culturally dominant group. The Nazi understanding of nation and *Volk* was based upon the negation of those who were different. Long before 1933, those differences had been defined along pseudoethnic lines.

These ethnocentric theories were a backlash against the trend toward assimilation that we find in western Europe in the late 19th century. In the tension between ethnocentrism and assimilation, emancipation became a double-edged sword for the Jews themselves. On one side, it meant assimilation, a process that epitomized the Enlightenment ideals of humanism and social equality, and which, it seemed, had finally ensured Jews a place within their native countries.

The other edge of emancipation, however, was that assimilation required the loss of Jewish identity: "even as Jews were emancipated, they were denied any recognition or distinguishing marks as a particular community. Citizenship required that Jews cease to be Jews in any traditional sense."[23] Because European cultures were still "Christian," assimilation implicitly denigrated Judaism as something to be gotten rid of. As Gershom Sholem has observed, those most in favor of assimilation "were precisely those who most consciously . . . considered the disappearance of the Jews as an ethnic group a condition for taking up their cause."[24]

Sholem's remarks highlight the fundamental tension that arises in any assimilative process. On the one hand, one prerequisite for a stable society is its ability to include different groups. For common ground to be created, some form of assimilation or accommodation has to occur. For the assimilating group, however, this process entails the relinquishment of a distinct cultural identity. Inherently, this distinct identity is devalued—leading to what Volf calls "exclusion by assimilation."[25] This phenomenon can be seen in Germany, where conservative Germans viewed the readiness of Jews to assimilate "as evidence of their lack of moral substance."[26] Yet, even when Jews converted to Christianity, they were still considered to be racially and culturally distinct.

It is striking to note that these developments converged with the emergence of modernity, which threatened to make the old distinctions (and their certainties) meaningless. Citing René Girard, Staub speculates that increased resentment of the Jews as "outsiders" may even have been one outcome of the new German concepts of nationhood that arose in the late 19th century:

Modern antisemitism was born not from the great difference between groups but rather from the threat of the absence of differences, the homogenization of Western society and the abolition of the ancient social and legal barriers between Jews and Christians.

Racist passions reach a climax precisely when the psychobiological differences on which they depend no longer exist . . . The racist will then rely on a science that has gone astray to justify biologically the charge of "differentness."[27]

In other words, racial anti-Semitism gained political respectability at precisely the historical moment when secularism and political liberalization were eradicating the barriers between ethnic and religious groups. Seeking to defend themselves against modernity, the nationalistically inclined looked for scapegoats. In the process, as Hannah Arendt has noted, Judaism was replaced by "Jewishness."[28] Theories about "Jewishness" were mainstream society's retaining wall to prevent full assimilation. Such theories ensured that even if Jews converted or became secularized, they still could never be "truly" German. "Jewishness," writes Bauman, was given the unchangeable status of natural law: "Man *is* before he *acts*; nothing he does may change what he is. This is, roughly, the philosophical essence of racism."[29]

The new modern identity was defined in negative terms: for the anti-Semite, the Jew was everything the Germans were not. As Theodor Adorno once observed, the key to understanding anti-Semitism is not an analysis of the Jews but of the anti-Semites: "It is they," he wrote, "who should be made conscious of the mechanisms that provoke their racial prejudice."[30] As Adorno's remark suggests, the question of "the other" is, ultimately, a question about identity—about who we think we are.

This is a crucial factor in understanding the behavior—in particular, the passivity—of bystanders. By embracing the identity that Nazism imposed upon them, they became part of the anonymous crowd. Arthur Cohen notes Sartre's statement in *Anti-Semite and Jew* "that the anti-Semite chooses to make himself nondescript, to attach himself to the solidarity of the miserable mob, to make himself mediocre precisely because he cannot make himself individual."[31] While Cohen disagrees with Sartre on other issues, he see this as an important point: "the perception of racism as an instrument of insulating and aggrandizing the empty man."[32]

This, perhaps, is the essence of what Bauman calls "the modernity of racism."[33] Given the long historical record of conflict and hatred between different ethnic or religious groups, he acknowledges that these aspects are not what distinguish the Holocaust from other instances of genocide. Those aspects of the Holocaust that make it unique, and which set the experience of its Jewish victims apart from that of the non-Jewish victims, are linked to modernity and totalitarianism.[34] Thus, he believes that the Nazi persecution of the Jews is not an aberration but an inherent part of modernity itself. For centuries in Europe, the Jews had been the quintessential outsiders, a group despised by all classes. With emancipation and the dawn of modernity, the Jews "were more than any other category vulnerable to the impact of new tensions and contradictions which the social upheavals of the modernizing revolution could not fail to generate."[35] They had became part of modern society because of the very possibilities of modernity. Their new status *"epitomized the awesome scope of social upheaval and served as a vivid, obtrusive reminder of the erosion of old certainties."*[36]

ANTI-SEMITISM, BYSTANDERS, AND THE HOLOCAUST

As the above discussion shows, prejudice is not merely the expression of personally held attitudes. It forms a common thread that runs through all levels of society; its manifestations can be either obvious or hidden. There is a relation between the personal prejudices of individuals and the cultural and political values that govern their societies. Society is built on the convictions and beliefs held by the majority of its members; where anti-Semitism is viewed with abhorrence, intolerant speech and action will not succeed. Conversely, however, dominant values in society can shape the beliefs of individuals or intimidate them into silence. Here, because of their role in shaping values and stabilizing (and "sanctifying") society, religious institutions play a powerful role.

This is why prejudice is so insidious, dangerous, and difficult to eradicate. Changing laws does not automatically change hearts. Some scholars, notably Elisabeth Young-Bruehl, argue that prejudice is rooted not so much in sociological/political factors as in deeply rooted psychological dynamics—ultimately, in the unconscious itself.[37] Conversely, the growth of tolerance or solidarity among some individuals does not necessarily lead to an overturning of prejudicial structures. There are numerous cases of people who privately offered kindness and help to the Jewish victims—and probably countless more of people who were privately troubled by what they witnessed. Referring to such people in 1943, Heinrich Himmler complained that every German had his "good Jew." Himmler spoke for the Nazi leadership's hope that it would eventually destroy all feelings of human solidarity with the Jewish victims. The examples of individuals who did help show that the Nazis did not succeed completely. But they succeeded too much, for we must assume that there were many people who, although troubled, were unable to turn their "concern into action," as the Oliners put it.[38] Without a change in social and political structures, good intentions often don't go very far.

ANTI-SEMITISM AND BYSTANDERS IN NAZI GERMANY

The myriad levels on which prejudice operates make it difficult to establish conclusively the degree to which anti-Semitism determined the responses of bystanders during the Holocaust. While most scholars agree that it played a role, the way in which it functioned is still being explored, because the historical details yield such different pictures.

Ian Kershaw's research uncovered a number of incidents that give a complex picture of bystander behavior. He found one instance of vicious anti-Semitism in the Franconian village of Gunzenhausen on Palm Sunday, 1934, when villagers, led by local storm troopers, brutally attacked and imprisoned local Jews. In the village of 5,600, some 1,000 to 1,500 citizens directly participated in the attacks.[39]

Even in Franconia, a province with a long history of anti-Semitism, Gunzenhausen was the exception. Nowhere else there did Kershaw find evidence of such an incident, and he cites several others that offer a different picture. In the town of Schwäbisch Fischbach, for example, the mayor prevented the burning of the synagogue in November 1938, and allowed Jewish services to be held there four days later.[40] In another village (Mainstockheim), the Nazi mayor stopped local crowds from attacking the synagogue, saying, "You don't have to talk to Jews, but otherwise you are to leave them in peace."[41]

The mayor's remark, Kershaw believes, shows the difference between "latent" and "dynamic" anti-Semitism.[42] The percentage of "dynamic" anti-Semites was small, he argues, even if the number of people who truly stood behind the Jews was even smaller. Still, Kershaw contends that "popular support for the Nazi movement and the social cohesiveness in the Third Reich were primarily based upon ideas and norms that had little to do with anti-Semitism and the persecution of Jews."[43]

Not all historians and scholars agree with Kershaw's conclusions.[44] Still, his research shows that the Bavarian population responded to the persecution of the Jews in different ways and gives us some insight into how prejudice worked in Nazi Germany. More importantly, his insights are substantiated by other studies. In the course of their study of rescuers, for example, the Oliners also interviewed seventy-two "bystanders"[45] and analyzed their values and motives. Most of the bystanders, they found, were characterized generally by a lack of relationship to others and the world around them: bystanders "were marked by constrictedness, by an ego that perceived most of the world beyond its own boundaries as peripheral. More centered on themselves and their own needs, they were less conscious of others and less concerned with them." Only a minority, they found, were "true ethnocentrics who perceived many people as alien to them, especially outsider groups."[46]

In examining the role of prejudice in Nazi society, the real question may be how it functioned. Historian Michael Kater, who studied anti-Semitism in pre-Nazi Germany, argues that anti-Semitism was widespread among Germans. Yet even he notes the incremental, almost haphazard nature of the anti-Jewish measures. Although the discrimination and persecution of the Jews were clearly a part of Nazism from the beginning, Kater contends that they did not occur "within the framework of a rationally conceived scheme nor according to a secret master plan." The anti-Jewish actions were "a pattern of interactions between private or personal initiative, semilegal activities . . . and, finally, governmental legislation."[47]

Despite disagreement over its significance, virtually every study makes it clear that prejudice shaped the beliefs and behavior of ordinary people in Germany, and influenced responses abroad to the plight of the European Jews. In some instances, it led ordinary citizens to join actively in violence against Jews, with apparent enthusiasm. In others, the evidence of anti-Semitism is more oblique. Deborah Lipstadt, for example, has noted how many foreign observers spoke of the "victims of Nazism" without ever mentioning that they were primarily Jewish—thus denying that it was the Jews, more than any other group, who had been singled out.[48]

The position of the bystanders is clear. Their very position as bystanders established that they had not been singled out as victims. Thus, although they wanted to remain on the sidelines, their silence clearly aligned them with the persecutors, not the victims. As Bauman writes, anti-Semitism renders people "foreigners" inside the country to which they belong—even if they are natives of that country and consider themselves assimilated.[49] The impact of someone becoming "the other" is that it creates an unbridgeable distance from those who still belong. That distance—between victims and bystanders, between people who had previously been neighbors—is one of the hallmarks of the Holocaust. The reaction of others to the genocide of the Jews, writes Otto Kulka, was "characterized by a striking abysmal indifference to the fate of the Jews as human beings. It seems that here, the 'Jewish question' and the entire process of its 'solution' in the Third Reich reached the point of almost complete depersonalization."[50]

Kulka's remark is not only true of people in Nazi Germany. There seems to have been little concern throughout the world about the people being murdered in Europe. There are a number of reasons for this. But one is certainly that, in their war against the European Jews, the Nazis drew on prejudices against the Jews that had existed for centuries.

In this context, it may seem odd to speak of "indifference." The word certainly does not fit the vicious brutality with which the Nazis tormented their victims or the ghoulish enthusiasm that we find in the letters and records of some perpetrators. Nor does it fit the jubilant crowds we see cheering Hitler in newsreels and the other historical evidence of the widespread support for many of the Nazi measures. It does not adequately describe the behavior of collaborators in the occupied countries, or the deliberate lack of response from the Allied countries.

On the contrary, the Holocaust offers countless examples of how "indifference" disguised other emotions. One Polish woman used the word to describe her own reactions toward the victims of Nazism, writing: "That guilt of mine, which bordered on cruelty, was my indifference to the Jewish fate. I was completely indifferent to the human beings who were perishing in the ghetto. They were 'them' and not 'us.' "[51]

Defending herself, she argues that this feeling was not anti-Semitic, but a rather normal generalized indifference to strangers. Yet, she goes on to argue that Jews are guilty of "many sins against the Polish people"[52] and that this "Jewish guilt" is the source of Polish anti-Semitism.[53]

The bottom line, as Raul Hilberg has put it, was that most people thought that, even if Jews shouldn't be killed, they weren't worth saving. Ultimately, there was nothing about the plight of the Jews that moved outsiders—bystanders—to see the Jews' fate as linked to their own.[54]

To speak of "indifference," or analyze the genocide of the Jews in the context of the larger brutality of the time, does not denigrate the enormity of that genocide, or deny the role played by anti-Semitism. The problem with looking at anti-Semitism in isolation is that this separates prejudice from the other factors that empower it. These other factors may be just as crucial in explaining the behavior of bystanders, for the fact remains that widespread cruelty and indifference was rampant. One of the most harrowing accounts in Horwitz's book on Mauthausen comes from the end of the war, when more than 300 Russian prisoners of war escaped from the camp. The Austrian farmers in the area even joined the SS in hunting down and murdering the escaped prisoners—who were not Jews. This, and many other examples, show that there was little compassion toward any of the victims of Nazism—Jews and non-Jews.

This suggests that the behavior we see among German bystanders and those in occupied countries is not solely the product of prejudice; other factors merged with prejudice to generate widespread apathy and brutality. The pervasive "indifference" of bystanders does not mean that they were innocent of prejudice or mere pawns of the Nazi leadership. "Indifference" and its various expressions is worth deeper examination, particularly if we are to draw lessons that can be used today.

NOTES

1. Marlies Flesch-Thebesius gives a moving portrayal of such reactions in her own family in her memoir, *Hauptsache Schweigen* (Stuttgart: Radius Verlag, 1988).

2. In Peter Melcher, *Weissensee. Ein Friedhof als Spiegelbild jüdischer Geschichte in Berlin* (Berlin: Haude & Spener, 1986), 73.

3. Ibid., 74–76.

4. Hecht, *Invisible Walls*, 30.

5. Cited in Polonsky, *My Brother's Keeper?*, 15.

6. In Richarz, *Jewish Life in Germany*, 25.

7. In Polonsky, *My Brother's Keeper?*, 4. See, too, Staub's discussion of this dynamics in *The Roots of Evil*, 18.

8. Staub, *The Roots of Evil*, 60.

9. In Bauman, *Modernity*, 62–64.

10. Three standard works dealing with this aspect are Lipstadt, *Beyond Belief*; Wyman, *The Abandonment of the Jews*; and Feingold, *The Politics of Rescue*.

11. See Tal, *Christians and Jews in Germany*. See also Randolph L. Braham,

The Origins of the Holocaust: Christian Anti-Semitism (Boulder, Colo.: Social Science Monographs and Institute for Holocaust Studies of the City University of New York, 1986).

12. Untitled document, written by "a small group of German refugees (of Aryan and non-Aryan descent)" in Geneva, sent by Church Refugee Director Adolph Freudenberg to Henry Smith Leiper at the Federal Council of Churches in New York in December 1943. This document is in the Henry Smith Leiper papers, Burke Library, Union Theological Seminary, New York. Quotation is made available by courtesy of the Burke Library of Union Theological Seminary in the City of New York.

For an analysis of this kind of thinking in the churches during the Nazi period, see Haynes, *Reluctant Witnesses: Jews and the Christian Imagination.*

13. Dietrich Bonhoeffer, "The Church and the Jewish Question," in *No Rusty Swords: Letters, Lectures and Notes 1928–1936* (New York: Harper and Row, 1965), 222.

14. Ian Kershaw, "Antisemitismus und Volksmeinung. Reaktion auf die Judenverfolgung," in Broszat, *Bayern in der NS-Zeit.* Vol. II: *Herrschaft und Gesellschaft im Konflikt,* 309.

15. Ibid., 311.

16. Ibid., 310.

17. Volf, *Exclusion and Embrace,* 49.

18. See Doris L. Bergen, *Twisted Cross: The German Christian Movement in the Third Reich* (Chapel Hill: University of North Carolina Press, 1996).

19. In Sanford Ragins, *Jewish Responses to Anti-Semitism in Germany, 1870– 1914* (Cincinnati: Hebrew Union College Press, 1980), 15–16.

20. Volf, *Exclusion and Embrace,* 49.

21. Kershaw, "Antisemitismus und Volksmeinung," in Broszat, *Bayern in der NS-Zeit.* Vol. II, 317.

22. See the chapter on this in Peter G. Pulzer, *Jews and the German State: The Political History of a Minority, 1848–1933* (Cambridge, Mass.: Blackwell, 1992).

23. Robert E. Willis, "The Burden of Auschwitz: Rethinking Morality," 275.

24. Gershom Sholem, "Jews and Germans," in Werner J. Dannhauser, ed., *On Jews and Judaism in Crisis: Selected Essays* (New York: Schocken Books, 1978), 76.

25. Volf, *Exclusion and Embrace,* 75.

26. Sholem, "Jews and Germans," 76.

27. Staub, *The Roots of Evil,* 103.

28. In Bauman, *Modernity,* 59.

29. Ibid., 60.

30. Adorno et al., *The Authoritarian Personality,* 128.

31. Cohen, *The Tremendum,* 13–14.

32. Ibid.

33. Bauman, *Modernity,* 56–60.

34. Ibid., 88–98.

35. Ibid., 45.

36. Ibid. Italics are Bauman's.

37. See Elisabeth Young-Bruehl, *The Anatomy of Prejudices* (Cambridge, Mass: Harvard University Press, 1998).

38. Oliner and Oliner, *The Altruistic Personality*, 187.

39. Kershaw, "Antisemitismus und Volksmeinung," in Broszat, *Bayern in der NS-Zeit*, 296.

40. Ibid., 331.

41. Ibid., 342.

42. Ibid., 343.

43. Ibid., 346.

44. See Marrus, *The Holocaust in History*, 91–92.

45. Oliner and Oliner, *The Altruistic Personality*, 4.

46. Ibid., 186.

47. Michael Kater, "Everyday Anti-Semitism in Pre-War Nazi Germany," in Marrus, *The Nazi Holocaust: Historical Articles on the Destruction of European Jews*, 160.

48. See Lipstadt, *Beyond Belief*, 205–263.

49. Bauman, *Modernity*, 34.

50. Otto Kulka, " 'Public Opinion' in Nazi Germany: The Final Solution," in Marrus, *The Nazi Holocaust*, Vol. 5.1: *Public Opinion and Relations to the Jews in Nazi Europe*, 47.

51. Janina Walewska, "In a Sense I Am an Anti-Semite," in Polonsky, *My Brother's Keeper?*, 131.

52. Ibid., 123.

53. Ibid., 131.

54. Hilberg, *Perpetrators, Victims, Bystanders*, 204.

CHAPTER 7

The Dynamics of Indifference

"Indifference" is a leitmotif of the literature of the Holocaust. It surfaces in historical documents; it is the theme of much of the fiction and poetry that emerged from that experience. It is an integral part of other issues, especially the theme of silence, which we will examine later in this chapter.

It is perhaps the most common form of behavior we see during the Holocaust. We encounter it in studies of perpetrators for whom murder became so routine that they seemed indifferent to it. It spreads among the victims themselves as, terrorized and fatigued into numbness, they are swept, apparently passive, to their deaths. Above all, however, "indifference" is the mark of the bystanders who remain passive, who avoid involvement and thereby step outside the wheel of history.

Whatever other emotions may be involved, indifference is essentially an expression of distance. "Responsibility, this building block of all moral behavior, arises out of the proximity of the other," notes Bauman.[1] But there are different kinds of proximity and distance. Psychological distance is more significant than purely physical distance: the psychological distance between bystanders and victims may be equally vast, whether they are next-door neighbors or live on different continents. The attitude that the Jews were "not worth saving" affected the actions of ordinary Germans, Poles, and other Europeans directly under Nazi occupation; but it was also an attitude shared by many people outside of Nazi Europe.

Indeed, a striking fact about much Holocaust literature is not just the frequency of "indifference," but the similarities of the rationalizations that are used to defend it. Ordinary Germans and people overseas alike claim that they were powerless, or that they didn't know what was happening until too late. The psychological mechanisms used to come to terms with the suffering of another appear to be very similar, whether the person is standing right before us or is 2,000 miles away.

As this suggests, a sense of moral urgency is distinct from physical immediacy: the urge to become involved stems not just from what we witness but from who happens to be involved. Long before we are called to help our neighbors, we have usually determined who our neighbors are. Confronted with a situation involving someone who has not been our "neighbor" up to now, a long, difficult process begins, in which we try to determine exactly what our stake in the matter is. Throughout this process, our prejudices about "the otherness" of the victims may have devastating effects on our readiness to help. Ideological and moral principles also come into play, as do self-interest and the weighing of the possible consequences of our actions. We try to establish what is or is not possible. In the end, our decision will be determined not so much by whether we actually have the power to change a situation, but whether we have the will to do so.

Because of all these factors, the indifference of bystanders is one of the hardest things to analyze. "Indifference" can describe a moral stance, a psychological attitude, or actual behavior. There were bystanders during the Holocaust who were genuinely indifferent, emotionally and ethically. Not only did they do nothing to help the victims, they remained unmoved by their plight. And there were other bystanders who, although they behaved indifferently, did so because they were afraid, or were unable to find options to help. For these people, indifference epitomized a failure of courage and clearsightedness, the triumph of pragmatism or fear over conscience. The letters and diaries they leave behind often reveal genuine anguish at what is happening around them.

A good starting point is to recognize that "indifference" can be used to describe observable behavior or emotional indifference. Each of these forms has ethical consequences for our understanding of bystanders. We often think of indifference as simply the absence of deep emotions like love or hatred. In reality, it is a complex, often unconscious mechanism that can hide a number of emotions, ranging from fear of the Nazis to silent approval for what the Nazis were doing.

While we must recognize this psychological reality, we must also acknowledge that, whatever emotions and motives lie under the surface, the effect of indifference was as devastating as active hatred would have been. For the victims, the "indifference" and silence of bystanders had the same consequences as the active hatred of perpetrators. Miroslav Volf writes of the "havoc wreaked by indifference," epitomized by the fact that, ultimately, bystanders "start to view horror and (their) implication in it as normalcy."[2]

Why, then, discuss indifference as a separate phenomenon? One reason is that "indifferent" behavior is prevalent throughout the Holocaust, inside and outside Nazi Germany. In various guises, it appears throughout the historical literature.[3] One guise was the emotional numbness witnessed among both bystanders and perpetrators, the "nonhuman blankness" described by George Kateb. Another of its guises was routine—the routine of the death camp guards, the Red Cross officials, the bureaucrats who signed forms ordering new shipments of poison gas, the train conductors who transported the victims to their deaths. The most frequent form of "indifference" was simply silence: among ordinary Germans, bureaucrats, diplomats, and people throughout the world.

The topic of "indifference," then, brings us to a different, more profound level of this history. We will first examine one rather controversial historical study that highlights the indifference of bystanders, and then explore how the scholars, artists, and writers who have wrestled with the Holocaust have interpreted "indifference."

THE INDIFFERENCE OF BYSTANDERS IN HISTORY

One of the most thorough studies of human behavior in Nazi Germany is Martin Broszat's study of Bavaria.[4] The Broszat study, based upon research by scholars under the auspices of the Institute for Contemporary History in Munich, studied the available documents from the Nazi era for the region of Bavaria, including records of arrests, Gestapo reports on public behavior and incidents, and the SOPADE reports (reports on public behavior, collected by the Social Democrats, a political opposition party). The work of Ian Kershaw, cited in the previous chapter, was part of this larger study.

The Broszat volumes are perhaps the most comprehensive study of *Alltagsgeschichte*—the history of everyday life under Nazism. Some historians and other scholars of the period find this form of scholarship controversial. Saul Friedlander, one of the most prominent scholars of the Holocaust, argues that Broszat's "historicization" and other attempts at *Alltagsgeschichte* come dangerously close to serving as apologetics. By focusing on the way most Germans perceived their everyday life, these historical accounts risk legitimizing such perceptions, including peoples' rationalizations and apologetics—for example, their contention that ordinary Germans didn't know anything about the persecution of the Jews or found out too late. Friedlander charges that the "everyday" aspects of German life documented by Broszat "possess the same moral and historical significance as Commandant Rudolf Höss's garden outside the enclosures of the crematoria"[5]; he fears that such details only distract us from the true nature of the history, and blind us to the complicity of the bystanders.

In discussing this point, historian Charles Maier acknowledges the danger of apologetics. Still, says Maier, at its best *Alltagsgeschichte* is an effort "to understand a regime in which Auschwitz and a lived normality (even if only as a species of false consciousness) could coexist. It endeavors to get at the simultaneity of banality and apocalypse, or, as Peukert says, 'barbarism and the everyday.' "[6]

The phenomenon of "barbarism and the everyday," of course, is at the heart of the Holocaust; it is the reason we talk about bystanders. And it must be noted that there are other examples of *Alltagsgeschichte* that reveal not only indifference, but blatant enthusiasm and complicity.[7] Indifference does not mean innocence, just as the question of "what people knew" concerns more than mere knowledge. Wiesel is correct that indifference was a form of complicity. It is not morally neutral; indifference furthers the cause of hatred, not reconciliation.

In analyzing the indifference of bystanders, our task is to interpret it, not rationalize it. Again, we are dealing both with historical fact and with ethical consequences. Only an examination of actual behavior can give us insight into what really happened, as well as into the subsequent interpretations of the Holocaust, both by scholars and by the victims themselves— who also, as we shall see, wrestled with the "indifference" they encountered. If we study Broszat's findings cautiously—and do not pretend that "indifference" signifies "innocence"—we can glean some insight into exactly how people behaved.

Broszat's study examines the behavior of the Bavarian population on a number of fronts, including their attitudes toward Jews and the measures against them. As mentioned previously, British historian Ian Kershaw looked at the records of measures against the Bavarian Jews and the public reactions to those measures.[8] He found instances of voluntary and spontaneous public participation in acts of anti-Jewish terror (e.g., in Gunzenhausen), as well as accounts of explicit public support for the Jews and opposition to their persecution. The records he studied showed a wide spectrum of behavior, ranging from open participation in anti-Jewish measures to refusal to comply with such measures—as in the case of a swimming pool manager, for example, who refused to yield to visitors' demands that Jews leave the pool, "giving the reason that the Jews were behaving quietly and that the director of the pool was in charge of maintaining peace and order."[9]

Not surprisingly, the earliest and most extreme incidents of public attacks on Jews occurred in regions with histories of pronounced anti-Semitism. Gunzenhausen in Franconia, where the villagers joined local storm troopers in attacking their Jewish neighbors, was an example.

Kershaw also discovered cases of opposition or outright disregard for the racial measures—including the two Bavarian villages whose leaders protected the synagogues from destruction in November 1938. Much of this opposition seems to have been based upon economic considerations. Throughout Bavaria, Jews were active in livestock trading and there was much opposition to moves against them, which local farmers feared would affect their business adversely. As a result, only in the district led by Julius Streicher (a leading Nazi ideologist and publisher of the propaganda sheet *Der Stürmer*) were Jews barred from livestock trading by the end of 1934. Elsewhere, Bavarian Jewish traders continued to work until the end of 1937, when the Gestapo took active measures to push the Jewish traders out. [10]

Much of this suggests that the Bavarian population was more interested in its own well-being than in waging a war against the Jews. Kershaw cites the 1937 report of a mayor who noted that only Nazi Party members were interested in getting Jews out of the livestock trade.[11] Among most farmers, he wrote, "the stance of rejection against the Jews is missing . . . Some of them are conspicuous for their friendliness to Jews."[12] Even in Gunzenhausen, an influential parish council member said, "We need the Jews because I can't get my cattle to the customer without them. The Christian traders always want to sell under price, which is not the case with the Jews."[13] As late as 1937, the police in Munich reported that Jewish businesses were still drawing customers.

All these instances reveal economic self-interest more than genuine solidarity. In addition to economic factors, public protest against Nazi authorities was often triggered by dissatisfaction on other points (such as the regime's moves against the churches, which aroused widespread protest). Kershaw acknowledges that public criticism of anti-Jewish measures represented "more an antipathy against the Party than empathy for the Jews or a rejection of the regime's Jewish policy."[14]

But all these nuances offer a more complex picture of what Kershaw terms "indifference." With few exceptions such as the Gunzenhausen incident, there was little spontaneous public initiative against the Jews or outright support for the regime's anti-Jewish measures. As one 1937 Gestapo report complained, "the deeper reasons" for the Bavarian farmers' support of Jewish cattle traders were "the farmers' attitudes, which are devoid of any kind of racial consciousness."[15] Throughout Germany, the population often reacted in a way that was unreadable to the Gestapo and others who were taking careful notes about public reaction.[16]

For this reason, scholars like Yehuda Bauer have cautiously concluded, on the basis of the Gestapo reports cited by Kershaw, Germans' attitudes were "characterized more by apathy, indifference, discomfort at the thought of what was happening to the Jews, and fear of the Nazi authorities, than by active agreement with Nazi policies."[17]

But what is the ethical significance of this "indifference"? Kershaw and Broszat do not get into this aspect, choosing to present the historical documentation without commentary. Others, however, have disagreed not so much with Kershaw's actual findings as with his use of the word "indifferent" to describe them. In addition to Daniel Goldhagen, Otto Kulka and

A. Rodrigue, for example, interpret this "indifferent" behavior more critically.[18] Citing the Germans' response to Hitler's speech on January 30,
1942 that promised "the annihilation of Jewry," they argue that Germans
knew exactly what was happening to the Jews: "Thus what was actually
reported to the regime should not be understood as 'indifference,' but as
an attitude that might best be characterized as passive complicity."[19]

Whether we agree with Kershaw or Kulka, it should be clear that both
scholars acknowledge that indifference was not benign; it is precisely what
enabled the genocide to proceed. Zygmunt Bauman has described the indifference of bystanders as "the paralysis of that public which failed to turn
into a mob."[20] This paralysis is not ethically neutral. Although they do not
join the mob, the silent bystanders form its foundation. "The masses sup-
plied volunteers: That is the inescapable fact. If not all in the majority were
eager, all those who were eager came from the majority," writes George
Kateb.[21]

The ethical significance of "indifference" is not confined to the complicity
it generates among bystanders. As Bauman has noted, the mechanisms that
make bystanders indifferent (e.g., the tendency to compartmentalize their
experience) are very similar to what we find among perpetrators.[22]

This raises the disturbing question of whether indifference signified the
inherent capacity to join the perpetrators. Did "indifference" make most
bystanders just as capable of atrocity as the career Gestapo guards? Is it
only chance that makes some people killers? Some incidents suggest this
(notably Gordon Horwitz's account of villager participation in the murders
of Soviet POWs[23]) and this question is a fundamental part of Goldhagen's
argument.[24]

The "indifference" of people outside of Nazi Germany gives us some
additional insights into the phenomenon. As in Nazi Germany, the "indifferent" world was a silent world, an informed but hesitant world, a world
that ultimately decided to opt for military defeat of Nazism as the best way
to rescue the victims. Even the Jews in Palestine, notes Michael Marrus,
reacted to news of the genocide in Europe much as the rest of the world
did: with a "reluctance to believe and a slowness to grasp the magnitude
of the destruction."[25]

The patterns of indifference we find among the international community
show not just disbelief and a general paralysis in reacting to the Jews' fate,
but a widespread sense that the fate of the European Jews was not a high
priority for most international institutions.[26]

Thus, "indifference" took different forms during the Holocaust. There is
the indifference of those who genuinely didn't care. There is the apparent
indifference (inaction may be a better word) of those who seemed paralyzed
but who, under the surface, suffered in anguish. There is the indifference—
with varying degrees of anguish—of organizations and world leaders who,
while they may have felt pangs of conscience about the plight of the Jews,

put those emotions aside in the interests of political and military pragmatism.

The various forms of "indifference" shaped what happened. Writing about the dynamics of victimization, theologian Christine Gudorf has observed how carefully (and deliberately) such patterns are created:

This is one of the most common aspects of victimization: the extent to which victimizers are unconscious of the evil they do. This lack of consciousness is seldom total, of course, and is often deliberately cultivated. Many of the religious rationales for victimization are just that—not the initiating cause of victimization, but carefully constructed defenses for continuing practices that benefit limited social groups at the expense of others. Ignorance of our common humanity is not random, but chosen and maintained through avoiding all that might lead us to identification with victims: physical proximity, common terms of address and description, shared institutions, knowledge of the other, and recognition of the injustice and unmerited and involuntary suffering present in our world.[27]

In other words, whatever else it signifies, indifference is also a tactic. It is the mechanism by which people—whether they are secretly troubled or genuinely don't care about the victims—choose to step outside the events occurring around them. Once such compartmentalization occurs and people have established their place in the scheme of things, the rationalizations begin and never end. Supported by mechanisms at every level of society, passivity requires less and less effort. It is activism—the fight against indifference, the rebellion against silence—that demands a monumental and courageous effort.

"INDIFFERENCE" AS A THEME IN HOLOCAUST LITERATURE

The stories of Tadeusz Borowski are related in a matter-of-fact tone, deliberately stripped of emotion. Graphic accounts of camp brutality are juxtaposed with equally detailed descriptions of the idyllic landscape surrounding Auschwitz.[28] The result is a cynical, surreal portrayal that underscores the utter depravity and dehumanization of the events he describes.

This may be because Borowski (who committed suicide in 1951) found himself in the dual position of victim and bystander. A member of the political resistance in Poland, he was arrested in 1942 and sent to Auschwitz. Not Jewish, he worked as a night watchman in the camp hospital; as a "kapo," he witnessed the continual disappearance of the Jews who arrived at the camp.

An example comes from his story "The People Who Walked On." One balmy late spring evening he and the other kapos play soccer:

A train had just arrived. People were emerging from the cattle cars and walking in the direction of the little wood. All I could see from where I stood were bright splashes of colour. The women, it seemed, were already wearing summer dresses; it was the first time that season. The men had taken off their coats, and their white shirts stood out sharply against the green of the trees. The procession moved along slowly, growing in size as more and more people poured from the freight cars. And then it stopped. The people sat down on the grass and gazed in our direction. I returned with the ball and kicked it back inside the field. It travelled from one foot to another and, in a wide arc, returned to the goal. I kicked it towards a corner. Again it rolled out into the grass. Once more I ran to retrieve it. But as I reached down, I stopped in amazement—the ramp was empty. Out of the whole colourful summer procession, not one person remained. The train too was gone . . .

Between two throw-ins in a soccer game, right behind my back, three thousand people had been put to death.[29]

Did such a scene truly happen or not? The story is apocryphal, haunting us not only because of its juxtaposition of tranquillity and horror, but because—like all of Borowski's writing—it seems to strip the scene of any deeper meaning. Describing the work of Tadeusz Borowski, Alvin Rosenfeld has observed,

Indignation is absent from this fiction for it implies distance or detachment, an attitude of moral separation. Shock, wonderment, revulsion, or compassion, likewise all absent, do the same. To keep these civilized responses alive would be to portray the savagery of the concentration camp as a thing apart, and Borowski, who is nothing if not the opposite of a sentimentalist, is intent on showing how terror quickly becomes domesticated . . . Of course that is to be complicitous, which of course means to be "an accessory to the crime," but there is only the crime.[30]

Borowski attempted to make a literary photograph of Auschwitz in its full horror and absurdity. In refusing to give it any meaning, he was insisting that there could be no interpretation of the Holocaust that could make any "sense" of it. The "indifference" in his stories strips the experience of all the trappings that different groups have tried to give it, of Nazi banners waving in the wind, and of the simple human dignity and decency that some victims tried to maintain. At the end of everything, as Rosenfeld says, "there is only the crime."

We may argue with this troubling portrayal, but it epitomizes a reality that confronts all students of the Holocaust. The phenomenon of bystander "indifference" is connected to the *meaning of indifference* in the Holocaust. Some scholars claim that the Holocaust is "indifferent" historically and ontologically—which does not mean that it does not matter, but that it matters so much that it falls beyond all human capacity to interpret it—that the very meaning of the Holocaust is its utter meaninglessness. Attempts to discern divine purpose or intent in the Holocaust, or to determine some long-term historical "good" that has come out of it, are an obscene insult to the victims.

It is on this level of interpretation that silence—the other leitmotif of Holocaust literature—is linked to "indifference." The behavior we observe as "indifferent" is predominantly characterized by silence: by people going about their business, refusing to talk about what is happening. Yet silence is more than the absence of protest or outrage. As theologian Robert McAfee Brown has observed, humanity's silence during the Holocaust is very much related to God's silence.[31] In the silence of the indifferent by-standers, we encounter the silence of God.

SILENCE

Several years ago, I interviewed an elderly German woman. She had an excellent memory, and had given me many details of what her life in the 1930s had been like. Then we turned to the subject of the Holocaust. Her family, she had told me, was not at all anti-Semitic, and had had many Jewish friends.

"What happened to the Jews you knew?" I asked.

"Why, I don't know." Her voice was surprised, as if the question had never occurred to her.

"Can you tell me something about what it was like when these people were taken away?" I asked. "How did you react, how did your family react?"

"We didn't see anything."

I tried again. "But you said that there were some Jewish girls in your school class. [she had been seventeen or eighteen years old at the time] What happened when they suddenly stopped coming? Did the teacher say anything? Did the other girls talk about it?"

"I really don't remember."

Suddenly, she had closed up, drawn a blank. Except that this is something that—in someone who otherwise had an astonishingly vivid memory—you wouldn't draw a blank on.

What struck me especially in this interview was that I had been confronted, firsthand, with a phenomenon that characterized the Holocaust as it was taking place. It appeared to me that the silence of this woman, forty years after the Holocaust, was linked to the silence that permeated Nazi society at the time. Those who did not speak out at the time remained silent decades later. Otto Kulka has observed that public reaction to the Nuremberg laws and the November 1938 pogrom in Germany "was widespread and varied, [but] during the war period the unquestionably dominant feature was the almost total absence of any reference to the existence, persecution and the extermination of the Jews—a kind of national conspiracy of silence."[32]

When we speak of "silence" during the Holocaust, the first thing that comes to mind is the silence of bystanders, inside and outside Nazi Germany. But it is intriguing to note how much Holocaust literature evokes the theme of silence through numerous images: the silence or absence of God; the silence of victims, bystanders, and perpetrators at the time; and the silence that characterized them all for decades afterward.

Rosenfeld notes that the silence imposed by the Holocaust became a theme of the literature written by the survivors, who all had to wrestle with their own silences.[33] In many ways, the survivors had been condemned to a silence without end. The world in which they had existed was gone. Particularly for Yiddish writers, notes Rosenfeld, the world of their culture and language had been decimated.[34]

Thus, there are different kinds of silence, but, as with indifference, these kinds of silence are linked. The silence of the witnesses as the victims disappeared was paralleled later in their silence of memory and speech. In the silence of bystanders, many victims felt abandoned, not just by their neighbors, but by God. And, finally, all these levels of silence created that desolate, silent world of the survivors, a world where the voices of loved ones—children, parents, brothers, and sisters—had been silenced, terribly. Silence—the absence of something—became a universe of its own. Years later, the poet Nelly Sachs wrote a poignant one-line poem about that world: "But silence is where the victims dwell."[35]

The theme of silence takes on particular significance when we examine bystanders. Silence, if you will, is what they did and who they were; it shaped their identity and their actions. It was part of the false language of "normalcy" described in the last chapter. The euphemism of normalcy depended upon silence; they were two sides of the same lie. The perpetrators murdered; the victims died; a few resisted. But the bystanders were silent, and when they began to speak after 1945, their words only gave shape to the silence. As my interview with the German woman illustrates, many people didn't talk so much about the Holocaust as around it. The horror of what had happened under Nazism remained nameless, vague, unspoken, a black hole in the center of consciousness: "I can't remember." Or, "we didn't know; we only found out later."

Denial of memory or of consciousness is one form of silence. The absence of protest, of course, is another form that existed during the Holocaust. Like denial, it persisted for years afterward. "We were victims, too," some people who lived through the Nazi era said, suggesting that protest had not been an option. Even those who broke their silence later could not undo the damage that had been done. In Germany, one of the most moving postwar confessions came from Lothar Kreyssig, the Brandenburg judge who had opposed the euthanasia program. At a 1950 meeting of Protestant church leaders, Kreyssig recounted an incident that continued to haunt him. He had a Jewish friend, he told his colleagues, who had received deportation orders to join one of the transports to the East. As a Christian, Kreyssig was determined to join him in solidarity and go with him to die in the camps. But at the last minute, Kreyssig weakened; "today," he admitted, "he is dead and I stand here."[36]

Kreyssig's failure to join the victims—in effect, to break away from the world of silence—led to his confession of guilt. He refused to be silent later. But his painful and forthright confession could not undo the earlier failure. This is one of the most painful realities that the bystander confronts: Silence at the time seals the deed. Speaking out later and breaking the silence is perhaps the only way to move on, to transform the future. It is certainly the only way to address the past honestly. But it cannot change the past world that was created and framed by silence.

The third form of silence that emerges in Holocaust literature, of course, is the silence of God. For many religious believers, the Holocaust altered the traditional perceptions of a divine and benevolent God. In both the Christian and Jewish religious traditions, the silence of God has always been one aspect of the divinity. When Moses encountered God in the burning bush, the Hebrew words describe God as "the sound of utmost silence." "Who is like unto Thee among the speechless, O God/Who can be compared with Thee in Thy silence?" as a medieval Hebrew poet expressed the dilemma."[37]

The silence of God expressed one of the fundamental mysteries of faith. It was not always perceived as a benign mystery, yet it was a mystery that contained some purpose. This sense of purpose—of meaning—vanished in the flames of the Holocaust. Before the Holocaust, the silence of God seemed profound, majestic, and mysterious. Afterward, this silence made God seem powerless, an accomplice to terrible crimes against humanity.

There is no way to separate God's silence during the Holocaust from the silence of the bystanders. As Arthur Cohen writes, "The silent God is treated by some of his critics as though speech were the only mark of affect or miracle the only modality of caring; hence silence is ineffectuality and the equivalent of the 'not-God.' "[38] In reality, however, "God's speech is really always man's hearing" and God's "speech and silence are metaphors for our language and distortion."[39]

There is another aspect of this silence, which Rosenfeld discusses. In his study of Holocaust literature, he notes that this silence exists in tension with the "necessities of language."[40] Mere language, Rosenfeld notes, fails to convey the reality of what happened in Auschwitz. Every writer who survived that experience has wrestled with the shortcomings of language, the impossibility of conveying what truly happened.

Thus, the silence of the Holocaust exposes the complicity of language at the time and its inadequacy thereafter. For the bystanders, silence *is* their language—sometimes as an absence of speech, at other times as a retreat into euphemism. The different forms of silence draw the line between the parallel worlds of bystander and victims.

PARALLEL WORLDS

In Elie Wiesel's novel, *The Town beyond the Wall*, the narrator catches a glimpse of a neighbor, a face behind a window that watches as the Jews are led away:

It was like a balloon. Bald, flat nose, wide empty eyes. I watched it for a long time. It was gazing out, reflecting no pity, no pleasures, not shock, not even anger or interest . . . The face is neither Jewish nor anti-Jewish, a simple spectator, that's what it is.

For seven days the great courtyard of the synagogue filled and emptied. He, standing behind the curtains, watched. The police beat women and children; he did not stir. It was no concern of his. He was neither victim nor executioner; a spectator, that's what he was. He wanted to live in peace and quiet . . . How can anyone remain a spectator indefinitely?[41]

The puzzle portrayed here is that the behavior of bystanders is no temporary lapse, no isolated action, but an indefinite, ongoing phenomenon. On one side of the curtain, women and children are beaten; on the other side, the impassive eyes of the bystander watch. The spectator does not turn away or withdraw; day after day, he watches.

The phenomenon of "parallel worlds" is a central reality of the Holocaust. The prisoner at Mauthausen looks longingly at the white houses; the victim in Wiesel's story sees a face watching from behind a curtain. In the altered universe in which the victims suddenly find themselves, the bystanders are the people who can, and do, withdraw to live as they did before. This separates them from the sufferings of the victims; they seem to live in a completely different world.

Under Nazism, the experiences of bystanders, perpetrators, and victims seemed so extremely different that they appeared to reflect totally separate worlds. At the Eichmann trial, prosecutor Gideon Hausner described "planet Auschwitz" as a place with different time, in which the people "had no names, no parents, no children . . . They breathed according to different laws. They did not live according to the rules of this world, nor did they die."[42]

Borowski evokes the vast chasm between this world and that of the bystanders in "A Day at Harmenz." In the story, an elderly Jewish kapo recalls his hunger in another camp:

Our camp, over there, was small . . . Right next to a road. Many people walked along that road, well-dressed men, women too. They passed on their way to church on Sundays, for instance. Or there were couples out for a stroll. And a little farther on was a village, just an ordinary village. There, people had everything, only half a mile from us. And we had turnips . . . good God, our people were ready to eat each other![43]

Later in the same story, Borowski described the young daughter of one of the camp commandants, playing with her dog on the veranda of a pictur-esque house, surrounded by ivy and roses. The inmates of the camp pass the house each day on their way back into the camp, and the description illustrates how visible these apparently separate worlds of the victims, per-petrators, and bystanders were to one another. It must have taken tremen-dous effort *not* to see the world of the other. The isolation and terror that characterized the world of the victims had to have some effect on that of the bystanders as well.

Thus, to speak of "parallel worlds" is not to suggest these were different worlds. The true significance of the parallel worlds of victims, bystanders, and perpetrators is that they were part of the same world. As Lawrence Langer notes, the presupposition that they were different worlds is ethically problematic:

Auschwitz wasn't the antiworld, but the world as Nazi Germany decided it should be. Removing its cosmology from our own by placing it in another universe is little more than an effort to sever ourselves from its acts and values in our ongoing search for what Brodsky calls mental comfort.[44]

In other words, we can only comprehend the full significance of these parallel worlds by recognizing that they are one: like silence and euphe-mism, two sides of the same lie. The phenomenon of "parallel worlds" depicts a fundamental reality of the Holocaust, in which the bystanders and perpetrators deliberately constructed and cultivated the illusion that the victims had disappeared from their universe. In one part, people suf-fered horribly; in the other, people continued to live normal lives, pursue careers, and raise their children. All Holocaust literature—both fictional and historical—shows us how close these worlds were to one another. The victims in Mauthausen and elsewhere could see the white houses; the by-standers—like the Mauthausen farmwoman whose window overlooked the camp—saw the victims.

Among the bystanders, what was missing was not knowledge or physical proximity, but the psychological and ethical sense of a link between these two worlds. This is the significance of "indifference." The "parallel worlds" were not just separated by physical walls and barbed wire; the real bound-ary was in the minds and hearts of the spectators. Tracing the development of parallel worlds in occupied Poland, Andrzej Bryk writes about the process that began with the establishment of compulsory ghettoes for Jews:

What is important is whether a psychological separation followed and whether it was taken for granted . . . There was a real mental confusion, an initial moral inability quickly and unequivocally to recognize the intentions and consequences of the Nazi policy. The separation between the two groups was reinforced by neither having any tangible, institutional means to cooperate which predated the terror. Each could turn culturally and morally to nationalistic or ethnic traditions which underlined their differences.[45]

As Bryk's description illustrates, a deep psychological division had already occurred between Jews and non-Jews in Poland; this led to a pervasive "psychological indifference" among Poles to the plight of the Jews.[46]

The proximity of the world of victim and bystanders is shocking because of how completely the bystanders abandon the victims. Describing the bystander in Mauthausen, Horwitz writes:

Neither raising his hand to help nor to strike, the bystander considers himself neutral. He abandons the inmates to their fate, forgetting that so removed are the inmates from any state of peace, so debased from the essence of their humanity, that to close one's eyes, to turn one's back upon them is to leave them concealed from the light of existence.[47]

SUMMARY

Ultimately, as Horwitz observes, the bystanders of Mauthausen were changed and corrupted by their own indifference. It is not possible to witness atrocities against other human beings and remain unchanged. In a universe divided into parallel worlds, those living in one sector lose all sense of relationship to the sufferings of others.

The creation of parallel worlds and its ethical consequences seems to be characteristic of all genocides. Decades later, writing about the rise of nationalism in eastern Europe after the end of the Cold War, Michael Ignatieff spoke of the "divided consciousness" of people who were trying to eliminate their enemies and, at the same time, could recall living peacefully with them: "In this divided consciousness, the plane of abstract fantasy and the plane of direct experience were never allowed to intersect."[48]

Inevitably, this leads the bystanders and perpetrators to compartmentalize their own reality—to distinguish between who they are and what they do. Parallel worlds arise within their own lives. This distinction has horrific ethical consequences. Ignatieff cites a news story about Serbian "ethnic cleansing," where a *New York Times* reporter quoted a Muslim victim of torture who recalled, "They told us nothing. They just said this is politics doing things to you, it is not us."[49] The retreat to a parallel world does

not just remove the bystander and perpetrator from emotional contact with
the victim. It disassociates the bystanders and perpetrators from their very
identity and the deeds of their own hands: "this is politics doing things to
you, it is not us."

It is striking to note how religious thinkers who have wrestled with the
Holocaust often focus on precisely this aspect: on the brokenness of the
post-Holocaust world, exemplified by the loss of a coherent ethical identity.
Any kind of honest confrontation with the past demands breaking the silence, removing the barriers between these parallel worlds, and reestablish-
ing the relationship between God and humanity, and of people with one
another. To affirm this relationship is to acknowledge the link between the
parallel worlds of victims and bystanders—which means recognizing the
relationship between the world of the victims and the silence and indifference of bystanders.

The use of the word "indifference" does not deny the evil and horror of
what really happened. A close examination of the phenomenon of "indifference" reveals a profound aspect about the Holocaust. The division of
human experience into parallel worlds resulted in a "broken world." The
brokenness of this world reflects not just the human lives that were shat-
tered, but many of our religious understandings about God and humanity.
The desolate, broken world that remains is evoked powerfully by the survivor and poet Jacob Glatstein in his poem "Smoke":

> God, wherever you may be,
> There all of us are also not.[50]

NOTES

1. Bauman, *Modernity*, 184.
2. Volf, *Exclusion and Embrace*, 77.
3. See, for example, Gordon, *Hitler, Germans and the "Jewish Question"*; Gellately, *The Gestapo and German Society: Enforcing Racial Policy 1933–1945*; Kershaw, *Popular Opinion and Political Dissent in the Third Reich: Bavaria 1933–
1945*.
4. Broszat, ed., *Bayern in der NS-Zeit*. Vol. I: *Soziale Lage und politisches
Verhalten der Bevölkerung im Spiegel vertraulicher Berichte*. Vol. II: *Herrschaft und
Gesellschaft im Konflikt*. See, too, Kershaw, *Popular Opinion and Political Dissent*.
5. In Maier, *The Unmasterable Past*, 92.
6. Ibid.
7. Two such books available in English are Ernst Klee, Willi Dressen, and
Volker Riess, *"Schöne Zeiten" (The Good Old Days): The Holocaust as Seen by
Its Perpetrators and Bystanders* eds., (New York: Free Press, 1991); and Bernt
Engelmann, *In Hitler's Germany: Daily Life in the Third Reich* (New York: Pantheon Books, 1986).

8. Kershaw, "Antisemitismus und Volksmeinung. Reaktion auf die Judenver-folgung," in Broszat, *Bayern in der NS-Zeit*, Vol. 2.

9. Broszat, *Bayern in der NS-Zeit*. Vol. I, 450.

10. Kershaw, "Antisemitismus und Volksmeinung," in Broszat, *Bayern in der NS-Zeit*, Vol. II, 301.

11. Kershaw cites a number of incidents and Gestapo files complaining of the lack of anti-Semitism among the population. Cf. Broszat, *Bayern in der NS-Zeit*, Vol. I, esp. 458–464.

12. Ibid., Vol. II, 301.

13. Ibid.

14. Ibid., 294.

15. Ibid., 301.

16. Ibid., 328.

17. Yehuda Bauer, "Jew and Gentile: The Holocaust and After," 19–63, in Marrus, ed. *The Nazi Holocaust*. Vol. 4.1: *The "Final Solution" Outside Germany*, 46.

18. Kulka and Rodrigue, "The German Population and the Jews in the Third Reich," in Marrus, *The Nazi Holocaust*, Vol. 5, *Public Opinion and Relations to the Jews in Nazi Europe*, 57.

19. Ibid., 59.

20. Bauman, *Modernity*, 74.

21. Kateb, *Hannah Arendt*, 72.

22. Bauman, *Modernity*, 101–103.

23. Horwitz, *In the Shadow of Death*, 124–143.

24. See especially his explanation of his methodology, *Hitler's Willing Executioners*, 463–468.

25. Marrus, *The Holocaust in History*, 170.

26. Again, see the discussion of this in Lipstadt, *Beyond Belief* and Wyman, *The Abandonment of the Jews*.

27. Christine E. Gudorf, *Victimization: Examining Christian Complicity* (Philadelphia: Trinity Press International, 1992), 2.

28. Borowski, *This Way for the Gas, Ladies and Gentlemen*.

29. Ibid, 83–84.

30. Rosenfeld, *A Double Dying*, 72.

31. Brown, *Elie Wiesel: Messenger to all Humanity*.

32. Kulka, " 'Public Opinion' in Nazi Germany; The Final Solution," in Marrus, *The Nazi Holocaust*, Vol. 5:1, *Public Opinion and Relations to the Jews in Nazi Europe*, 148.

33. Rosenfeld, *A Double Dying*, 115.

34. Ibid., 116.

35. In Rosenfeld, *A Double Dying*, 112.

36. From minutes of *Berlin-Weissensee Synod* (Berlin: EKD Kirchenkanzlei, 1950), 339, cited in Barnett, *For the Soul of the People*, 235.

37. Rosenfeld, *A Double Dying*, 114.

38. Cohen, *The Tremendum*, 80.

39. Ibid., 97.

40. Rosenfeld, *A Double Dying*, 114.

41. Elie Wiesel, *The Town behind the Wall*, 160–161.

42. In David Moss, "The Shibboleth of Modernity: Reflections on Theological Thinking after the *Shoah*," in *Literature and Theology*, 6: 61, March 1992.

43. In Borowski, *This Way for the Gas*, 54–55.

44. Langer, *Admitting the Holocaust*, 6.

45. Bryk, "The Hidden Complex of the Polish Mind: Polish-Jewish Relations during the Holocaust" in Polonsky, *My Brother's Keeper?*, 165.

46. Ibid., 166.

47. Horwitz, *Mauthausen*, 123.

48. In Baillie, *Violence Unveiled*, 265.

49. Ibid.

50. In Rosenfeld, *A Double Dying*, 26.

CHAPTER 8

A Broken World: Religious Interpretations of the Holocaust

If the Holocaust is nothing more than a historical event, says Arthur Cohen, "its life is as long as the life of memory." But if it is something more than history—if it is "metaphysical evidence that discloses something new about our relation to God and God's relations to creation," then "it acquires an ineffaceable eternity."[1]

The deeper implications of the Holocaust haunt every scholar who studies it. This is especially true for those of us who try to understand "what happened" from a religious perspective. Is the Holocaust indeed "metaphysical evidence"? Or should it be understood more as an ethical catastrophe—the outcome of human, not divine, failure? However we answer these questions, both interpretations affect our understanding of bystanders.

To study the Holocaust as ethical catastrophe means to determine "what happened" primarily on the basis of the historical, sociological, and psychological evidence. It assumes that human behavior during that era—ranging from the failures of people to stop the genocide to actual participation in the murders—was behavior that, while extreme, still falls within the general spectrum of explicable human experience and behavior.

To see the Holocaust as a theological *tremendum* or a *caesura* (in Cohen's words) is to view "what happened" as something radically new in human history—as a historical and metaphysical break with all that has preceded it, a rupture between the earthly and the metaphysical realms. This interpretation takes us into the realms of philosophy and religious belief, beyond what we can ever know for certain. When we wrestle with the Holocaust as *tremendum*, we must go beyond our study of the historical facts to reflect more deeply on "what happened." To see the Holocaust as an ethical failure raises questions about morality, socialization, and psychology; to reflect on it as *tremendum* poses us with fundamental questions about God and human nature itself.

In an essay about religious language after the Holocaust, Isabel Wollaston offers some insights that may help us distinguish between these two religious interpretations of the Holocaust.[2] Wollaston divides post-Holocaust religious language into three categories, giving examples of each category from the work of different Christian and Jewish religious scholars.

The first category assumes the *continuity* of religious tradition, and draws on traditional doctrine and language to understand the ethical dilemmas posed by the Holocaust. This is the category into which most of the scholarship on "Holocaust as ethical failure" falls. It views the Christian and Jewish traditions as essentially intact, despite the Holocaust. Christian complicity, for example, is seen more as an ethical failure than as a sign of inherent problems in Christian doctrine. The Jewish experience is interpreted as a historical catastrophe, but not one that tears at the covenantal fabric that binds God and the people of Israel.

The second category includes scholarship that deliberately proclaims the *discontinuity* of religious tradition. It interprets the Holocaust as a *caesura* that makes it impossible to speak about God, religion, and humanity as before. This sense of discontinuity exemplifies the "Holocaust as *tremendum*" category. It compels us to wrestle with the reality of evil in a new way. Theologically, it has moved some Christian thinkers to focus on particularly problematic Christian dogmas and texts: the notions of atonement and supersessionism, for example, or biblical passages traditionally interpreted as anti-Judaic. Also included in this category are scholars who view the Holocaust as such an extreme ethical failure that the usual categories don't apply (Wollaston cites the early work of Richard Rubenstein as an example of this).

The third category is characterized by an acceptance of continuity and discontinuity in post-Holocaust religious belief, seeing them in tension with one another. Here, for example, Wollaston cites the work of Berkowitz and Fackenheim. While Fackenheim acknowledges the profound destruction wrought by the Holocaust, he also links it to the survival (and even deepening) of central aspects of Jewish faith. He writes, for example, that "a new dimension to piety" marked by "a fidelity and a will-to-live" can be seen in the fact that the Jewish people "has experienced exile in a form more horrendous than ever dreamt of by the apocalyptic imagination."[3]

Most religious thinkers who have chosen to remain within their tradition fall into this third category. They affirm the viability and integrity of their faith as Christians or Jews, even in the wake of the Holocaust. Such affirmations of faith, however, cannot afford to evade or deny the challenges the Holocaust poses for religious believers. As Catholic scholar John Pawlikowski writes, "Christianity cannot equivocate regarding its responsibility for the spread of Nazism if it is to enter authentically the continuing debate about the broader theological implications of the *Shoah*."[4]

Wollaston's subject is religious language, but her categories are helpful for examining the different religious interpretations of the Holocaust. The language of Cohen, Rubenstein, Fackenheim, and others reflects some fundamental differences in how they interpret what happened theologically. Her insights also illustrate how totally different the Holocaust's religious legacy is for Jews and Christians—particularly with regard to the significance of the bystander for each tradition.

For many Jewish thinkers, the silence of the bystander has theological implications. The betrayal of the victims by their neighbors, colleagues, friends, and even strangers epitomizes God's apparent abandonment of the victims. In the silence of humanity, writers from Wiesel to Cohen hear the silence of God. The theological reflections of Jewish thinkers are marked by the themes of silence, the post-*Shoah* nature of God (or God's absence), and the question of whether religious faith is even possible in a world of burning children. As Martin Buber wrote:

How is a life with God still possible in a time in which there is an Auschwitz? . . . One can still "believe" in a God who allowed these things to happen, but how can one still speak to Him? . . . Dare we recommend to the survivors of Auschwitz, the Job of the gas chambers: "Call on him, for He is kind, for His mercy endureth forever?"[5]

Similar questions confront Christians. Yet for Christians, the silence of the bystanders is an accusation, not just against God or humanity, but against themselves, their church, and its tradition. Emil Fackenheim writes:

Where would Jesus of Nazareth have been in Nazi-occupied Europe? If he was who he is said to have been, he would have gone to Auschwitz or Treblinka voluntarily . . . A Jesus that goes voluntarily reveals the scarcity of his disciples in the great time of testing—that saints, those Christian included, were few.[6]

While some Christians were indeed persecuted by the Nazis, many more stood passively on the sidelines as the Jews were tormented and murdered. For the most part, the churches were silent. In Germany, the courage of the few clergy who protested openly on behalf of the victims—such as Catholic priest Bernhard Lichtenberg and Protestant pastor Paul Schneider—is in painful contrast to the failure of their church superiors to support them publicly (Lichtenberg died as a result of his imprisonment in Dachau;

Schneider was murdered in Buchenwald). Moreover, its long history of preaching against Judaism implicates the Christian religious tradition itself in the persecution of the Jews. For a religion that emphasizes love of neighbor and puts obedience to God above allegiance to the Caesars of this world, the behavior of the churches during the Holocaust is a scandal that challenges both Christian credibility and its very belief.

Thus, Christians and Jews confront very different issues when they reflect on the role of bystanders. The parallel worlds created by the bystanders' indifference continue to exist; the post-Holocaust landscapes of Christians and Jews are not the same. These parallel worlds—the divisions between perpetrators, bystanders, and victims—represent a broken world in theological terms as well.

One aspect that both traditions share, however, is the tension between continuity and discontinuity that characterizes Wollaston's third category. Members of both faiths must search for ways not just to understand what happened, but how to worship God in its wake. What religious concepts are still viable? Which parts of our traditions have become ineradicably tainted or altered? Whatever their religion, most scholars recognize that the Holocaust poses troubling questions for how we think about God and humanity: about who we really are, and who God really is, and how we should live our lives as religious people after the Holocaust.

WHAT HAPPENED: THE HOLOCAUST AS ETHICAL CATASTROPHE

One need not be a religious scholar to see the Holocaust as an ethical catastrophe. The period between 1933 and 1945 was characterized by a widespread lack of compassion, courage, and concern for the victims and for the greater good of humanity. Still, religious scholars have drawn different conclusions about the *nature* of the Holocaust's ethical lessons.

Particularly in the period immediately following the Holocaust, Christian thinkers tended to view the ethical questions raised by the Holocaust within the framework of traditional ethics. Throughout the Christian world, the reply to "What happened?" was that Christians had not been good enough Christians. They had failed to live up to Christian precepts of love and mercy, and had failed to recognize that God's law had precedence over state law. In the words of the German Protestant Church's 1945 Stuttgart Declaration, Christians should have "confessed more courageously, prayed more conscientiously, believed more joyously, and loved more ardently."[7]

In the decades that followed, this perspective began to change. As the historical details of the churches' role during the Holocaust emerged, it became clear that the churches' sin often had not been one of omission, but of actual complicity. Christian leaders, even some of those who came into conflict with the Nazi regime, had made anti-Semitic statements. The Christian community not only failed to stop the Holocaust; to a horrifying degree, it had passively watched and even participated. The German churches had emphasized obedience to the Nazi state, not resistance on behalf of its victims. Internationally, while there were a few courageous Christian leaders who spoke out against the persecution of the Jews, many more remained silent. This silence was amplified by the passivity of most members of their churches.

Most importantly, the long history of Christian preaching, doctrine, and actual violence against the Jews showed that the problem went beyond a lack of courage or faithfulness. "If Christianity hadn't taught anti-Semitism and hatred of the Jews, the Holocaust wouldn't have happened," charged Elie Wiesel.[8] The inherent problems of traditional Christian teachings about Judaism became evident in the aftermath of the Holocaust itself, when some Christian theologians continued to interpret the fate of the European Jews as a sign of divine intent. One example is the German theologian Franz Mussner, who wrote that "the terrible events of the *Shoah*" had occurred "by God's will":

If the Jews were not God's chosen people, then they would not be those unique people who are out of place among the Goyim, and for which the Gentiles cannot forgive them. Herein, up to the present day, lies the true roots of antisemitism . . . the Cross rises in the dark mystery of the deity; its mystery is inexplicable, seen in a theology after Auschwitz.[9]

As Mussner's words make clear, an understanding of Christianity's ethical failure between 1933 and 1945 is not enough. The theological foundations of that failure must be challenged. An early work that wrestled with the implications of this was Rosemary Ruether's 1967 book *Faith and Fratricide*, in which she explored Christian doctrine, Christology, and traditional interpretations of the early Christian break with the Judaic tradition. Her controversial conclusion was that the Christian tradition itself had laid the foundation for the Holocaust: that the church's guilt was not that it failed to be Christian enough, but that it had been too Christian.

Debate on this point has continued ever since. In recent years, this has led to new theological thinking about Christianity's roots in the Judaic tradition.[10] That is not the topic of this book, but it indicates one direction taken by the Christian discussion about "what happened" during the Holocaust in religious terms.

Jewish thinkers who reflect on the nature of the Holocaust as ethical catastrophe confront other questions. Many of them have entered into an argument with God. In a world after Auschwitz, the understanding of divine purpose and existence are radically different from those in the world before Auschwitz, when many religious people could assume that God's purpose was being fulfilled. The world of the victims was destroyed; for the survivors, their children and grandchildren, the world can never be the same. The ethical lessons drawn from this concern not just the nature of the spectator, but the nature of God and the universe. Non-Jews, writes Arthur Cohen, can never completely grasp the full impact of the Holocaust, while

every Jew who has endured to this hour is a survivor in fact or an accidental survivor at least, whereas for the non-Jew the genocide of the Jews is an objective phenomenon which, on the face of it, by its definition appears to exclude him . . . the non-Jew is able to contemplate but not share in either the fate of the victims or the perpetual unease of the survivors.[11]

For non-Jews, says Cohen, the death camps will always be an "epiphenomenon," "a paradigm of human brutality." For Jews, "it is historically real."

The bystanders epitomize this difference. As Cohen's distinction between Jews and non-Jews indicates, their respective experiences during the Holocaust—as different as they were—were inherently connected: the Jews were victims because of the active involvement and passive complicity of non-Jews.

This means that our understanding of what happened ethically touches on a number of levels; perhaps this is why "what happened" under Nazism raises questions that don't seem to fit the usual ethical categories. Part of the Holocaust's horror is its message about what "ordinary" human beings are capable of doing and tolerating. The central ethical question is "why?" Did people become bystanders because of prejudice and hatred, or because they had become "amoral"? Did they actively promote this evil, or passively tolerate it?

Because it is impossible to answer these questions completely, much post-Holocaust ethical reflection has actually abandoned the realm of individual ethics and focused instead on the larger factors that characterized the Holocaust. This explains why much of the scholarship in this field up to now comes from sociologists and political scientists. It is tempting to conclude that individuals are impotent in the face of collective evil, "mass society," or a totalitarian state. The ethical implications of Milgram's experiments were that it is possible to structure an experiment (and, by extension, a society) in such a way that individual ethics become irrelevant. In situations where individuals feel they have little control, they also feel relieved of responsibility for their actions. When Milgram varied his experiments so that the experimenter's authority was weakened, his subjects assumed more responsibility and acted more independently. Milgram's results suggest that most people have a weak ethical or moral center that can be manipulated by outside factors, especially the presence of a strong authority.

A central ethical question, then, is whether the bystander behavior is essentially active or passive. Is complicity the product of free will, individual conviction, and prejudice? Or is the bystander a passive figure, and complicity the result of greater systemic forces that very few people can withstand? Psychological or sociological insights into human behavior can answer these questions only in part. In the wake of the Holocaust, these questions compel us to decide whether we still believe in a divinely created order, whether Good and Evil exist (and in what form), and whether an essential human morality exists that overrides all socialization and ideological precepts. What are the foundations of human morality? What are the foundations of resistance to evil?

These questions are especially difficult because Nazi ideology was so successful in relativizing moral values on a widespread scale. The Nazi understanding of morality was epitomized in the contention of Adolf Eichmann's defense attorney that, as Zygmunt Bauman writes,

Eichmann committed acts for which one is decorated if one wins, and goes to the gallows if one loses. . . . Actions have no intrinsic moral value. Neither are they immanently immoral. Moral evaluation is something external to the action itself, decided by criteria other than those that guide and shape the action itself.[12]

This plea for moral relativity is troubling not only because it was made at the Eichmann trial, but because it exemplifies the ethical distortions that characterized Nazism. To say that people like Eichmann were just following orders is too simple. The question is whether they believed that what they were doing was right, not just in terms of expedience, but as a "higher good." Or whether—as the defense attorney implied—they viewed their duties as "amoral," as morally irrelevant, and considered themselves exonerated because they had not given the orders?

In his book *Morality after Auschwitz*, philosopher Peter Haas explores these issues. He argues that Nazism represented a new ethical system, in which the "elimination" of Jews and other "undesirables" was viewed as a moral "good" that was necessary to create a better Germany. Accordingly, he says, Germans began to tolerate behavior that was otherwise viewed as immoral (such as attacks on individuals, homes, and businesses). Traditional moral considerations no longer applied to Jews and others deemed to be "inferior"; in turn, this new reality reshaped the moral convictions of most Germans.

What Haas is saying is that Nazi society basically functioned like any other society. People continued to have a sense of right and wrong, of decency and duty. What had changed was not the way they thought ethically, but the *content* of that new ethics. From their point of view, most citizens of Nazi Germany were not doing anything wrong; Eichmann, says Haas, was an example of this.[13]

In some ways (though not all), Haas's systematic interpretation of what happened to the Germans under Nazism parallels that of Goldhagen. Like Goldhagen, Haas attributes the redefined morality of Nazism to the legacy of 19th-century racial theories and centuries of anti-Semitism. The Jews had already been singled out as the enemy of the German people. Once the Germans decided to wage "racial war" on the Jews, they simply incorporated the "just war" theory as part of their new racial ethic.[14] As in "just war theory," the Nazis thought they were behaving ethically as long as they obeyed the rules—despite the fact that most of us would consider those rules to be criminal. Thus, writes Haas, the Nazis epitomized "not the banality of evil but the human ability to redefine evil . . . They were fully aware of what they were doing and displayed principled acquiescence. The difference is that for them such deeds were simply no longer understood to be evil."[15]

Haas extends his conclusions to include the outside world, among whom the "Nazi ethic was able to win broad public acceptance because it bore formal similarity to an already-understood ethic."[16] Because Nazi anti-Semitism and anticommunism were sentiments shared by most international leaders, he argues, the Allies opposed Germany only after it became a military threat. Thus, even outside Nazi Germany, the Holocaust emerged from coherent ethical presuppositions that resembled other ethical systems:

The Holocaust became ethically possible because the basic character of ethical argumentation remained unchanged. This is the reason that Germans, and others, could tolerate the utter destruction of Jews and Judaism in Germany over a period of at least twelve years while in other ways continuing to be thoughtful, intelligent, charming people. It is not that they had lost the ability to behave ethically; they simply evaluated certain activities in a different, yet still ethically coherent, way.[17]

Haas's analysis of "what happened" employs traditional ethical terms, and he contends that most Germans themselves understood it that way. The difference was that their values had been "redefined" by Nazi ideology.

There are some historical problems with Haas's analysis. As has been noted in previous chapters, the actual historical record shows more ambiguity in behavior and motives, inside and outside Germany, than Haas acknowledges. It is difficult to reconcile Haas's portrayal of German behavior with the details that come to light in the work of Kershaw and others. The historical development of the resistance in Germany and the phenomenon of rescue, there and elsewhere, raise additional questions. Haas acknowledges that it is possible, although exceptional, for individuals to withstand the pressures of a new value system. But he argues that people were capable of resistance or rescue only to the degree that they were outsiders in Nazi society, and thus removed from the social pressures described above. Yet a sizable number of the members of the German resistance that did eventually try to overthrow Hitler and undermine the regime's policies were very much insiders: civil servants, bureaucrats, diplomats, and intelligence officers. Many of them were moved by serious ethical opposition to Nazi ideology and policies.[18] Moreover, given the protests from abroad that did greet Nazi measures, the claim that the "Nazi ethic" had "broad public acceptance" throughout the world is problematic. The international response to the Holocaust was shaped more by cold-hearted pragmatism than by enthusiastic support for the genocide of Jews.

Still, Haas's book offers a useful framework for examining the intersection between individual ethics and greater influences, since he is exploring the central question outlined above: is the bystander essentially a passive or an active phenomenon? Haas is really tracing how a new ethic is constructed, how it functions ideologically, how it takes hold and begins to shape the behavior of individuals. In an intriguing exercise, he compares the behavior of an SS officer named Martin Luther with that of French Pastor Andre Trocmé, who led his village to rescue 2,500 Jews. In ethical terms, argues Haas, the behavior of both men was

internally coherent and correct, depending on the judge's perspective. . . . Each did what in his context was the appropriate thing to do. . . . Each career trajectory began in a simple way: the decision to step into an administrative impasse [for Luther], the decision not to raise the flag [for Trocmé]. From these very first steps, each trajectory is smooth and predictable. The first, almost inconsequential decisions made by these two individuals set them on tracks that moved in widely different directions. It is probably fair to say that neither man realized the momentousness of his first innocent decisions . . . Only in retrospect do we see clear heroes and villains; only in retrospect can we make evaluations as to good and evil.[19]

The ethical implications of this theory are profound. For example, Haas includes a horrific account of an incident where Jewish boys were beaten and chased before being murdered by SS guards in a camp. The incident, he says, epitomizes the extent to which the redefined Nazi ethic "was capable of socializing people into supporting it. It is tempting at this point to fantasize that German Nazis were simply not like all other people in the world. The truth is that they were like precisely like everyone else."[20] In their own eyes, argues Haas, they were behaving ethically because their actions conformed to the dominant norms and values in Nazi society—even when those actions included something as abhorrent as the murder of children.

Was this "orgy of killing" logically coherent in a society that had redefined its ethics (as Haas argues)? The issues are complex. It is difficult to interprets the torture and murder of children as "normal" behavior even within the context of a "redefined" ethic. Even some of the Nazi perpetrators had trouble doing so. In some cases, those carrying out atrocities showed symptoms of stress like illness, excessive drinking, and fighting; indeed a regular and abundant supply of alcohol was part of the rations among SS troops. In addition, there seem to have been various psychological mechanisms (such as Robert Jay Lifton's theory about "doubling") by which individuals learned to live with such behavior.

Developing the psychological mechanisms that enable someone to live with such behavior, however, is different from affirming it as a "good" value within a new moral system. Other questions arise about bystanders and "ordinary people" who were not involved in atrocities. Some caution is needed when we attempt to generalize from the motives and behavior of the perpetrators to the bystanders. While there are certainly similarities, there may also be differences that are relevant for our ethical conclusions. Did the Nazis successfully really redefine evil for this group? Or did they only succeed in creating a society in which all values were relativized, in which people could be part of it and survive, really, only by becoming amoral? It may be that the behavior of most bystanders simply illustrates the inevitable dehumanization and brutalization of those who are part of a profoundly *amoral* society—one in which more and more matters, even the treatment of children, are removed from the jurisdiction of any kind of ethical judgment.

This would suggest that the persecution of Jews was not so much a "good" to be pursued, but that the bystanders simply put it outside the realm of ethics altogether. There can be little doubt that other factors, particularly prejudice, helped this process along—that the Jews were excluded from the moral universe, as Helen Fein says. But the central ethical event may be that the bystanders came to understand their own situation as an amoral one. The compartmentalization of public and private, the creation of parallel worlds, the silence and euphemisms were all symptoms of a system in which human ethics had become irrelevant: "amoral." If conformity to the Nazi ethic was not based upon conviction but other reasons, then on some level, the bystanders could or should have known that what was going on was wrong. Haas writes,

In any case, Nazi Germany illustrates that people's moral inhibitions are easier to overcome than we might hope. . . . Moral inhibitions against atrocious violence will be overridden when that violence is given official authorization by those in power, when it is given ethical sanction. People committing the violence may at the beginning feel some moral resistance, but this will almost always be compartmentalized, trivialized, and then ignored.[22]

Whether we agree with his entire theory or not, Haas gives us two clear options for interpreting bystander behavior ethically. We can view the ethical behavior of Germans as intentional and "ethical" (from their perspective) within the context of a system that had decided to kill Jews. The other option is to view it as the incremental construction of "amoral" behavior that had a pervasive effect on the behavior of individuals and institutions. Both interpretations have the same components: prejudice, some degree of voluntary complicity, the influence of authority and totalitarianism, and various mechanisms for psychologically adjusting to the situation. The question is how we fit these components together.

Up to now we have focused on what people thought they were doing ethically. At the most fundamental level, the *relationship* between the bystanders and victims was betrayed: neighbors, colleagues, and friends were suddenly divided into victims, bystanders, and perpetrators. A consistent characteristic of those who resisted Nazism or rescued its victims was their acknowledgment of relationship, both to what was happening around them and to the victims. The denial of relationship (culminating in the creation of parallel worlds) characterized the bystanders in Sonderburg, Mauthausen, and elsewhere.

This betrayal of relationship is at the heart of understanding the Holocaust as ethical catastrophe. The bystander symbolizes that betrayal. As Robert McAfee Brown writes, "It is lack of relationship, indifference, that characterizes the spectator, and it is the most dehumanizing of all human acts, for it destroys both the observer and the observed."[23] The victims perish; the bystanders, too, are changed and diminished. The only "moral survivors" of the Holocaust, writes theologian Robert Willis, were those who were able to "rise above indifference."[24]

Many who write about the Holocaust can only rise above indifference by expressing outrage and anguish—not just at the silence of bystanders, but of God. The connection between the silence of humanity and the silence of God is a motif in the writings of many survivors. In his poem "Psalm," Paul Celan "addresses and affirms God as 'No one,' yet a 'No one' whose presiding Absence seems to embody the fullness and majesty of omnipotent Presence."[25] Because there was "no one" to cry out for the victims, God and humanity alike are negated. Relationships, society, and creation itself are "radically and systematically undone."[26]

Thus, our reflections on the nature of the Holocaust as ethical catastrophe inevitably take us into the territory of those scholars who view the Holocaust as *tremendum*. The studies of Mauthausen and Sonderburg showed that, despite the bystanders' denial of their relationship to the genocide and its victims, they were indeed connected to it. They were also changed by it, for the nature of the sin alters the soul of the sinner.

The nature of that sin is what those who view the Holocaust as *tremendum* are exploring. The dilemma they confront was expressed by Tadeusz

Borowski in his story "The People Who Walked On." "Will evil be punished?" one of the women in the concentration camp asks the narrator. "I mean in a normal, human sense!" The narrator's reply is haunting: "Can a crime committed on one level be punishable on a different one?"[27]

THE HOLOCAUST AS RELIGIOUS *TREMENDUM*

As Borowski suggests, the Holocaust takes us beyond the "normal, human" sense of things. It raises haunting ethical and theological questions about how we understand our world and ourselves, and how we think about God.

The traditionally progressive view of the world and human history was based upon the assumption, as Arthur Cohen notes, that reason ruled history and that there was a steady progression toward human enlightenment. This led to a more universal sense of responsibility, within the limited context of what one had (or had not) to do. There is a moral and philosophical coherency in Donne's statement "no man is an island" that no longer exists in our time, even when we affirm his words as an expression of the solidarity of human existence. The difference between Donne's time and ours is that "the God of classical theism . . . has disappeared finally into the folds of mystery, where reason cannot make meaningful the relativity implicit in God's involvement with creation and faith cannot make cogent the remoteness and impassivity that God's absoluteness requires."[28]

The *Shoah* has sealed the door to the kind of faith that existed for centuries. This is Arthur Cohen's assertion in describing the Holocaust as *tremendum*.

Theologically and historically, of course, this development is not solely a result of the Holocaust. Scholars like Zygmunt Bauman argue that the *Shoah* is more a symbol of this change than its cause—that it is not so much *tremendum* as the climax of modernity. The Enlightenment and the spread of democratic ideas introduced dynamics that gradually eroded a fixed sense of place in society, even if these changes didn't really take hold until the 20th century. Long before Auschwitz, people had begun to think differently about God and the relevance of religious faith. It was Nietzsche, not Hitler, who proclaimed that God is dead, and Marx who viewed mainstream religion as the opiate of the masses. They helped initiate the age of ideology, an age in which people of faith were confronted with new challenges and new options.

Soviet Communism and Nazism were systems that embraced ideology as the new religion. Most church leaders responded by trying to retreat behind the certainties of traditional faith and doctrine. The third option—which confronts people who try to think religiously after the Holocaust—is to try to understand the nature and possibilities of belief in this new situation. The most striking example of this, during the Nazi era and afterward, was the German theologian Dietrich Bonhoeffer, who was hanged in April 1945 for his resistance to Nazism. In his famous concept of a "religionless Christianity" in a "world come of age," Bonhoeffer was addressing the ideological realities of his time—not just the reality of Nazism, but the legacy of Nietzsche, Marx, Heidegger, and Hegel.

The Holocaust is not the sole cause of this religious dilemma, but it makes it impossible for us to avoid it. In the wake of the Holocaust, there is no way around the fact that concepts of "both God and man are in need of rethinking and redescription."[29]

The question for people of religious faith is "how can God be affirmed meaningfully in a world where evil enjoys such dominion?"[30] The challenge that faces us is not how to explain this evil, but "to estimate what consequence it has for our thinking about the nature, existence, and action of God."[31]

Concepts of Evil

After Auschwitz, theology must be done in a universe "whose human history is scarred by genuine evil."[32] The question of evil is central in religious reflection about the Holocaust, and our concept of evil is very much linked to what we think happened. Was the evil of the genocide an ontological event? Or was it the absence of good—the result of good people doing nothing?

Here, too, the scholars offer different answers. Haas contends that the Holocaust is not "an example of utter evil" but an "ethic."[33] In a similar fashion, Fred Katz argues for a view of evil as something "that can be known and, therefore, eventually curbed, rather than dealing with mysterious, basically unknowable forces that are essentially beyond us or consist of a convergence of historical circumstances entirely unique to each event."[34] The root of evil, says Katz, is not ontological, but occurs in the dehumanization and objectification of others: "Depriving a person of dignity is a critical starting point in the genesis of evil."[35]

One reason that evil is so often viewed as mysterious or beyond all human control is its complexity. Where does it begin? How (or can) we withstand and prevent it? Drawing on the recent work of Christian theologians like Walter Wink and Marjorie Suchocki, theologian Miroslav Volf argues for a multifaceted understanding of evil. Only this, he believes, truly describes what happens in genocidal situations. Volf speaks of the "background cacophony of evil," a "complex transpersonal and systemic reality of evil which dominates, ensnares, and lures persons to dominate others."[36]

This is closer to Cohen's understanding of evil, which is that evil is not divinely planned and orchestrated, but expresses the reality of the monstrous power of this world.[37] Still, he argues: "Evil exists. It is no longer understood as the absence of good, privation, a lapsarian abnegation, a void of conscience, a characterological defect."[38] It is important to recognize evil "as substantive, as ontologically affirmative, as real presence."[39] Evil, writes Cohen, "is a real force. . . . Evil has ontic reality no less than the good."[40] It is not simply misbehavior or the expression of a psychologically explicable flaw (this echoes Améry's criticism of Arendt's "banality of evil," mentioned in an earlier chapter).

Concepts of God

The related question is, Who is God after the Holocaust? The question is linked to reflection about who (and where) God was during the Holocaust. The argument with God is an ongoing theme of Wiesel's writings, where he confronts, charges, and pleads with God:

Why and how survive in a universe which negates you? Or: How can you reconcile yourself with history and the graves it digs and transcends. . . . And then, the big question, the most serious of all: How does one answer the person who demands an interpretation of God's silence at the very moment when man—any man, Jew or non-Jew—has greater need than ever of His word, let alone His mercy?[41]

Wiesel's argument is part of the Judaic tradition of wrestling and arguing with God—in Fackenheim's words, the tradition of "protest which *stays within* the sphere of faith."[42] This tradition, notes Darrell J. Fasching, is what makes post-*Shoah* Judaism possible; the argument itself is an affirmation. Fasching argues that Christians and Jews alike must engage in this argument if they want to do theology after the Holocaust. The only legitimate post-*Shoah* faith is "a questioning faith, a faith prepared to call even God into question. . . . The test of authentic faith is the possibility of dissent against all authority in the name of human dignity."[43]

In confronting God, we confront and question our understanding of God. This, too, is an essential theological act if we are to acknowledge our relationship to the victims. Does God's silence signify indifference? It does if we put God on the side of the bystanders and perpetrators. As Robert McAfee Brown notes, "Traditional orthodoxies are perilously close to affirming God as executioner."[44] Omniscient, omnipotent, and triumphalist images of God become problematic. In his study of Wiesel's work, Brown explores the post-Holocaust options of God as victim, executioner, spectator, and participant.[45] The only theologically viable role, he concludes, is of God as participant—as a God who engages "in the ongoing struggles against the forces of evil."[46] In removing God from the side of the perpetrators, this theological conclusion reminds us that we cannot remain bystanders. What has happened to the victims—and our response to that—has direct relevance for who we are.

From this perspective, our salvation, theologically and personally, is exemplified not just by a God who is involved, but by our own involvement. As Dorothee Sölle writes:

God has become vulnerable and only thus is still God. . . . God has left asceticism behind, and lives as a relationship, a proximity, a dependency on us. "In the beginning was the relationship," says Martin Buber. A theology that takes the pain of God seriously should give something to God, to this suffering, growing, caring God, who should not have to regret having created the world.[47]

It was the option formulated by Bonhoeffer in his theology for "a world come of age." It is intriguing that it echoes some of Arthur Cohen's conclusions as well:

This is the optimism and hope of being created in the image of God: . . . that God describes the limits but man sets them, that God engenders possibility but that man enacts them, that God's freedom to be eternally open to his own nature is our freedom to speak and enact in time.[48]

SUMMARY

Where do we go from here? All the interpretations we have reviewed— historical, psychological, political, and theological—portray a world that is profoundly altered. Even those scholars who disagree with the more ontological and religious interpretations of the Holocaust wrestle with issues that do not arise in other historical events. In many ways, the post-Holocaust world is a broken world. It has been tainted by the failure of faith, the corruption of language and culture. The most damaging corruption, however, is of ourselves. We now know that ordinary human beings are capable of doing and tolerating terrible things. We cannot rule out the possibility that other societies in the future will build concentration camps, gas chambers, and crematoria. Nor do we have any guarantees that the world will react any differently than it did in the past.

Thus, the Holocaust has changed the way we think about human nature, existence, God, and the world in a way that other cataclysmic events in history have not done. "In a terrible but undeniable way," writes Alvin Rosenfeld, "the Holocaust marks out our time, so much so as to alter radically our conception of the human."[49]

It is difficult to arrive at any optimistic conclusions about bystanders. History, sociology, and psychology all suggest that human behavior is unpredictable, at best, and that what we call "civilization" is only a fragile veneer. Again and again, we find scholars of the Holocaust coming up against the issue that Rosenfeld addresses. Christopher Browning, concluding his study of "ordinary men" who became members of a killing squad, asks, "If the men of Reserve Police Battalion 101 could become killers under such circumstances, what group of men cannot?"[50] Writing about the [...]g the perpetrators, historian Charles Mai[...] at the moral self is a fragmented self, and [...] the sanctity of life, at least for those outs[...] y and friends, does not exist."[51]

Th[...] is development is that our notions of mor[...] egenerated as well: "What civilization once [...] cruelty or sadism has in our day become a useless rhetoric . . . Words no longer command us, precisely because they no longer reflect concepts and convictions which directly govern and thereby agitate conscience."[52] Decades after Allied soldiers liberated the camps, we remain horrified by the sights that greeted them. Yet there is little doubt that we are less horrified than they were. We have become too familiar with the details of the Holocaust to be genuinely shocked. While pictures of the horrors in Bosnia, Rwanda, and elsewhere are terrible to look at, we do look at them, and we live with the knowledge of them. The significance of evil—as Jean Améry put it—is that it does not simply shape behavior; it transforms and changes people. This is why the Holocaust is a theological event.

Thus, the confrontation with evil demands of us not just an ethical response, but a theological one, based upon our understanding of who we are as members of a world in which God, Auschwitz, the victims, bystanders, and perpetrators all exist. In the words of Robert Willis, we must recover "a usable image of the human condition."[53] Willis believes this can be found in images of "moral survivors"—those "who managed, against all odds, to remain human until the end, whether that proved to be death within or life beyond the camps."[54]

Among the bystanders, what is required is the emergence of what the Catholic philosopher René Girard calls "disruptive empathy"—a wonderful phrase because it describes very accurately *what can happen* to change the bystander. Imagine, for only a moment, that the people in the white houses of Mauthausen had been so outraged by the death marches that they had run into the streets, beaten back the SS guards, and taken the victims into their homes. Moved by "disruptive empathy," the bystander is not only changed within, but compelled to break with the world as it is—and thus to change the very movement of history. Disruptive empathy shatters the illusion that the world is whole, that life is normal. It is the opposite of what Staub calls "empathic joining," in which peoples' perceptions of reality become defined by the attitudes and goals of the group.[55]

"Disruptive empathy" does not heal the broken world; on the contrary, it recognizes how broken the world is and refuses to acknowledge it as whole. It refuses to deny, to lie, to pretend that all is "normal." Thus, it brings the bystander back into history—not as a passive observer, but as protagonist.

NOTES

1. Cohen, *The Tremendum*, 52.

2. Isabel Wollaston, "What Can—and Cannot—Be Said: Religious Language after the Holocaust." *Literature and Theology* 6: 47–56, March 1992.

3. Emil Fackenheim, "The Holocaust: A Summing Up after Two Decades of Reflection," in Jacobs, *Contemporary Jewish Religious Responses to the Shoah*, 74.

4. John Pawlikowski, "The Shoah: Continuing Theological Challenge for Christianity," in Jacobs, *Contemporary Christian Religious Responses to the Shoah*, 140.

5. Martin Buber, "The Dialogue between Heaven and Earth," cited in Fackenheim, *To Mend the World*, 196.

6. Fackenheim, *To Mend the World*, 280–281.

7. *Stuttgart Declaration of Guilt*, reprinted in Barnett, *For the Soul of the People*, 209.

8. Wiesel, "Freedom of Conscience: A Jewish Commentary," 638–649.

9. In Haynes, *Reluctant Witnesses*, 176. See also Haynes' discussion of this on pp. 88–89, 175–178.

10. The list of scholarly and popular works dealing with this issue is increasing rapidly. Two of the first scholars to wrestle with the significance of Judaism for Christian theology were Friedrich-Wilhelm Marquardt in Germany and Paul van Buren in the United States.

11. Cohen, *The Tremendum*, 22–23.

12. Bauman, *Modernity*, 18.

13. Haas, *Morality*, 108–109.

14. Ibid., 58.

15. Ibid., 2.

16. Ibid., 191.

17. Ibid., 7.

18. There are a number of books (and perspectives) on this. Regarding the ethical perspectives of some of those in the resistance, see Helmut Gollwitzer, ed., *Dying We Live* (New York: Pantheon, 1956).

19. Ibid., 190.

20. Haas, *Morality*, 154–155.

21. See, for example, Browning's discussion of Wilhelm Trapp in *Ordinary Men*, as well as pp. 114–120. See also Ernst Klee, *"Euthanasie" im NS-Staat* (Frankfurt: Fischer Verlag, 1985), 336–340.

22. Haas, *Morality*, 90.

23. Brown, *Elie Wiesel: Messenger to All Humanity*, 73.

24. Robert E. Willis, "The Burden of Auschwitz: Rethinking Morality," 282.

25. In Rosenfeld, *A Double Dying*, 107.

26. Ibid., 87–88.

27. Borowski, "The People Who Walked On," in *This Way for the Gas*, 90.

28. Cohen, *The Tremendum*, 83.

29. Ibid., 34.

30. Ibid., 34.

31. Ibid.

32. Ibid., 86.

33. Haas, *Morality*, 9.

34. Katz, *Ordinary people*, 137.

35. Ibid., 146.

36. Volf, *Exclusion*, 87.

37. Cohen, *The Tremendum*, 30.

38. Ibid.

39. Ibid.

40. Ibid., 33.

41. Elie Wiesel, *One Generation After* (New York: Random House, 1970), 166.

42. In Fasching, *Narrative Theology*, 55. See also Brown, *Elie Wiesel*, 184–149.

43. Fasching, *Narrative Theology*, 72.

44. Brown, *Elie Wiesel*, 157.

45. Ibid., 156–157.

46. Ibid., 158.

47. Dorothee Sölle, "God's Pain and Our Pain: How Theology Has to Change after Auschwitz," in Otto Maduro, ed., *Judaism, Christianity, and Liberation: An Agenda for Dialogue* (Maryknoll, N.Y.: Orbis Books, 1991), 120. This insight is the impetus for some of the Christian theology of liberation, which emerged not just in the wake of the Holocaust but as an attempt to respond theologically to injustice and oppression throughout the world. Some Jewish scholars such as Susannah Heschel and Leon Klenicki have critiqued Christian liberation theology for its anti-Judaism—for example, in some of the supercessionist thought that persists or its interpretation of Jesus' ministry as a battle against Jewish patriarchy. Some of the critique, in my opinion, is legitimate; some liberation theologians were more successful than others in rethinking those aspects of doctrine that are anti-Judaic. Nonetheless, the critique of the traditional ties between the Church and political authority, and the new interpretations of scripture that allow us to understand God in a new way, are important insights that are necessary for any post-Holocaust Christian theology.

48. Cohen, *The Tremendum*, 93.

49. Rosenfeld, *A Double Dying*, 5.

50. Browning, *Ordinary Men*, 189.

51. Maier, *The Unmasterable Past*, 97.

52. Cohen, *The Tremendum*, 10.

53. Willis, "The Burden of Auschwitz," 278.

54. Ibid.

55. Staub, *The Roots of Evil*, 238.

CHAPTER 9

Acts of Disruptive Empathy: One Village

One would hardly have expected our third village, Le Chambon, to be involved in any way with the historical cataclysm that swept through Europe. Located on a plain in the mountains of southwestern France, it was far removed from Berlin and Munich. Yet this village of 3,000 people saved the lives of 2,500 Jews, most of them children. Philip Hallie tells the town's story in *Lest Innocent Blood Be Shed: The Story of the Village of Le Chambon and How Goodness Happened There.*

The villagers of Le Chambon were hardly "bystanders," since the entire population, led by Pastor André Trocmé, became actively involved in rescuing Jews. Yet precisely because of this, it is worth exploring the similarities and differences between Le Chambon and the two villages discussed earlier, Sonderburg and Mauthausen. The villagers of Mauthausen, confronted directly with evil, accommodated themselves to it in silence. In Sonderburg, the non-Jewish villagers drifted passively through the Third Reich while the lives of their neighbors were destroyed. Le Chambon could have become like these towns and most villages in Vichy France. What made it different?

The most obvious difference seems to have been the decisive role of its religious leader, Pastor André Trocmé. Cosmopolitan and educated abroad, Trocmé arrived there in 1934 to serve as pastor of the local Protestant church. He had studied in Paris and joined the Fellowship of Reconciliation after World War I. He received a scholarship to study theology at Union Seminary in New York, an institution on the forefront of the activist social gospel movement at the time. Yet Trocmé found the social gospel too secular; it lacked "the person-to-God piety . . . For Trocmé, only this intimate relationship between a faithful person and God, only a person's conscious obedience to the demands of God, could arouse and direct the powers that could make the world better than it is."[1]

Perhaps this is the key to understanding the culture of rescue that Trocmé helped create in Le Chambon. A devout Christian and charismatic preacher, he had already sparked a revival in his first parish in a poor, working-class town. It was the kind of revival that "raises people above their ordinary levels of energy, so that, celebrating, they rush out to meet and to change the world around them . . . They had what Trocmé called a *morale de combat* (an ethic of combat), an active way of living in the world."[2] It was remarkably similar to what happened later in Le Chambon, which became a community of committed Christians whose horizons of faith extended beyond the narrow portals of their church.

Trocmé began by establishing an alternative school, designed to help prepare students for their university exams, in the fall of 1938. It started with four teachers and eighteen students, but grew rapidly because of the influx of refugees from the east. The number of refugees increased steadily throughout the early war years.

The growth of the school coincided with Trocmé's determination to help the persecuted Jews. His membership in the Fellowship of Reconciliation and his studies in the United States had given Trocmé contacts with foreign church leaders in France. In the winter of 1941, Trocmé visited Burns Chalmers of the American Friends Service Committee in Marseilles.

The two men began to meet once a month in the town of Nimes. Outraged that French Jews and refugees from the east were being incarcerated in concentration camps in southern France, Trocmé considered joining them in the camps voluntarily, as an act of witness. But after Chalmers explained that the Quakers were trying to find safe refuges for the children of those inside the camps (which French authorities at that point permitted), the two men decided that Le Chambon would be that place. With some financial help from the Quakers, Trocmé's school began to serve a new function.

Such a task was too big for one person alone; the entire village had to be involved. Its readiness to do so can be traced in part to its history; most of the villagers were direct descendants of the French Huguenots, who had been persecuted themselves in the 16th century. It was a region, as Philip Hallie wrote, shaped by a tradition of "solidarity and resistance" against persecution.[3]

Trocmé's active resistance began in 1940. Vichy officials had ordered schools to begin their days with a fascist salute to the French flag. Together with Roger Darcissac, the principal of the local public school, Trocmé developed a plan by which his own students could avoid the salute. Darcissac and Trocmé placed the flagpole between the two schools and made the salute optional. Within weeks, everyone had stopped saluting the flag.

It was a simple act—but, as Hallie puts it, once the villagers saw the bird of resistance, they knew this bird existed. Trocmé had created a dynamic of resistance; his "originality *generated originality* in others."[4]

Beginning with this first step, the movement toward resistance in Le Chambon was incremental—as was the movement toward apathy in Mauthausen and Sonderburg. Trocmé may have revived the legacy of resistance among his parishioners, but the village was hardly a hotbed of radicalism when he arrived in 1934. At that time, he wrote in his diary, the village was "moving toward 'death, death, death,'" and the pastor was entrusted with helping the village die."[5] The first refugee, a barefoot woman who arrived in midwinter 1940, was greeted with suspicion. Only Trocmé's wife, Magda, was willing to take her in, and the town council even ordered the Trocmés to send the woman away, fearing repercussions from Vichy authorities. Magda Trocmé refused.[6]

Thus, despite the obvious differences in the histories of Le Chambon, Sonderburg, and Mauthausen, the three towns were not that different at the onset of the Nazi reign of terror. What subsequently happened in Le Chambon could not have been predicted. The people of Le Chambon did not begin with a mature readiness to accept refugees. Trocmé "had started something, as a battery may start a motor, but he had not known when he started it what would be the result of his impulse to resist evil, nor had he known exactly how to bring about that result."[7]

In all three villages, the first steps seemed insignificant at the time. In Sonderburg, they hung out the swastika flag; in Le Chambon, they refused to give the fascist salute. In Mauthausen and Sonderburg, those early, apparently innocent compromises eventually destroyed the whole fabric of the townspeople's ethics. With time, the people of Sonderburg and Mauthausen learned to tolerate evil. As the evil increased, the villagers themselves became diminished morally. In contrast, Le Chambon began to move in the opposite direction, toward goodness. Its residents became more sure of themselves, more reliant and trusting of each other. Trocmé himself "was always growing, always becoming stronger while he gave strength to those around him—he grew *with* them."[8]

The movement toward resistance in Le Chambon was not accidental or spontaneous; it was deliberate, nurtured by regular meetings and Trocmé's preaching. Every two weeks Trocmé met with thirteen "responsables" to study a biblical passage; in turn, they met with their own neighbors to talk about their scriptural readings.[9] A number of religious ethical assumptions, underscored by Trocmé's sermons and the Huguenot hymns, played an important role in the daily lives of the villagers of Le Chambon. Many of them were guided by a devout faith; having chosen to resist, they could find sustenance from their religion. It affirmed a deep commitment to offer refuge and help to anyone who sought it, based upon the commandment in Deuteronomy 19:10 to shelter the persecuted "lest innocent blood be shed in your land . . . and so the guilt of bloodshed be upon you." Others, like Trocmé's wife, Magda, were not explicitly religious but possessed a remarkably clear sense of moral duty. She felt "responsible," as she told Hallie, to anyone who approached her for help.[10]

Eventually, a number of houses in the countryside around Le Chambon either hid refugees or served as way stations for those trying to reach Switzerland. Through Trocmé's ecumenical contacts, some of the refugees were helped by the French *Cimade*, the Quakers, Catholics, World Council of Churches in Geneva, and the Swedish and Swiss governments.[11] Although it received support from outside, the village itself was the heart of the serious resistance. Inevitably, it became the focus of Nazi pressure.

In fact, the people of Le Chambon faced a situation similar to that in Mauthausen after the escape of Russian prisoners from the Mauthausen camp. In 1942, Vichy police arrived in Le Chambon, looking for Jews to hand over to the SS. The people of Le Chambon quickly helped the refugees hide in the woods around the village; even a house-to-house search by police officials failed to discover a refugee or intimidate the villagers. In Mauthausen, the townspeople and farmers had joined the SS guards in hunting down the prisoners and brutally murdering them. In Le Chambon, not one refugee was turned in or captured.[12] When Trocmé was forced to flee the village during the last year of the Occupation (he returned after the Normandy invasion in June 1944), the village continued to shelter Jews, despite increased Gestapo pressure on the region. There are several indications that local police officials decided to ignore the village's activities, implicitly protecting it.

Le Chambon was liberated by French troops in September 1944. The village had rescued approximately 2,500 people. The villagers never attempted to convert the Jewish children in their care to Christianity.[13] No one in Le Chambon ever turned away, denounced, or betrayed a refugee.[14] By coincidence, Albert Camus was writing *The Plague* in a nearby village during 1942. There are similarities, Hallie observes, between André Trocmé and the character of Dr. Rieux in Camus' book: "Both men knew that the plague of mankind is man's desire to kill, or, more usually, man's willingness to allow killing to happen without resisting it."[15]

THE ATMOSPHERE OF RESISTANCE

René Girard's notion of "disruptive empathy" does not just describe a force that can withstand evil. Empathy gives us the strength to resist, but the foundation of that strength is the act of reaching out to the other.

Disruptive empathy is the opposite of passivity and indifference; it is an active force that changes the very atmosphere. Hallie's comparison of Trocmé and Dr. Rieux highlights the active nature of rescue by contrasting it to the passivity of bystanders—to "man's willingness to allow killing to happen without resisting it." Disruptive empathy is an "unwillingness" to let things happen; passivity disguises a "willingness" to permit history to take its course. Passivity is not inaction, but "an *act of harmdoing* . . . from the point of view of that refugee, your closed door is an instrument of harmdoing, and your closing it does harm."[16]

It is tempting to look at the more obvious differences between Le Chambon, Mauthausen, and Sonderburg, and to attribute the behavior of each town's residents to these differences. The most striking difference, of course, is that the villagers of Le Chambon were clearly influenced by their religious faith. The French Huguenot tradition of nonviolence and the town's own history of religious persecution obviously contributed to a very different mentality among the people in the region. In Sonderburg and Mauthausen, religion is only part of the background; there is no evidence that people in either village were deeply religious or that their church leaders tried to move them toward resistance or rescue.

Yet this, in and of itself, cannot explain what happened in Le Chambon. A neighboring village, Le Mazet, had a similar history, yet the people there did not join the efforts to help refugees. Another obvious difference is the presence of Le Chambon's charismatic and strong-willed leader, André Trocmé. But Trocmé was not acting alone; the story of Le Chambon is the story of the involvement of an entire village.

More than anything else, the story of Le Chambon shows the movement, of individuals alone and in community, along the spectrum of involvement. One decision led to another; the intention to rescue was not there from the beginning, but developed over a period of time. Hallie describes it as a kind of "atmosphere. . . . People shared a dangerous and helpful atmosphere the way people share physical air; it was all around them, and yet each drew it into his or her own life, the way we share and divide the air we breathe."[17] Whenever a new refugee arrived in Le Chambon, the papers for a forged identity card appeared in the houses of those who needed them. No one was able to tell Hallie later how this had happened.

The notion of "atmosphere" describes the interaction between the lives of individuals and the institutions with which they are involved. As we saw earlier, the development of totalitarianism in Nazi Germany is an example of how a certain atmosphere both fosters and is fostered by individual and institutional complicity. The story of Le Chambon shows how an atmosphere that nurtures resistance can be created. The resistance of Le Chambon depended upon the villagers' relationships with each other and with the people they were rescuing. One of the most amazing things about this "conspiracy of good" was that everyone was involved. Everyone either sheltered a refugee or helped others do so; only in this way was it possible for a village to save 2,500 lives.

In contrast, the atmosphere in Mauthausen and Sonderburg was tainted by fear and passivity. This, in turn, made it that much harder for individuals to help others. In Sonderburg, the twelve Jews who remained in the village after 1939 were kept alive by friendly neighbors who brought them food late at night and cared for them.[18] Yet these acts of charity were necessarily done in complete silence and isolation; it was a case of "good neighbors showing kindness often without committing themselves to any action which could have landed them in trouble."[19] Most of the rescuers during the Holocaust were similar to the people who helped in Sonderburg: they were individuals, often acting alone, secretly and in stark contrast to the behavior of their neighbors. Ultimately, the efforts of individuals acting alone were not enough to stop the Holocaust, although they were able to save individual lives.

Thus, the significance of what happened in Le Chambon is not just that the villagers rescued hundreds of individuals. The miracle of Le Chambon was that it showed that something else was possible: that the refusal of individuals to remain bystanders can change the ethical patterns of an entire community. All three communities—Sonderburg, Mauthausen, and Le Chambon—were a composite of individuals, institutions, and leaders. In Sonderburg and Mauthausen, the sum of the villagers' behavior, prejudices, and fear worked to create an atmosphere of tacit "moral permission" for what happened. Only in Le Chambon did the local institution of the church and its pastor take a leading role in propelling the community from passivity to resistance.

RESCUE AND RESISTANCE

This is the social context in which we must understand the motives of individual rescuers during the Holocaust. It is striking that none of the studies done on rescuers have arrived at a standard "profile" of a rescuer. The story of Le Chambon might lead us to assume that rescuers in general were strongly influenced by religious beliefs. Yet those who have studied the behavior of rescuers (notably the Oliners and Nechama Tec) have been unable to establish any consistent factors, including religious beliefs, that predict peoples' behavior. Religious beliefs were apparently not a significant factor for most rescuers. In her study of Polish rescuers, Nechama Tec discovered only 27 percent who cited religious conviction as a motive; the Oliners found only 15 percent.[20] Michael Marrus notes that in the two countries (Italy and Denmark) where there was significant popular opposition to Nazi policies against the Jews, "religious factors" don't seem to have played a role.[21]

The Oliners began to look at other factors, including rescuers' personalities. They concluded that there were generally four types of rescuers, each shaped by various "experiences, relationships, values, and personality characteristics."[22] One group was characterized by strong family bonds; another by consistent and close relationships with Jews; another by more abstract principles and a general sense of responsibility; and the fourth by strong sentiments of egalitarianism and empathy. The distinguishing feature of all these groups was "their stronger sense of attachment to others and their feeling of responsibility for the welfare of others, including those outside their immediate familiar or communal circles."[23]

In some cases, this orientation was based upon the rescuers' close relationships with others, which nurtured their sense of empathy; other rescuers were more influenced by the moral or political principles that had been instilled in them. Examining the same data, Staub distinguishes between a "prosocial value orientation" that focuses on human welfare, and a "rule-oriented morality" that emphasizes duty and the importance of living by certain principles.[24] Staub and the Oliners agree that this is where bystanders differ significantly from rescuers. Marked by their sense of relationship to others, rescuers felt a responsibility for them. Bystanders, in contrast, were "centered on themselves and their own needs."[25]

Before 1933, these differences did not have a noticeable effect on the lives of rescuers and bystanders. In social and historical circumstances that demanded little of them personally, the two groups were indistinguishable from one another. After 1933, however, these good citizens began to move in opposite directions. It was difficult for rescuers, moved by empathy, a sense of responsibility, and principles of right and wrong, to remain passively on the sidelines under a system like Nazism. Their natural tendency was to help its victims and resist the dictatorship's demands upon them. They felt a personal stake in what was happening around them—either based upon their own relationship to the victims or upon their involvement in the policies or actions of an institution.

The bystanders, who had little sense of greater responsibility and whose lives had always been centered around their own needs, withdrew. Even those who had qualms about what was happening under Nazism chose to remain silent. They evaded the intentionality that is the prerequisite for rescue or resistance; the marks of this evasion were "indifference," passivity, and the creation of "parallel worlds." They denied any connection between their own lives and what was taking place around them. "The majority of bystanders," the Oliners write, "were overcome by fear, hopelessness, and uncertainty. These feelings, which encourage self-centeredness and emotional distancing from others, provide fertile soil for passivity. Survival of the self assumes paramount importance. This was the characteristic of most bystanders."[26]

Thus, rescuers were characterized by a sense of commitment that took them beyond the boundaries of their private concerns, based upon either empathy for others or their principles of justice. They also seemed to have a sense that their own individual behavior was important and could make a difference. By refusing to simply proceed with their lives, by avoiding the temptations of "normality," they—like the people of Le Chambon—began to live on a different level, not skimming along the surface of history, but living fully within it. In the process, they changed it.

THE SIGNIFICANCE OF RESCUE AND RESISTANCE

If we compare the dynamics in Le Chambon with those that developed in Mauthausen and Sonderburg, it becomes obvious that what happened in the French village did not result simply from the absence of hatred or indifference. Resistance and rescue are active forces that change the people involved and the world around them.

There were differences between rescuers and resistance members. Rescuers, discovered the Oliners, tended to believe "that ethical principles were at stake."[27] The motives of resistance members tended to be more abstract and political. They felt strong opposition to Nazism or patriotic feelings; "for rescuers, however, such reasons were rarely sufficient."[28]

In an essay, "Empathy and Protest: Two Roots of Heroic Altruism," Krzysztof Konarzewski analyzes the subtle differences between the rescuers and resisters.[29] Empathy, he reflects, is on behalf of someone; protest is against something or someone. Yet both rescue and resistance express a sense of *relationship* to what is happening, and both seem to require some degree of inner independence.

They also produce a strong sense of external freedom. Bystanders remained paralyzed by their belief that "nothing could be done"—that they were "powerless" and had few options. For those who began to resist, resistance was an act of internal liberation:

The moment of decision has often been described by Resistance intellectuals as a private victory, an inner rejection of constraints in defiance of the state. Alfred Andersch wrote in 1952 of his desertion from the German army: "I simply thought, with a tremendous sense of triumph, of the freedom that I had created for myself."[30]

At its very core, resistance was the opposite of "indifference." In the chapter on totalitarianism, we have examined the phenomenon of "inner emigration"—the private resistance that many bystanders cited later to justify themselves; their silence (so they claimed) only "appeared" to be indifference. Rescue, writes Lawrence Blum, was the assertion of "a different way of living and different values than those of the Nazis—an assertion not made by bystanders (those who did nothing to help), whatever their actual disagreements with the Nazi regime and philosophy."[31] In this sense,

Blum notes, rescue was very much a form of resistance. In comparisons between bystanders, rescuers, and resistance members, the focus is often upon their acts and the outcome of those acts. This is understandable; action or inaction, after all, is the most obvious way to distinguish between these groups. Yet the more we examine rescuers and bystanders, the clearer it becomes that what defined them was not just their actions, but the way they were.

It is difficult to pinpoint the moment when a bystander becomes involved—the moment of "disruptive empathy." This moment marks the beginning of a new way of connecting with the situation. Once people feel connected to the injustice of what is happening and, more importantly, to the fate of the victims, they begin to see everything in a new light: family, work, their options, and the very purpose of their lives.

From this point on, the bystander is no longer a bystander. Resistance is genuinely disruptive—not just of the surrounding situation, but of the bystander's own life. It connects the "parallel worlds" of the bystanders, perpetrators, and victims; it shatters the illusion of "normality" that enables the bystanders to pursue their own lives in isolation from that happening around them. Suddenly, all the pieces in the puzzle—historical factors, prejudice, psychological factors, the political situation—begin to fit together differently. Things we think of as unimportant in the greater scheme of things—upbringing, our relationships with others, the principles with which we have been raised—prove to be the most important of all; "it is out of the quality of such routine human activities that the human spirit evolves and moral courage is born."[32]

These are the factors that build "character." In his study of Le Chambon, Philip Hallie emphasized the role of character in the behavior of the villagers: "Ethics is inwardly experienced self-control. When the moral law within you rules your passions, you are good. When your inward government is in chaos, in anarchy, you are bad. In short, ethics is only a matter of character."[33]

Using the language of law and government to describe the internal workings of individual ethics helps us understand how individual ethics affect the greater society. "Ethical communities," Hallie writes, "are as real as legal institutions. To call ethics personal is not to call it anarchic. It, like the law, can bring people together."[34] His examination of the resistance in Le Chambon showed Hallie how a strongly expressed sense of individual ethics creates an atmosphere in which people become more than bystanders and how, in turn, this atmosphere continues to foster such behavior.

While character is often viewed as an individual attribute, it has much broader implications. The content of our character determines how we approach the world and relate to others. What the people of Le Chambon did was create an ethical community that mirrored their "inward government"—i.e., that reflected their character. The creation of an ethical community is what saves people; its absence is what dooms them. Ultimately, "ethical community" can be created only by individuals who see the purpose of their lives as connected to more than the private realm of their own lives.

Yet character means something more, for we cannot attribute the difference between Le Chambon and Sonderburg simply to the fact that the people of Le Chambon were involved in something greater than themselves. The same could be said of the bystanders of Sonderburg, and of millions of Germans, the purpose of whose lives was indeed determined by something greater—but that something greater was Nazism. The incredible power achieved by Nazi Germany was created by the complicity of millions of bystanders who linked their personal destinies to the totalitarian force of Nazism.

The central distinction is that the individuals who lived in Le Chambon retained a kind of ethical freedom. They acted in community, but were not swept up in a mass movement. The atmosphere of Le Chambon did not make its citizens cogs in the wheel, or compel them to become part of a greater force that eradicated their own individuality and freedom. A "moral society," writes Robert McAfee Brown, "will be a society of *participants* rather than *spectators*."[35] The nature of that participation cannot be determined by the dominant social or ideological values, or commanded by political leaders. It must be created by the choices each person makes, as an ethical being.

NOTES

1. Hallie, *Lest Innocent Blood*, 62.
2. Ibid., 69.
3. Ibid., 26.
4. Ibid., 92.
5. Ibid., 77.
6. Ibid., 119–125.
7. Ibid., 91.
8. Ibid., 138.
9. Ibid., 172.
10. Ibid., 153.
11. Ibid., 176.
12. Ibid., 107–112.
13. Ibid., 54.
14. Ibid., 196.
15. Ibid., 248.
16. Ibid., 122.
17. Ibid., 199.
18. Henry, *Victims and Neighbors*, 84.
19. Ibid., 98.

20. Nechama Tec, *When Light Pierced Darkness* (New York: Oxford University Press, 1986), 145; and Oliner and Oliner, *The Altruistic Personality*, 155.

21. Marrus, *The Holocaust in History*, 105.

22. Oliner and Oliner, *The Altruistic Personality*, 183–184.

23. Ibid., 249.

24. Staub, *The Roots of Evil*, 145.

25. Oliner and Oliner, *The Altruistic Personality*, 186.

26. Ibid., 146.

27. Ibid., 170.

28. Ibid.

29. In Oliner et al., *Embracing the Other*, 22–30.

30. In Wilkinson, *The Intellectual Resistance in Europe*, 263–264.

31. Lawrence A. Blum, "Altruism and the Moral Value of Rescue." In Oliner et al., *Embracing the Other*, 41.

32. Oliner and Oliner, *The Altruistic Personality*, 260.

33. Hallie, *Lest Innocent Blood*, 278.

34. Ibid., 271–272.

35. Brown, *Elie Wiesel*, 206.

CHAPTER 10

The Individual as Ethical Being

For centuries, most people were born and died in the same community. Their entire lives were spent in a relatively contained social environment, with established rules and a degree of social stability that is difficult for many of us to imagine today. This made people's ethical responsibility for their neighbors very concrete. Individuals were aware of their socially appropriate role, and watched closely to ensure that others fulfilled their roles as well. The limits of freedom and responsibility were clear, as were the guidelines that meted out charity, punishment, approval, and disapproval.

Because these lines seem to have been so clearly drawn in the past, we sometimes long for simpler times, when communities were smaller, more cohesive and homogeneous, consisting of people who (we assume) were more willing to help one another. When we examine the numerous problems that confront us today in modern urban societies, it is easy to assume that these problems, including the phenomenon of "bystanders," are the outcome of modernity and all that goes with it.

Yet the more stable societies of our ancestors did not automatically lead to greater charity or social conscience. Our longing for earlier, simpler times (and the mechanisms we use to recreate the illusion of such simpler times, such as retreating into our private worlds) really indicates an assumption that our ancestors faced simpler ethical issues. Yet a sober look at human history, whether in biblical times, the Middle Ages, the Industrial Revolution, or the 20th century, shows that the response to the question "Who is my neighbor?" has always been bound by the rules of social convention, class distinction, and popular prejudice. The notion that we are obligated to help a stranger from another class or ethnic group was a radical one when Jesus of Nazareth told the story of the good Samaritan to his followers in Galilee. It remains radical today.

Our situation does differ in several ways, however, from that of our ancestors. The range of what people in earlier ages could know about and the immediacy with which they were confronted with it was limited. They were certainly familiar with the local alcoholic, with who was poor and who was rich, and with the vices and virtues of their neighbors. But nothing else would have seemed immediate in the sense that they felt personally responsible (or able) to intervene. The plight of people on another continent—or even in other cities—was far removed. Their ethical responsibilities were confined to the immediate realm of their own experience.

Today, the human situation is quite different. Modern developments have made us all too familiar with suffering elsewhere in the world. Technology has made us witnesses—and thereby bystanders—to much horror. Even people who spend their entire lives in a small, relatively stable community are exposed to the suffering of people elsewhere. The growth of international trade and modern communications has brought people in different countries and cultures in touch with one another, and given us the ability to know about events as they unfold in other parts of the world.

We live in a "global village." The phrase suggests that our world today somehow resembles the small, insulated villages of the past and, to some degree, this is true. Through technology, we are as familiar with events in other parts of the world as our ancestors were with news from neighboring towns. Famines, wars, and atrocities elsewhere in the world confront us with almost as much immediacy as the homeless people on the streets of our cities. Like our ancestors, we employ various mechanisms—psychological, social, and political—to insulate ourselves from the suffering of others.

There is an important difference, however: unlike people in earlier times, *we do not have to turn our eyes away in order to withdraw*. We can, and do, continue to look at what is happening, in the knowledge that there is a physical distance of thousands of miles between ourselves and those suffering elsewhere. Passivity to the suffering of others is eased (some would say even necessitated) by the fact that they are miles away, out of reach. And yet we see.

Thus, while the bystander is not a new phenomenon, some of the questions we face today are new. What happens to us when we witness atrocity and suffering throughout the world? What happens when we feel an emotional response to such events but are unable to respond? What does this mean for our ethics? What have we become accustomed to? Do we, like the bystanders during the Holocaust, come to define ourselves as "powerless" and hence, on some level, innocent? But can we be innocent of a crime that we know about? What insights does our situation today give us into the behavior of bystanders during the Holocaust? What insights can we derive from the history of the Holocaust for our responsibilities today?

These questions add up to the central question: what does it mean to be an ethical being? If, as Zygmunt Bauman said, the Holocaust is a window through which we can learn much about human existence, what does the Holocaust suggest about our nature as ethical beings?

Many people, when asked about their ethical responsibilities for one another, offer some version of the Golden Rule or the story of the good Samaritan. The lesson of the good Samaritan has been incorporated into the social contract of many societies. Witnesses to an accident are expected, for example, to remain on the scene until help arrives. Society expects them to render assistance to injured parties to the extent possible. This precept is law in many countries; in much of Europe, these laws are even called "Samaritan laws."

Such laws do more than just define who our "neighbor" is. They presume a connection between the responsibility of individual citizens for one another and the greater good of society. The failure of bystanders to aid someone in need is not just an individual sin; ultimately, it undermines the viability of society as a whole. In 1964 a young woman, Kitty Genovese, was murdered on a Brooklyn street. Although she repeatedly cried for help, numerous people watching from their windows did not even call the police. The Kitty Genovese murder is still cited as an event that profoundly unnerved people at the time, for it made them aware of the breakdown of U.S. society. It was a signal that the human involvement, commitment, and shared sense of responsibility necessary for the healthy ethical life of a society had disappeared from modern cities.

We know all too well that modern society is filled with examples of apathy. It has become a commonplace that most bystanders do not offer assistance, but look away, even when victims plead for outside help. In modern cities, anything else is considered foolish; the bystander who renders help is newsworthy. Still, it is shocking and disturbing to read about people who remain passive or turn away when approached by someone who needs help. Despite our awareness of the realities of modern life, we sense that people should know better.

This is one reason why the behavior of bystanders during the Holocaust haunts us. In our awareness of what they failed to do then, we are compelled to reflect on our responsibilities today. Like them, we move along a continuum of human behavior. How and in what direction we move is shaped by the kind of people we are and the circumstances in which we find ourselves. Then and now, the mechanisms we use to avoid our responsibilities are similar. Mentally, we compartmentalize our world into public and private realms, and retreat into the private sphere. We distinguish between our world and that of the victims, between "us" and "them," by creating various forms of distance between our situation and that of others. Faced with situations where it is difficult or risky to intervene, we consider ourselves "powerless." Prejudice, fear, and conformity remain powerful motivations. The "courage to care" remains as elusive a quality today as it was between 1933 and 1945.

Aside from its historical relevance in helping us understand what happened in the Holocaust, the real significance of bystander behavior during that era is that it tells us something about how we function as ethical beings. Its message is both bleak and empowering. The passivity of bystanders allowed the brutality of the Holocaust to flourish. At the same time, the potential of bystanders to become involved remained till the very end. For that reason, the bystanders haunt us precisely because we sense that we should do better. In retrospect, and particularly when we look at the stories of rescuers, we see that they could have done better.

In drawing lessons for our own times, we recognize that the moral involvement of citizens is crucial for a society to thrive. Even today, most of us still consider altruism, not apathy, a virtue. Altruism is not just something we expect of saints; we know it is necessary, to some degree, in all societies. As the Oliners write, "No society could exist unless its members acknowledge and make sacrifices on behalf of each other. Thus, said Durkheim, altruism is not merely 'a sort of agreeable ornament to social life' but its fundamental basis."[1]

Such expectations are part of our religious understanding as well. Historically, there is a strong tradition within both Christianity and Judaism of bearing responsibility for one another. It begins with God's question to Cain: Where is Abel your brother? The history of the human denial of that responsibility begins with Cain's reply: Am I my brother's keeper? This story is at the heart of Jewish and Christian religious ethics. It bears early witness to our human potential for brutality and for denial. Cain's words— Am I my brother's keeper?—are a denial both of the murder of his brother and of his greater responsibility.

This greater responsibility is at the heart of all religious ethics. As human beings present in the world, we bear responsibility for what happens in it. We find this throughout Jewish and Christian scriptures, in God's question to Cain; the injunction to Moses and the people of Israel to welcome the strangers in their midst, since they themselves were once strangers in Egypt; the parable of the good Samaritan. All these stories are a call for us to become involved in the world in a different way. The question faced by bystanders is not a modern dilemma, but epitomizes the problem that has existed since the beginning of human history: Who is my neighbor? What are my obligations?

Discussions of ethics often focus on basic precepts and principles. Not surprisingly, in much of the literature on the Holocaust, the ethical failures of bystanders and perpetrators alike are identified in very specific terms: anti-Semitism, or nationalism, or traditions of subservience to authority. Each of these factors can obviously affect ethical judgment; any of them could be identified as a primary cause of the Holocaust.

But the historical details of the Holocaust give a far more complex picture, one that makes it difficult to attribute the Holocaust or the behavior of bystanders to any single factor. We are clearly looking at a combination of factors, and it was the interaction between them that affected the responses of individuals, institutions, and the international community. The nature of the sin is individual—it is individuals who turn away, refuse to help, and offer alibis for their inaction—but the Holocaust shows us how very profound the social and historical implications of this failure are.

One way of thinking about this is to consider the *moment* of "exclusion" or "embrace." Let us suppose that there really is a decisive moment, a turning point when the bystander decides (even unconsciously) to move in one direction along the spectrum or the other.

In many accounts about rescuers, there is such a moment: a knock at the door, an acquaintance who approaches another, a concrete request for help. In some cases, it was not the victim who approached the neighbor, but the rescuer who took the initiative: who saw someone who needed help and reached out, who perceived the Nazi injustice and decided to do something about it.

Let us begin with a scenario in which the bystander, in this crucial moment, acts to exclude the other. An example from Henry's study of Sonderburg was that of Joshua Abraham, the long-time member of a card-playing club that excluded him immediately after the Nazis came to power.[2]

Abraham's story haunts us. How could long-time friends, literally from one week to the next, treat someone this way? How could they have a relationship with someone and suddenly change simply because the political circumstances around them changed? The logical conclusion is that Abraham's friends were obviously *not* morally grounded like the "altruistic personalities" studied by Samuel and Pearl Oliner.

But because this kind of weakness was the norm during the Holocaust, not the exception, the social ramifications are worth exploring. The reaction of Abraham's card club illustrates the interplay between the individual level of ethical decision and the social level of dominant values. What happened to Joshua Abraham shows that peoples' perceptions of another person—even a friend, someone with whom one has a relationship and a history of shared common experiences—can shift when there is a change in the situation or (more importantly) in the social categorization of the other. For his friends in Sonderburg, Joshua Abraham was no longer some-one they played cards with, but a Jew, and his identification as a Jew had become all-important in Nazi Germany.

Frances Henry gives another example: the case of S., a Jewish teacher who lost his job immediately after Hitler came to power in 1933. After he had stood at his apartment window one day to watch the local SS parade, a young acquaintance, a member of the SS, visited him to both apologize for the parade and to warn him. His interpretation of the encounter years later is intriguing; he told Henry that he had never blamed the young SS man or the other citizens in Sonderburg, *"since he knew that they were simply following orders and had lost their personal freedom to act with decency."*[3]

Is the "personal freedom to act with decency" utterly dependent upon the values imposed or supported by society? Are social pressures so pow-erful that they invariably neutralize individual ethics, even when people know better? This is the disturbing conclusion drawn by Milgram and many others. But if this is the case, what does "personal freedom"—or any notion of ethical free will—mean?

The frightening thing is that, as we grow more familiar with the details of what happened in Nazi Germany, the reactions of Abraham's friends and the young SS man become easier to understand. Self-interest is the clearest of all motives, and it was in every German's self-interest (in the limited sense, at least) to conform to the new Nazi way of life, even if this meant abandoning former friends and neighbors.

The real mystery is what leads the individual, in the decisive moment, to "embrace" the other. On some level it means that such individuals are ethically "grounded" in such a way that their spontaneous reaction is to do the right thing. This "moral grounding" can be the result of very dif-ferent factors such as religion, family upbringing, or political conviction; no single factor is predictable. But the Oliners' work convincingly shows that, whatever the combination of factors, the end result is an "altruistic personality": a person capable of feeling empathy and of acting on it.

A crucial function of such moral grounding in situations like that of Nazi Germany was that it enabled the individual to withstand the social pres-sures to conform to a different set of values. But its function went beyond that; in Nazi Germany, those who stood by their Jewish friends and refused to conform became part of a small but firm resistance. There were severe political consequences even for actions which, in ordinary times, would have been nothing more than simple acts of friendship.

We might imagine that an "ethical society" is one that largely consists of such people, a society that operates collectively the way its members do individually. Its culture and institutions would reflect an ethic of caring for one another and a general refusal to tolerate injustice or violence against individuals. Its institutions—schools, religious bodies, governmental bureaucracies—would reflect this as well.

Yet our vision of this imaginary society is essentially just a mirror of the virtues of its individual members. Is an "ethical society" simply the composite of its citizens? This, of course, is the question that philosophers and ethicists have wrestled with since Plato and Aristotle. It was the subject of Reinhold Niebuhr's *Moral Man and Immoral Society*. His conclusion was that there wasn't such a thing as an "ethical society"—that the outcome of human beings acting together on the social level is different from the outcome of one individual acting ethically. Sociologist Gordon Allport affirmed this insight when he visited South Africa in 1956. As his colleague Thomas Pettigrew noted, Allport had viewed sociological factors as "distal" when he wrote *The Nature of Prejudice*. He changed his mind after visiting South Africa:

It shook him not only in his conception of the nature of prejudice but in his conception of the nature of personality. There he saw men who met his definition of the mature adult, but who nevertheless were doing evil things regularly and routinely as part of their lives in an evil social system.[4]

The connection between the private and public, between our own behavior and its consequences for society, has been part of history from the beginning; the mystery has always been how the connections work. This is a complex matter but one very relevant to what happened in Nazi Germany. The genocide of the Jews shocked the world precisely because it raised moral issues, not just political ones. Yet in the wake of that genocide, it was precisely these moral issues that were so difficult to address. At the heart of the postwar debate about collective guilt, for example, was the philosophical distinction (made by Arendt, Jaspers, and at the Nuremberg trials) that guilt ultimately could only be ascribed to individuals. It was individuals, not the German nation, who were held accountable and tried in Nuremberg.

Yet the implications of the Nuremberg trials do not merely concern individual sin or guilt. The underlying presupposition of the charge of "crimes against humanity" is that individual sin has social implications because individuals are socially and politically accountable. This is what Philip Hallie meant when he spoke of the importance of character[5]; it is what theologian Robert Willis means when he defines conscience as the "moral self *in its wholeness*."[6] As both writers make clear, the definitive aspect of conscience or character is not a certain set of principles, but a strong sense of responsibility for the whole.

In Trocmé's case, this sense of responsibility extended not just to his society but to history itself. He and his Quaker friend Burns Chalmers were not just trying to save the lives of the children they sheltered; they consciously "wanted to give the children of the refugees a strong feeling and a solid knowledge that there were human beings *outside their own family* who cared for them. Only by showing them that human beings could help strangers could they give those children hope and a basis for living moral lives of their own."[7]

For Trocmé, the *moral* aspect of this sense of relationship was exemplified by *how* he fulfilled the obligation to the stranger (the "other"), and the consequences of his actions for society and for history. Most people are capable of helping those whom they know or who are like them. Going beyond that—reaching out on behalf of those we don't know, those who are different from us, even people whom we may view with distrust or prejudice—is different. It goes to the very heart of the word "altruism," which is derived from the Latin word for "other."

The "otherness" of the stranger is a central aspect of what happened during the Holocaust not just because it was such a significant principle in Nazi ideology, but because it is a crucial element in any genocide. Those who refused to participate in the ideological scapegoating of others were able to through the false distinctions between "Aryans" and "others": to see, in the face of the stranger, another human being.

This capacity can be fostered by religious convictions or by secular principles of democracy, justice, and tolerance. But it is not just based upon individually held values, but on their concept of what kind of society they want. During the Holocaust, rescuers and resistance members were distinguished not just by their character, but by their vision of a different kind of society and their commitment to that vision. Altruism is not simply based upon peoples' moral convictions or kindness; it is linked to how they see the world around them, and to where they see their place in that world. As Darrell Fasching notes, this capacity is an intrinsic part of the Christian and Judaic understandings of charity. In both religious traditions, to welcome the stranger is a metaphor for welcoming God. Both the stranger and God represent "otherness": "In encountering the stranger, one encounters a witness to the transcendence of God, one who, like God, cannot be domesticated in order to legitimate one's life, religion, or cultural-national identity—one who by his or her very differentness or otherness calls one's identity into question."[8] The motif of welcoming the stranger recurs throughout the Hebrew *Tanach* and the Christian New Testament; it appears in the stories and texts of all major religions. And the consequences of compassion and charity are never entirely confined to the giver or recipient: "a holy community has its center outside itself, in a transcendence whose social analogue is the stranger. Thus a holy community defines the human in terms of an otherness that gives birth to an ethic of hospitality. . . . Compassion binds the individual within the holy community to the individuals in the society beyond its borders."[9]

Compassion does not just establish a relationship between the individuals immediately involved. Acts of compassion connect *everyone* involved in a new way, and thus alter the very dynamics of society. Conversely, when the individual's moral range of vision becomes restricted to his or her own private realm, the realm where one is *not* involved increases; the scope and efficacy of individual ethics are diminished. This, in effect, is how parallel worlds are created. This is the context in which we must understand Zygmunt Bauman's comment: "Moral behavior can exist only in a social context."[10]

What does it mean to be an ethical being? It means, as Bauman suggests, that the private and public realms of morality are ultimately one. The ethical being, says Miroslav Volf, is a "re-centered self"—not in the form of "self-obliterating denial of the self" in the name of some greater purpose, but in actions that establish the self as a responsible ethical being in relation to surrounding society.[11] The ethical being no longer thinks of character or conscience as purely individual characteristics. Ultimately, such people help create a society in which conscience (the "moral self in its *wholeness*"[12]) has an active and powerful voice.

Much of the growing fascination with the Holocaust revolves around the questions that arise about bystanders. The initial emotional response of many students is to avoid the bystander entirely: to feel solidarity with the victims and outrage at the criminals. But these emotions impel us to ensure that such things do not happen again—and this confronts us with the bystander, the figure in the shadows of history.

In this book, we have attempted to bring the bystander out of the shadows, to examine some of the factors that led most people during the Holocaust to remain bystanders. All too often, the historical details show a shocking degree of apathy toward the reports of atrocity and suffering. Yet the details also reveal other emotions, ranging from hatred to silent anguish. Numerous forces shaped human behavior throughout the world during that awful period; the universal failure to stop the Nazi genocide was caused by a number of motives and emotions. There were people who hated the Jews, others who tried desperately to save them, others who felt terrible at what was happening but did not even try to do anything. There were those who did try to do something but failed, and those who cautiously tried to compromise or work behind the scenes. There were people who wanted to help, and yet could not break away from their prescribed role. In the pages of Holocaust scholarship, we encounter all the rational grounds for hesitation that are given today in the editorial pages about Bosnia, Rwanda, and other places.

In other words, the failure of bystanders to help was not always the product of hatred or apathy, but often reflected a profound sense of helplessness. Yet the ethical failure of so many during the Holocaust was that they equated "helplessness" with "powerlessness." Even today, we have failed to construct an ethic that can deal with evil on such a magnitude. Despite the prevalence of terms like "global village," for most individuals our world resembles a village only in terms of knowledge. We know what is happening throughout the world, yet knowledge is not enough. The solution is to discover a new way of connecting ethically, of changing both individual and societal ways of thinking about our ethical responsibilities.

Ethics encompasses what we choose to live with, and this is one reason that the Holocaust remains so troubling. The Holocaust was the outcome not just of human powerlessness or passivity, but of the moral arrangements people made to survive, physically and psychologically. From the request of the simple Mauthausen farmwoman that the camp keep its murders "out of sight" to the deliberately cautious policies of the International Red Cross, these moral accommodations signified death for millions of innocent people.

Perhaps the central issue is the *nature of goodness* that we see in Le Chambon. A different kind of goodness, of ethics, was necessary to confront the genocide. It changes something in us, and in others, when we help. It changes something in us, and in others, when we *don't* help. This is what comes across very strongly in all the studies of rescuers—but it is a truth that is evident in all histories of the Holocaust.

The "mystery of the good"—the spark that moves people to help another, to resist evil, to risk their lives for principles—remains elusive. Religious and political convictions are obvious influences. Yet there were thousands of people—good, decent people of religious faith and moral convictions—who nonetheless failed, in the moment of crisis, to be anything more than bystanders.

In the final analysis, what seems to have moved people to deeds of courage and compassion was a sudden glimpse of their profound connection to the world around them and all who inhabit it: the same vision that inspired Donne. They sensed that they were part of something greater, and that it was possible for them to act in a way that could change the fate of another. The miracle is that, where individuals sensed this, they did succeed in rescuing others. The numbers saved are pitifully small; of the 500,000 Jews living in Germany in 1933, 14,574 were hidden in Germany and survived the Holocaust.[13] Yet each rescued individual is not just testimony to the courage and kindness of another, but witness to a commitment to the kind of human community that too often eludes us.

The words "no man is an island" are simple, but Donne was really describing a complex human ecology, one in which our actions and beliefs not only affect those whom we encounter directly but literally create the world in which we live. Centuries later, the same thought was inscribed at the Yad Vashem memorial in Israel, which commemorates those who saved the lives of Jews during the Holocaust: "Whoever saves one life saves the universe." The value of each individual life is precious. The loss of each individual life shakes the universe and changes the course of history. In this way, the conscience of each individual has the power to reach far beyond the private realm, and create the fabric of a progressively greater whole: of family, society, nation, history, and humanity itself.

NOTES

1. Oliner and Oliner, *The Altruistic Personality*, 5.

2. Henry, *Victims and Neighbors*, 95.

3. Ibid., 107–108.

4. "Gordon Allport: His Unique Contributions to Contemporary Personality and Social Psychology," in Richard I. Evans, ed., *Gordon Allport: The Man and His Ideas* (New York: E. P. Dutton, 1970), 122–123.

5. Hallie, *Lest Innocent Blood*, 278.

6. Willis, "Auschwitz and the Nurturing of Conscience," 435.

7. Hallie, *Lest Innocent Blood*, 134.

8. Darrell J. Fasching, *Narrative Theology After Auschwitz: From Alienation to Ethics* (Minneapolis, Minn.: Fortress Press, 1992), 82–83.

9. Ibid.

10. Bauman, *Modernity*, 179.

11. Volf, *Exclusion and Embrace*, 71.

12. Willis, "Auschwitz and the Nurturing of Conscience," 435.

13. Sarah Gordon gives the figure 500,000 (Gordon, *Hitler, Germans and the "Jewish Question,"* 8). The number rescued is from Bruno Blau, "The Last Days of German Jewry," *YIVO Annual of Jewish Social Sciences* 8: 189–90, 1953.

Selected Bibliography

Adorno, T. W., Else Frenkel-Brunswik, Daniel Levinson, and R. Nevitt Sanford. *The Authoritarian Personality*. New York: Harper & Brothers, 1950.

Allen, William Sheridan. *The Nazi Seizure of Power: The Experience of a Single German Town 1930–1935*. New York: Quadrangle Books, 1965.

Allport, Gordon W. *The Nature of Prejudice*. 1954. Reprint, Reading, Mass.: Addison-Wesley Publishing Company, 1979.

Arendt, Hannah. *Eichmann in Jerusalem. A Report on the Banality of Evil*. Revised and enlarged edition. New York: Viking Press, 1964.

———. *The Origins of Totalitarianism*. New edition. San Diego: Harcourt Brace Jovanovich, 1979.

Baillie, Gil. *Violence Unveiled: Humanity at the Crossroads*. New York: Crossroad Publishing Company, 1995.

Bauman, Zygmunt. *Modernity and the Holocaust*. Ithaca: Cornell University Press, 1989.

Borowski, Tadeusz. *This Way for the Gas, Ladies and Gentlemen*. Selected and translated by Barbara Vedder. New York: Penguin Books, 1976.

Broszat, Martin, ed. *Bayern in der NS-Zeit. Soziale Lage und politisches Verhalten der Bevölkerung im Spiegel vertraulicher Berichte*. Munich: Oldenbourg Verlag, 1977.

Brown, Robert McAfee. *Elie Wiesel: Messenger to All Humanity*. Notre Dame: University of Notre Dame Press, 1983.

Browning, Christopher R. *Ordinary Men: Reserve Police Battalion 101 and the Final Solution in Poland*. New York: HarperCollins, 1992.

Charny, Israel W. *How Can We Commit the Unthinkable?* Boulder, Colo.: Westview Press, 1982.

Chorover, Stephan L. *From Genesis to Genocide: The Meaning of Human Nature and the Power of Behavior Control*. Cambridge, Mass.: MIT Press, 1979.

Cohen, Arthur A. *The Tremendum. A Theological Interpretation of the Holocaust*. New York: Crossroad Publishing Company, 1981.

Dietrich, Donald. *God and Humanity in Auschwitz. Jewish-Christian Relations and Sanctioned Murder*. New Brunswick: Transaction Publishers, 1995.

Dimsdale, Joel E., ed. *Survivors, Victims, and Perpetrators: Essays on the Nazi Holocaust*. Washington: Hemisphere Publishing Corporation, 1980.

Fackenheim, Emil. *To Mend the World: Foundations of Post-Holocaust Jewish Thought*. New York: Schocken Books, 1982.

Fasching, Darrell J. *Narrative Theology after Auschwitz: From Alienation to Ethics*. Minneapolis: Fortress Press, 1992.

Feingold, Henry L. *The Politics of Rescue: The Roosevelt Administration and the Holocaust, 1938–1945*. New York: Schocken Books, 1970.

———. "The Witness Role of American Jewry: A Second Look." In Michael Ryan, ed., *Human Responses to the Holocaust: Perpetrators and Victims, Bystanders and Resisters*. New York: Edwin Mellen Press, 1981.

Frankl, Viktor E. *Man's Search for Meaning*. 4th edition. Boston: Beacon Press, 1992.

Friedlander, Henry. *The Origins of Nazi Genocide. From Euthanasia to the Final Solution*. Chapel Hill: University of North Carolina Press, 1995.

Gellately, Robert. *The Gestapo and German Society. Enforcing Racial Policy 1933–1945*. New York: Oxford University Press, 1990.

Genizi, Haim. *American Apathy: The Plight of Christian Refugees from Nazism*. Ramat-Gan, Israel: Bar-Ilan University Press, 1983.

———. *America's Fair Share: The Admission and Resettlement of Displaced Persons, 1945–1952*. Detroit: Wayne State University Press, 1993.

Gerlach, Wolfgang. *Als die Zeugen schwiegen. Bekennende Kirche und die Juden*. Berlin: Institut Kirche und Judentum, 1987.

Geyer, Michael and John W. Boyer, eds. *Resistance against the Third Reich 1933–1990*. Chicago: University of Chicago Press, 1994.

Girard, René. *The Scapegoat*. Baltimore: Johns Hopkins University Press, 1986.

Gordon, Sarah. *Hitler, Germans and the Jewish Question*. Princeton, N.J.: Princeton University Press, 1984.

Gushee, David. *The Righteous Gentiles of the Holocaust: A Christian Interpretation*. Minneapolis: Fortress Press, 1994.

Haas, Peter J. *Morality after Auschwitz. The Radical Challenge of the Nazi Ethic*. Philadelphia: Fortress Press, 1988.

Hallie, Philip. *Lest Innocent Blood Be Shed: The Story of the Village of Le Chambon and How Goodness Happened There*. New York: Harper & Row Publishers, 1979.

Hausner, Gideon. *Justice in Jerusalem*. (reprint.) New York: Schocken Books, 1968.

Haynes, Stephen R. *Reluctant Witnesses: Jews and the Christian Imagination*. Louisville: Westminster John Knox Press, 1995.

Hecht, Ingeborg. *Invisible Walls: A German Family under the Nuremberg Laws*. New York: Harcourt Brace Jovanovich, 1985.

Henry, Frances. *Victims and Neighbors: A Small Town in Nazi Germany Remembered*. South Hadley, Mass.: Bergin & Garvey Publishers, 1984.

Hilberg, Raul. *Perpetrators, Victims, Bystanders: The Jewish Catastrophe 1933–1945*. New York: HarperCollins, 1992.

Hoffmann, Peter. *The History of the German Resistance 1933–1945*. Cambridge, Mass.: MIT Press, 1977.

Horwitz, Gordon. *In the Shadow of Death: Living Outside the Gates of Mauthausen*. New York: Free Press, 1992.

Human Rights Watch. *Slaughter among Nations: The Political Origins of Communal Violence*. New Haven, Conn.: Yale University Press, 1995.

Hunt, Morton. *The Compassionate Beast: The Scientific Inquiry into Human Altruism*. New York: Anchor Books, 1990.

Jacobs, Steven L., ed. *Contemporary Christian Religious Responses to the Shoah*. Lanham, Md.: University Press of America, 1993.

———. *Contemporary Jewish Religious Responses to the Shoah*. Lanham, Md.: University Press of America, 1993.

Jaspers, Karl, *The Question of German Guilt (Die Schuldfrage)*. (reprint.) Translated by E. B. Ashton. Westport, Conn.: Greenwood Press, 1978.

Kateb, George. *Hannah Arendt*. Totowa, N.J.: Rowman and Allanheld, 1983.

Katz, Fred E. *Ordinary People and Extraordinary Evil: A Report on the Beguilings of Evil*. Albany: State University of New York Press, 1993.

Kelman, Herbert C. "Violence without Moral Restraint: Reflections on the Dehumanization of Victims and Victimizers." *Journal of Social Issues* 29, 4, 1973.

Kershaw, Ian. *Popular Opinion and Political Dissent in the Third Reich. Bavaria 1933–1945*. Revised edition. Oxford: Clarendon Press, 1983.

———. *The "Hitler Myth": Image and Reality in the Third Reich*. New York: Oxford University Press, 1987.

Koshar, Rudy. *Social Life, Local Politics, and Nazism. Marburg, 1880–1935*. Chapel Hill: University of North Carolina Press, 1986.

Langer, Lawrence. *Admitting the Holocaust: Collected Essays*. New York: Oxford University Press, 1995.

Large, David Clay. *Contending with Hitler: Varieties of German Resistance in the Third Reich*. Cambridge: German Historical Institute and Cambridge University Press, 1994.

Lifton, Robert Jay. *The Nazi Doctors: Medical Killing and the Psychology of Genocide*. New York: Basic Books, 1986.

Lipstadt, Deborah. *Beyond Belief: The American Press and the Coming of the Holocaust, 1933–1945*. New York: Free Press, 1986.

Lookstein, Haskiel. *Were We Our Brothers' Keepers? The Public Response of American Jews to the Holocaust, 1938–1944*. New York: Vintage Books, 1985.

Maier, Charles S. *The Unmasterable Past: History, Holocaust and German National Identity*. Cambridge, Mass.: Harvard University Press, 1988.

Marrus, Michael. *The Holocaust in History*. Hanover, N.H.: University Press of New England, 1987.

———, ed. *The Nazi Holocaust: Historical Articles on the Destruction of European Jews*. Westport, Conn: Meckler Corporation, 1989.

Milgram, Stanley. *Obedience to Authority: An Experimental View*. New York: Harper & Row, 1974.

Niebuhr, Reinhold. *Moral Man and Immoral Society.* New York: Simon & Schuster, 1995.

Oliner, Samuel and Pearl Oliner. *The Altruistic Personality.* New York: Free Press, 1988.

Oliner, Samuel and Pearl Oliner, with Lawrence Baron, Lawrence A. Blum, Dennis L. Krebs, and M. Zusanna Smoleska, eds. *Embracing the Other: Philosophical, Psychological, and Historical Perspectives on Altruism.* New York: New York University Press, 1992.

Payne, Stanley G. *A History of Fascism 1914–1945.* Madison: University of Wisconsin Press, 1995.

Peukert, Detlev. *Inside Nazi Germany: Conformity, Opposition and Racism in Everyday Life.* New Haven: Yale University Press, 1987.

Polonsky, Antony. *My Brother's Keeper? Recent Polish Debates on the Holocaust.* London: Routledge, 1992.

Richarz, Monika, ed. *Jewish Life in Germany. Memoirs from Three Centuries.* Translated by Stella P. and Sidney Rosenfeld. Bloomington: Indiana University Press, 1991.

Rosenberg, Alan and Gerald E. Myers, eds. *Echoes from the Holocaust: Philosophical Reflections on a Dark Time.* Philadephia: Temple University Press, 1988.

Rosenfeld, Alvin H. *A Double Dying: Reflections on Holocaust Literature.* Bloomington: Indiana University Press, 1980.

Roth, John K. and Michael Berenbaum, eds. *Holocaust: Religious and Philosophical Implications.* New York: Paragon House, 1989.

Ryan, Michael, ed. *Human Responses to the Holocaust: Perpetrators and Victims, Bystanders and Resisters.* New York: Edwin Mellen Press, 1981.

Staub, Ervin. *The Roots of Evil: The Origins of Genocide and Other Group Violence.* New York: Cambridge University Press, 1989.

———. "Moral Exclusion, Personal Goal Theory, and Extreme Destructiveness." *Journal of Social Issues* 46, 1, 1990.

Sunga, Lyal S. *Individual Responsibility in International Law for Serious Human Rights Violations.* Dordrecht, Holland: Martinus Nijhoff Publishers, 1992.

Tal, Uriel. *Christians and Jews in Germany: Religion, Politics, and Ideology in the Second Reich 1870–1914.* Translated by Noah Jacobs. Ithaca, N.Y.: Cornell University Press, 1975.

Volf, Miroslav. *Exclusion and Embrace: A Theological Exploration of Identity, Otherness, and Reconciliation.* Nashville, Tenn.: Abingdon Press, 1996.

Wiesel, Elie. "Freedom of Conscience: A Jewish Commentary." *Journal of Ecumenical Studies* 14: 638–649, 1977.

Wilkinson, James D. *The Intellectual Resistance in Europe.* Cambridge, Mass.: Harvard University Press, 1981.

Willis, Robert E. "Auschwitz and the Nurturing of Conscience." *Religion in Life* 44: 432–447, Winter 1975.

———. "The Burden of Auschwitz: Rethinking Morality," *Soundings* 68, 2: 273–293, Summer 1985.

———. "Bonhoeffer and Barth on Jewish Suffering," *Journal of Ecumenical Studies* 24: 598–615, Fall 1987.

Wyman, David. *The Abandonment of the Jews: America and the Holocaust, 1941–1945.* New York: Pantheon Books, 1984.

Index

About the Author

VICTORIA J. BARNETT is a consultant for the Department of Church Relations, U.S. Holocaust Memorial Museum. She has written numerous scholarly articles on religious topics. An authority on the history of the churches during the Holocaust, she is the author of *For the Soul of the People: Protestant Protest against Hitler* (1992).

Recent Titles in
Contributions to the Study of Religion

Church and Synagogue Affiliation: Theory, Research, and Practice
Amy L. Sales and Gary A. Tobin, editors

Presbyterian Women in America: Two Centuries of a Quest for Status, Second Edition
Lois A. Boyd and R. Douglas Brackenridge

The Druids: Priests of the Ancient Celts
Paul R. Lonigan

Thomas K. Beecher: Minister to a Changing America, 1824–1900
Myra C. Glenn

From the Unthinkable to the Unavoidable: American Christian and Jewish Scholars Encounter the Holocaust
Carol Rittner and John K. Roth, editors

Holocaust Education and the Church-Related College: Restoring Ruptured Traditions
Stephen R. Haynes

Protestant Evangelical Literary Culture and Contemporary Society
Jan Blodgett

Competing Visions of Islam in the United States: A Study of Los Angeles
Kambiz GhaneaBassiri

Bodies of Life: Shaker Literature and Literacies
Etta M. Madden

Toward a Jewish (M)Orality: Speaking of a Postmodern Jewish Ethics
S. Daniel Breslauer

The Catholic Church in Mississippi, 1911–1984: A History
Michael V. Namorato

Holocaust Scholars Write to the Vatican
Harry James Cargas

ISBN 0-313-29184-5

90000>

EAN

9 780313 291845

HARDCOVER BAR CODE